# BUCKET LIST OF AN IDIOT

# BUCKET LIST OF AN IDIOT

FOREWORD BY THE PRIME MINISTER

## DOM HARVEY

ALLEN&UNWIN
SYDNEY·MELBOURNE·AUCKLAND·LONDON

First published in 2012
Copyright © Dominic Harvey 2012

All rights reserved. No part of this book may be reproduced or transmitted in any form or by any means, electronic or mechanical, including photocopying, recording or by any information storage and retrieval system, without prior permission in writing from the publisher.

Allen & Unwin
Sydney, Melbourne, Auckland, London

Level 3, 228 Queen Street
Auckland 1010, New Zealand
Phone: (64 9) 377 3800

83 Alexander Street
Crows Nest NSW 2065, Australia
Phone:   (61 2) 8425 0100
Email:   info@allenandunwin.com
Web:    www.allenandunwin.com

National Library of New Zealand Cataloguing-in-Publication Data

Harvey, Dominic, 1973–
Bucket list of an idiot / Dominic Harvey.
ISBN 978-1-877505-17-1
1. Harvey, Dominic, 1973– —Anecdotes. I. New Zealand Wit and humor. II. Title.
NZ828.302—dc 23

ISBN 978 1 877505 17 1

Photograph of McDonald's plane, page 335, courtesy of Betsy Prujean

Set in 12.5/16 pt Bembo by Post Pre-press Group, Australia
Printed in Australia by McPherson's Printing Group

10 9 8 7 6 5 4 3 2 1

**Mixed Sources**
Product group from well-managed forests, and other controlled sources
www.fsc.org  Cert no. SGS-COC-004121
© 1996 Forest Stewardship Council

The paper in this book is FSC certified. FSC promotes environmentally responsible, socially beneficial and economically viable management of the world's forests.

# CONTENTS

Foreword by Prime Minister John Key   vii
I am an idiot . . . and this is my bucket list   1
Convince the prime minister to write the foreword   7
Fight a girl   11
Release an original song   27
Go skinny-dipping with my older sister in broad daylight   41
Visit a dominatrix   49
Hire a granny stripper for my boss   65
Get suspended from work   86
Bury the hatchet (the big apology)   92
Kiss a celebrity's arse (literally)   112
Eat at a buffet until I throw up   119
Stick it all on black   135
Go pool crashing   151
Have a midlife crisis (get Botox)   164
Run the Boston Marathon   177
Prank my mum   192
Go to a gay sauna   203
Be a life drawing model   219
Cross-dress   232
Get a bad tattoo   244
Jump off the tallest building in New Zealand   265
Learn to meditate   277
Arm-wrestle an All Black   290
Track down my first kiss   300

Ask for a threesome   315
Do it on a plane   328
Run the paintball gauntlet   336
Have a crack at writing erotic fiction   344
Write a book   347

# FOREWORD
## BY PRIME MINISTER JOHN KEY

Dom,

Top of the bucket list

- ☑ Party Vote National.
- ☑ Do a sky dive
- ☑ Do a bungee jump without the bungee.

P.S Do this last.

*John Key*

# I AM AN IDIOT...
# AND THIS IS MY BUCKET LIST

Hello, my name is Dominic Harvey and I am an idiot.

I am comfortable with that now. I have managed to carve a pretty good career and make a decent living out of being an idiot on the radio. So, far from taking it as an insult, I consider it a sort of compliment.

I have always been one, too. Even in the days before I went professional and became paid to be an idiot. My long-suffering parents were among the first to recognise it:

```
'Get off the clothes line, you bloody
 idiot!'
```

That was Mum when I was nine and probably more than old enough to know better.

We had one of those old rotary clothes lines and I thought it would make an awesome ride, a bit like a home-made merry-go-round. So I held on to one of the four arms that came off the trunk and ran until I built up a bit of speed, then took my feet off the ground, which usually gave me a couple of seconds of fun. Mum stopped the ride . . . on that occasion. Eventually I was forced to retire that activity when one of the aluminium arms designed for wet towels bent and then eventually snapped.

Granddad was another family member to recognise my gift for doing foolish things:

```
'Dominic, stop being an idiot! Pull your
togs up and sit down or get out!'
```

This came after an awkward incident in Granddad's spa pool when I was twelve years old. Granddad's spa, complete with artificial grass on the ground, was in a conservatory with a ranch slider. Conservatories were all the rage in the mid eighties—anyone who was doing well for themselves had this bizarre extra room added to their house. The artificial grass was not so popular—I believe Granddad selected that based on price more than appearance. This particular day I had my back facing the ranch slider and because the jets and bubbles were making considerable noise I had not heard Granddad come in.

My poor old granddad, so meticulous with his spa pool maintenance, had walked in to see me with my togs partially down and my little white bottom half out of the water as I attempted to put my penis into one of the water jets. After that an extra rule was added to Granddad's already thorough list of rules on the wall—NO SHENANIGANS! I did appreciate his subtlety.

When I left school and got my very first job in radio the name-calling continued:

```
'What sort of an idiot puts dirty dishes
 back in the cupboard?!'
```

Luckily, I'd made it to the end of my three-month trial period before Steve Rowe, the radio station manager, came to the conclusion his most recent hire was an idiot. Since I was seventeen and employed to work the midnight to six am 'graveyard shift', Steve had given me a lengthy job description which included things like 'clean the staff kitchen every night'. This pissed me off—I wanted to be a DJ, not a bloody cleaner! I didn't do any of my own dishes at my flat, I reasoned, so why the hell should I have to clean up other people's mess at work?

So once my trial period was up I started to cut corners. I would just put any real dirty dishes I came across away in the back corner of the cupboard, still dirty.

My cunning plan was discovered when one of the staff members saw a giant rat in the kitchen one morning. That rat was executed. I was lucky not to be.

Even my first proper girlfriend, Kim, recognised that her first true love was a fool.

```
'Are you trying to burn the house down,
 you idiot?'
```

That came after she arrived home from work one day and found me squatting totally naked in front of the oven with my underpants dangling on the end of a wire coathanger that I had fashioned into a rod. In my defence, what was I supposed to do? I had no clean undies and no dryer. Desperate times call for desperate measures.

My old personal trainer in Palmerston North, Graeme Sciascia, had to agree with everyone else:

> 'What sort of an idiot doesn't wear underpants under his gym shorts?'

Graeme is a man with a big heart—and even bigger pectoral muscles—but the alarm bells started ringing for him this one session where he had me doing squats. This is where you have a bar loaded with weights behind your neck and you crouch down until your thighs are parallel with the floor, then you push the weight up again.

On this particular day Graeme had me squatting and lifting 140 kilos, a tremendous amount of weight and way more than I was realistically capable of. I told him this but he said he believed in me. I put the bar on my shoulders, psyched myself up with some deep breaths, then slowly lowered the weight until I was crouching not far from the floor. That was the easy bit done. Then I started to push to get the weight back up again. I pushed with everything I had. My face was red, veins were popping out in my neck, I could feel my eyes watering from the strain, and then it happened. My bowels spontaneously expelled gas from the force and, along with it, a small, perfectly formed poo, bigger than a Malteser but smaller than a scorched almond, which fell from my shorts and rolled across the floor. I was mortified. I put the bar up and, without saying a word, I grabbed a handy-towel, picked up the evidence and walked to the toilet to dispose of it. When I went back to the squats area, Graeme shook his head and uttered that sentence above, which did little to put my mind at ease. Had I been wearing undies or lined shorts I would have still had 'the accident'. The only difference is it would have saved me considerable embarrassment. I have not done a squat or defecated on a gymnasium floor since that day.

Ever since the Morgan Freeman and Jack Nicholson movie *The Bucket List* came out in 2008, people have been creating their own lists of things to do before they kick the bucket. No two bucket lists are the same, but each list has the same ultimate goal—to make the list-maker feel like they are doing something useful with their life instead of just sitting around writing lists and watching Morgan Freeman DVDs.

Every person's list is different. I've seen some of them and they look so difficult that I wonder if dying would be a better option than actually ticking off the items. I mean, where is the fun in writing 'climb Mount Everest' on your list? Bring it up on Google Earth, have a good look around, then get back to Facebook. This way you will get to experience the world's highest mountain and you shouldn't lose any of your fingers to frostbite.

Also, I am a life member of a cool little place called the comfort zone. People always go on about the importance of getting out of your comfort zone. It seems these days everyone is all about personal challenges and setting goals, all that Eat-Pray-Love stuff. Not me. My comfort zone is just that—a zone that is incredibly comfortable. And any day I can stay inside it is a good day.

People might say this is lazy but I don't care.

For no real good reason (other than an obligation I had to write a book) I decided to complete a bucket list of my own, kind of like a reverse bucket list. A bunch of stuff that I could have happily passed away without actually putting myself through. Reluctant to challenge myself, I reached out to some family and mates to suggest items for the list. I'm not sure what your best friends are like, but mine are the sort that take great delight in seeing me suffer or squirm. Asking them to help me out is possibly just more proof that I am an idiot. The sort of things they wanted me to do were not the sort of things I would ever want to do. Some of the stuff was fun. Most of it was not. I was even left traumatised by a few of the things.

So here it is—my pain, discomfort and humiliation for your pleasure. THE BUCKET LIST OF AN IDIOT. Read it from start to finish, or go to a chapter that sounds interesting and read that. Read it any way you want. It is a perfect book for people with short attention spans. None of the chapters are too long so if, like me, you enjoy taking some reading material into the loo, it could be perfect for those visits.

Thanks for giving it a read. I hope you like it. Even if you don't, you'll probably still enjoy it more than I enjoyed actually doing some of these things.

# ☑ CONVINCE THE PRIME MINISTER TO WRITE THE FOREWORD

Book forewords always seem a bit show-boaty to me. It seems like a cheap ploy by the author just to sell a few extra copies of their book by getting someone far more famous than him or herself to make a guest appearance at the start of the book. And if the person who has written the foreword is enough of a drawcard, you can even use it as a selling point by advertising the fact on the cover.

Like Bob Greene did with his book *The Best Life Diet*. Even though Oprah only occupies a couple of pages at the very start of Bob's book, her name on the front is in a font size not much smaller than the book's title.

Bob's not alone either. Heaps of people have tried to earn a bit of instant credibility for their book by convincing an A-list celebrity to write the bit at the beginning. Here are a few books I found where the writer of the foreword is far more popular than the writer of the actual book:

> *The Family Chef* by Jewels and Jill Elmore—foreword by Jennifer Aniston
>
> *Letters from a Nut* by Ted L. Nancy—foreword by Jerry Seinfeld
>
> *Unforgettable Steve McQueen* by Henri Suzeau—foreword by Brad Pitt
>
> *Do Hard Things: A Teenage Rebellion Against Low Expectations* by Alex and Brett Harris—foreword by Chuck Norris

Does anyone even bother reading them? I suspect a lot of people probably just cut straight to the first chapter, like skipping through that ad about movie piracy at the start of a DVD.

But rather than try to fight this, I was going to play the game. I needed a heavyweight to write my foreword. This book was not going to sell itself, so I needed to aim high—I wrote up a letter to the prime minister of New Zealand, John Key.

> Dear Mr Key,
> I hope you are having a nice day. I am writing a book and I would love it if you would write the foreword for it. The book will be called *Bucket List of an Idiot* and is basically just a bunch of stuff that most people would probably

avoid doing before they kick the bucket.

I intend to do things like dress up as a lady and participate in a women-only fun run, get a regrettable tattoo and model nude for a life drawing class.

Having the current prime minister write the foreword for my book would be great for sales and give it the credibility it would otherwise lack.

Your advisers will tell you not to do it. And they are probably right. But here is a list of all the reasons why I reckon you should do it:

1. I voted for you in the last election.

Okay, that is the only reason I could think of. Stink.

I have already been turned down by other high-profile New Zealanders including the bloke on the five dollar note, Sir Edmund Hillary. Did you know that Sir Ed died a while back? I seem to have missed the memo on that one, which made for a very awkward conversation when I called about the foreword:

*Is Sir Edmund Hillary there, please?*
*He's not?*
*Well could you pass a message on?*
*You can't?*
*Why not?*

*Wow, when did that happen?*
*Oh, I see.*
*No, of course I was not aware of that.*

So, how about it? You've got nothing to lose (other than your reputation, credibility and the next election).
Thanks in advance!
Dominic Harvey
Author

P.S. I heard you have a bit of a sweet tooth so I have sprinkled some icing sugar in the envelope.

I did not get round to sending the letter to parliament. John Key came into our radio studios for an interview so I plucked up the courage to ask him in person.

The conversation went like this:

**Me:** I'm writing a bucket list book—can you write my foreword for me?
**John Key:** Yep.

And just like that, I managed to tick off the first item on my bucket list. That was easy. You've already seen the foreword at the beginning of this book. Unfortunately, the rest of my misadventures would not be quite so straightforward.

# ☑ FIGHT A GIRL

Like most people, I want others to like me. But sometimes in my line of work you end up upsetting people along the way. It happens, and it sucks when it happens. Incredibly, though, my big mouth has only put me in physical danger once.

It was at my first radio job in Palmerston North, on the local station, 2XS FM. My on-air partner at the time was Mike West, and we were the kings of Manawatu radio. Well, Mike West was and I just happened to be there for the journey. The name of the show was *Mike West and Baldrick*. I was Baldrick. It was a nickname given to me by one of the sales reps at the station when I was a schoolboy doing work experience—it came from the Rowan Atkinson TV show *Blackadder*. The somewhat unflattering nickname caught on and ended up becoming my radio name because, just like the *Blackadder* character, I was essentially the radio station's slave and sidekick. If you compared us to the Swedish pop-rock duo Roxette (though I don't think too many people ever did), Mike was like the hot lady who sings and I was the unremarkable guy who just stands in the background playing the keytar.

This one morning, the big story in Manawatu was about a local sports star who was in trouble with the police—it was something to do with marijuana. Mike and I had some fun with this, goofing on a little bit, making some obvious pot jokes and then holding a very dodgy mystery-sound contest, with a really blatant and obvious sound effect that was supposed to be someone toking on a joint—all against a backdrop of Bob Marley music. It was 1990s regional radio at its finest. After a couple of minutes of this we moved on to the next thing and forgot all about it. Just a throwaway bit which, in breakfast radio, you do a dozen of every morning.

A good couple of hours after that, closer to 10 am and the end of the show, Mike and I were sitting in our swivel chairs with our legs stretched out and our feet on the desk. It was about as relaxed as any man could ever hope to be in the workplace. There was a song playing and we were exhausted from another morning of clowning around and making jokes about people we had never met.

Unknown to us, one of these people—the local sports star we had been making fun of—had just arrived to see us. He told Vanessa—our lovely, if a bit too trusting, receptionist—that he was here to see the boys. Instead of asking him his name and inviting him to take a seat while she paged our extension to tell us who was here to see us, Vanessa told the agitated visitor we were in the studio, gave him directions, then sent him around to us unaccompanied.

As he burst in on us we had no time to register what the hell was going on. I was closest to the door and he lunged at me with a closed fist, clobbering me on the left side of my face. You know that bone just in front of your ear? That's where he hit me. It knocked me right off my chair. Looking around for something to defend himself with, Mike picked up the most suitable item he could find. In a radio studio, the options on hand were limited, so he went for a metre-long rack we used to store sound-effect cartridges. In fact, the sound effect labelled 'marijuana puff' was possibly stored in the very rack now being used to fend off the very man the segment was about. What a curious twist of events.

So there I was, cowering on the ground, bewildered and startled, as my assailant stood over me, his fists still clenched and his angry eyes looking all . . . you know . . . angry. Mike was to my right, protected by the desk in front of him, and using the heavy cart rack he managed to keep our local sporting hero at arm's length and a wee bit more until some other staff from round the office got wind of what was going on. Luckily for us, the guy was done, and saw himself out before the situation got any worse, but on his way out he said, 'You pricks have had this coming for a long time,' and he was dead right. We had. It was a well-deserved thumping.

The police were called in but we didn't press charges. I wasn't really that keen to give the cops a detailed statement explaining what we did to provoke this guy and then how I ended up falling off my chair into a heap on the floor. It wasn't a story I wanted to share in a courtroom, especially since the one strike hadn't left any cut, mark or bruise. The ear stopped ringing after a couple of days and the only long-term damage was a fractured ego.

Thankfully, I had not been punched again since then. In fact, apart from a couple of fairly low-key schoolyard scuffles, that was the only time I had been hit in my life. And the total number of punches I'd thrown was even smaller. I truly had no idea if I was even capable of physically hurting another human being.

It was time for me to get in a fight. A proper fight too—not some street brawl outside a kebab shop while waiting for a taxi at 3 am, but in a boxing ring.

And I wanted my opponent to be a lady. There were a couple of reasons for this. Firstly, I wanted to find out if I could actually bring myself to throw a punch at a lady—even if she was giving me her greatest hits. I despise men who hit or bully women. I think this stems from the environment I was raised in. In 1970s New Zealand, belting kids with the jug cord was all right if they deserved it—but it was a complete no-no for men even to swear in front of the women.

Secondly, if I'm being completely honest, I thought that a punch thrown by a female fighter would probably hurt a lot less than a punch from any male boxer. It sounds like a reasonable theory . . . but that was before I met 'Diamond' Daniella Smith. ('Diamond' my arse! I can assure you that on the women's boxing circuit this particular Diamond is anything but a girl's best friend. If she was being more truthful she would have gone with 'Rough Diamond' or 'Blood Diamond'.)

It was my friend Monty Betham who put me onto Daniella.

Monty is a retired rugby league player. He used to play for the Warriors and the Kiwis. He retired from league to concentrate on boxing. Nicest bloke you'll ever meet, Monty, but he really does enjoy hurting people. As long as it is done in a sporty kind of way. He currently spends his days training people at a gym called Boxing Alley in the Auckland suburb of Parnell.

I told Monty about my bucket list and how I wanted to fight a girl. I also made a point of telling him I was unsure if I would be able to bring myself to hit a girl. Monty laughed at this. He assured me I would have no problem hitting a girl once I got into the ring with Daniella Smith.

Daniella was the number one women's boxer in New Zealand at the time and had a world ranking of number six. Monty told me that Daniella only trained with male boxers, because she was just too good to have a serious sparring session with any female boxers. She would kick my arse. No question about that. The big question for me was, how badly? And how angry would she be if I punched her in the boob? I was about to find out.

The fight was set down for a Friday at the Boxing Alley gym where Monty trains Daniella. It would consist of three one-minute rounds. Monty offered to give me a

'Boxing 101' lesson, just a crash course in fighting and blocking, prior to setting foot in the ring, but I declined. It was probably incredibly stupid to turn him down but I was determined to be totally unprepared and untrained. This way I would learn if I was a fight, flight or freeze type of person. Because I had never fought before, I had no idea.

The week leading up to the fight I was bloody nervous. Not constantly. Not crippled with fear. But whenever I thought about it I had a sick feeling in my stomach.

Also I was wrestling with a lot of internal conflict as I recalled a saying I'd once heard. I have no idea about the origins of this quote but it does make a lot of sense:

```
'There is no honour in beating up a girl
 but there is a whole lot of shame if a
 girl whips your ass!'
```

A whole lot of shame was really the only outcome we were going to have here.

When my co-hosts Mike Puru and Jay-Jay Feeney got wind of what I was doing they pissed themselves. They were adamant that the fight should take place live on the air during the breakfast show. I was a bit iffy about this. I mean it's one thing to get humbled/humiliated in a boxing gym with a small handful of spectators. It's another thing to have it broadcast live to a nationwide radio audience.

Jay-Jay and Mike invited and encouraged spectators to come along, promoted the fight time with enthusiasm, decided my fighting name would be the rather pessimistic 'Dead Man Dom' and convinced TV3 sports presenter Hamish McKay to call the match. All of a sudden we had a very public fight on our hands.

I got to Boxing Alley at 7.30 am on the Friday morning, half an hour before my fight. Diamond Daniella Smith was already there. We met. I kissed her on the cheek and we chatted. You know, it really is an odd situation to be in—having a pleasant conversation with someone only half an hour before you are going to be punching each other.

I stood a lot taller than Daniella and after looking at my arms she commented on my 'reach'. She actually seemed

*Given my massive advantage in height, weight and reach, Daniella looked nowhere near as petrified as she should have.*

a little nervous. She was nowhere near as intimidating as I expected. I was still bloody nervous myself but all of a sudden I wondered if things would perhaps not be as bad as I had been building them up to be.

My hands were bound tight with tape, another first for me in this whole fish-out-of-water experience. It made me feel a little bit tougher, a little bit more like a fighter. Then the gloves went on, a lovely feminine pink pair. It's an odd feeling, losing the use of your hands. I was reliant on my mate, Sharyn, to help me put my protective headgear on, give me water, put my mouthguard in and even scratch an itch—thanks for that, Sharyn!

The boxing ring is a terrifying place to be. No exits, no hiding places. It's a fairly big area when you inspect it from the outside but once you get in there to fight it appears so much smaller.

I was standing in my corner, my arms numb with fear. Monty was yelling instructions at me: 'Keep your hands up! Always keep your hands up.'

The theory is that your hands will protect your face and head while your arms keep your body covered—but I was so paralysed with fear, even lifting my gloved hands and keeping them up felt like hard work.

Monty Betham agreed to referee the fight. He called both fighters—Diamond Daniella Smith and Dead Man Dominic Harvey—to the centre of the ring.

'I want a good clean fight, especially you, Dom. Protect yourself at all times, especially you, Dom. Ready? Box!'

And with that we started. I looked the part, I think.

*Monty Betham does up my headgear. When your brain cells are down to the final couple of thousand it is important to protect them.*

We danced around for the first two seconds of the round before I went in and threw the first punch—if you could call it that—a fairly feeble jab which hit Daniella's glove. I think I was reluctant to hit her with any real force for fear of making her angry. Something I learned seconds later: you don't need to hit Daniella to make her angry.

Daniella threw a punch with her left hand which got me just below my rib cage. It hurt. Then immediately after that she took a big swing with her right hand which I managed to back away from. It just glanced off the corner of my headgear but knocked me off balance. I remember thinking to myself, 'Shit. That was close.'

I stood up and tried to use my long arms, my reach, to jab away at her. Literally keep her at arm's length. Then she came at me again. A right hand to the side of my body followed by a right hand to the side of my head.

These blows hurt but I was still able to focus and keep composed. I was just wondering when the hell the one minute would be up. I had never known time to go so slow.

**Hamish McKay:**
```
She is looking to go to that rib cage
early.
   He's copped a right hand! Harvey has
copped a big right hand to the head that
stunned him. Boom. A right hand to the
head again. With that leading left from
the champ Daniella, that seems very
effective.
```

> Oh no. He's just copped another one.
> Four beauties right on the kisser!

Daniella kept coming at me swinging, hitting. I kept moving backwards trying to avoid being hit. Finally my back scraped against the ropes on one side of the ring. Then she unleashed fury. Bang. Bang. Bang. Bang. Blow after blow. She had me trapped and there was nothing I could do about it. I was getting weaker with each punch. I could feel my eyes rolling into the back of my head. I remember thinking, 'Why isn't anyone coming to stop this? Monty, I thought you were my mate. What the hell are you doing?'

I know this is the sport of boxing. But I'm not a boxer. I'm just a guy writing a book. My legs and feet gave way beneath me. My arms slung over the ropes were the only thing that stopped me from falling to the canvas floor. Diamond Daniella showed her compassionate side and stopped punching me. Or maybe it was just that the first sixty-second round was over. I had a mouthful of blood and felt physically drained. Already I was dazed and exhausted. The thought of another two minutes like that was daunting.

There were thirty seconds of downtime before the next round would begin. In my corner, Sharyn reiterated what I had to do—keep my arms up and my face covered, advice I had successfully ignored in the first round. Then the bell rang—from the world's slowest minute into the world's fastest thirty seconds.

**Hamish McKay:**
What can we expect? The second round is underway. And Dead Man Dom has started better this round, actually! He's looking a bit more confident. Just moving around a bit better, trying to avoid the punches.

When you realise you are all alone and nobody is going to save you, survival becomes the key. I was trying to box her, fend her off. But I was also trying to avoid being hit. My unorthodox technique was to basically just keep moving back as she stalked me around the ring. Hardly courageous-looking... but I was not too concerned with how things looked at this point.

Monty's suggestion of keeping my hands up in front of my face failed me miserably. No matter where my hands and arms were, my opponent managed to find a gap, a way to get my head or body. This method may work for other fighters but I really needed a third arm to give me adequate shielding.

**Hamish McKay:**
She is working him towards the corner. Looking to go towards the body. And she does. Gets him a beauty and now she's gone upstairs with two huge rights. And another one. The fight has been stopped. Surely it's all over. He can't carry on.

Monty came over to get Daniella off me. I was still on my feet but I was stumbling around, bewildered. As exhausted and beaten as I was, I wasn't going to stop the fight—I didn't feel it was my place. But I was clearly not in a good way—why the hell didn't Monty or Sharyn in my corner make that call? Throw in the towel on my behalf? I suspect they were all enjoying this a bit too much. Daniella had not actually knocked me out yet so until that occurred, this top-quality entertainment at my expense would continue.

**Hamish McKay:**
Let's start the third round. Dead Man Dom took a terrible hiding midway through the second round. And this is where it gets very dangerous. She's got him up against the ropes again and Monty Betham steps in to pull the two fighters apart. And it's a left to the head. A swinging right arm to the body. Ooh! Low blow! I think he might have copped it on the you-know-where. And the mouthguard has been spat out.

I doubled over in agony. I had been hit in the genitals. The blast of pain was excruciating. In my opponent's defence, the low blow was not intentional. She didn't need to resort to dirty play to get the edge on me in this tussle! I think it had to do with the awkward angle I had got my body into, in an attempt at self-preservation. Boy, did that plan backfire!

Monty Betham came over to me to ask if I was okay. Through gritted teeth I spat back at him that my dick was burning, a heat-of-the-moment comment that Hamish McKay heard ringside and repeated in his live radio commentary.

**Hamish McKay:**
```
He's got a burning dick!
```

The dull, sickening pain of testicular damage engulfed me, and my penis felt like it was on fire. This was a first for me and, men, I can assure you a dick-punch does not feel all that good.

I paused for a few seconds to compose myself and let the burning subside. Monty encouraged me to jump up and down on the spot to alleviate the pain. Fat lot of good that did.

The fight continued. I was hoping that the time I had spent doubled over nursing my jewels would have been taken off the third round. Sadly that was not the case. But it was the home stretch now. It had been a feeble effort on my part, but if I could get through to the end of this third and final round without being knocked over, it would allow me to leave the ring with just a tiny bit of dignity.

**Hamish McKay:**
```
Daniella the champ looking for that body
again. Watch the way she comes upstairs
and cracks him! Ouch, that must have
hurt! And that one, another big right
```

> hand. I'll tell you what, he is going to have a very sore rib cage when he wakes up tomorrow morning, this young man.
>
> We are just about ten seconds away from the end of the fight. Can he hang in there and go the distance? Remarkable effort from Dead Man Dom. Wind up the *Rocky* music, he's almost there. And that is it! The end of the fight.

It had not been pretty. But I had survived. I'm not sure how much effort Diamond Daniella Smith was putting in. But if she wasn't hitting me with her best shots, I shudder to think just how dangerous she is when she goes all out on an opponent.

Our fight had been the perfect role reversal, really. I was a man fighting like a girl, fighting a girl who was fighting like a man.

I woke up the morning after and felt like I had a bad hangover. My head and neck ached. My right shoulder was sore. There was blood in my urine. And the bottom of my left rib cage was unbelievably agonising, making essential tasks like getting dressed, coughing and putting a seatbelt on very difficult.

Out of courtesy, I texted Diamond Daniella Smith to make sure she was not feeling too beat up. She put my worried mind at ease—she was fine. So fine that after I left, her coaches made her do some more training! Way to make a guy feel good about himself. And to add insult to injury, I signed my text off with an 'x' to represent a friendly kiss, which she didn't return in her text. I'm pretty certain she hates me. Imagine if I'd actually managed to punch her!

I was hoping to learn a thing or two about myself by fighting a girl and I did. I realised that your own mind, your own imagination, can be your biggest enemy. Leading up to the fight I was crippled with nerves. And the three minutes in that ring were pretty damn scary. Then it ended and I had time to reflect. And that's when I gained a bit of perspective and realised that even though it was bad, maybe even worse than I'd anticipated it was going to be, it was still manageable. I had survived. And that feeling right there—getting through something I wasn't sure I would be able to—feels pretty damn good.

I also found out my boxing technique resembles a newborn giraffe attempting to walk on hind legs.

# ☑ RELEASE AN ORIGINAL SONG

I can't sing. Not one note. In a lot of people the inability to hold a tune is due to tone-deafness. Not so with me! I am the complete opposite of tone-deaf. When I sing, I can hear the tone in my ears and I find the sound just as offensive as those unfortunate enough to be around me.

It really is a pity, because I like to sing. So out of courtesy to others I only sing when I am alone these days. And out of courtesy to my own ears I make sure I turn the song I am singing along to up really loud to drown myself out.

I am okay with this impediment now. I have had years to deal with the disappointment.

I first got wind of it when I was nine and joined the Riverdale Primary School choir. Back then I was a big fan of David Bowie and held aspirations of one day being a famous singer like him. In the choir we practised for a whole term singing two songs: 'The Lion Sleeps Tonight' and 'Yellow Submarine'. We were working towards a goal—at the end of the term the choir was going to go on the road and visit rest homes around Palmerston North to sing to the elderly.

By the way, the poor old people! Here they are paying good money to be looked after in their twilight years and this is all they have to look forward to—shitty lunchtime concerts from primary school kids. Then again, maybe the rest-home staff member in charge of entertainment intentionally books crap acts so the old people don't feel so bad about their imminent death. If I was eighty-seven years old and the highlight of my week was a group of children butchering a Beatles classic, I would probably start to look forward to the prospect of dying.

I was so eager to be a great singer that I used to position myself in the front row of the choir and sing with as much effort as I could. Singing made me so happy. I even got a blank cassette and taped 'Lion Sleeps Tonight' off the radio so I could practise it at home. This was the only way to get a song back in 1982. There was no YouTube or iTunes. There was not even a music TV station. There was a half-hour chart show on TV2 every Saturday night called *RTR* and that was it. So most kids had a blank tape on stand-by in case a song they liked came on one of the limited range of AM music radio stations.

The version I taped had been recorded by an American group, the Tokens, in the sixties. Listening to it over and over, I noticed our choir was putting in nowhere near as much effort as the Tokens put into it. So I took it upon myself to add some falsetto harmonies:

'Weeeeeeeeee oh weee ohhhh weeee umm ummm awaaaaay.'

I was so excited. I thought Mrs McGrath, who was running the choir, might single me out for some praise, let the other kids know I was the standard, the benchmark, they should all be trying to reach.

Just as I predicted Mrs McGrath did single me out. She pulled me aside and asked me if I would like to stand in the back row of the choir and try to 'not sing so loud'.

I was only nine but I wasn't stupid. You don't put someone in the back row and ask them to sing quieter because they are too awesome. I knew what she was up to and I was devastated. I don't resent her, though—she was right on the money. The fact she even let me stay in the back row was charitable.

After that tour of the retirement villages I stopped singing in public—my dreams of rock stardom shattered, all before I had even turned ten.

Subconsciously, maybe this is why I opted for a career in music radio. This would allow me to be in the music industry, albeit very much on the fringes.

The opportunity arose in December 2010 to get this tick on my bucket list by releasing an original song. It was suggested by my boss at The Edge radio station, Leon Wratt. He came up with an idea for our radio show called 'X-mas Factor'—a Christmas time piss-take of the talent quest TV show *X Factor*. Mike Puru, Jay-Jay Feeney and

I were each issued the challenge of coming up with an original Christmas song. Given our severe lack of any sort of musical talent, and to ensure this would not be a complete embarrassment, we were told we could work with an established artist if we could convince anyone to put their reputation on the line.

Jay-Jay approached an incredibly talented but relatively unknown guy by the name of Seth Haapu. He agreed to take part and within a couple of days had written a catchy innuendo-laden pop track called 'XXXmas'. The chorus went like this:

```
Oh oh oh!
Do I hear ho ho ho?
Kissing all year long under mistletoe
Don't send an STD down my chimney-ee
I've been a naughty girl
Santa, be nice to me
I've been a bad, bad girl
I've been a bad, bad boy
```

Mike Puru called up one of New Zealand's best singer-songwriters and *New Zealand's Got Talent* judge, Jason Kerrison from the group Opshop. They are old mates who went to radio school together. After graduating, Mike used his diploma to get a job in music radio. Jason went on to have a wildly successful music career. He had an old Christmas song he had written years earlier that he told Mike he was welcome to use, an epic ballad called 'Nothing More for Christmas'.

```
I need nothing more than being with you
I could want for nothing more
I need nothing more than to be with you
I could wish for nothing more
No room, no view
[Whispered] This Christmas
Only you
Only you-oo-oo
```

I don't know what it all means but I bet any guy who can write stuff like that never goes to bed alone at night.

My own genre would have to be rap. I've already explained that I can't sing—a fact recognised decades earlier by Mrs McGrath. But I could talk as well as the next bloke, so I would have to play to my strengths.

I approached Scribe, arguably New Zealand's most successful rapper. I say 'arguably' because these hip-hop people all look quite menacing and I don't really fancy getting on the wrong side of Savage and his friends at the Dawn Raid music label, who could also arguably be the best.

Scribe is famous for being difficult to track down. Had Saddam Hussein and Osama bin Laden just stuck close to Scribe it's possible that US Intelligence would still be scratching their heads looking for them to this very day.

I was warned by my boss that Scribe was hard to pin down and reminded that the deadline for the song was not far away. No pressure! It was a long shot, trying to get Scribe, but you don't know if you don't ask. I sent him a tweet:

> Yo! @mcscribe I need to come up with a Xmas song for a work competition. I want to do a rap. LOVE to do it with you my man. Holla if U keen.

With words in my tweet like 'my man' and 'yo' and 'holla', how could he turn me down? Clearly, I had some hip-hop 'cred' (that's a quick way of saying credibility, FYI).

I sent my tweet and assumed I would probably not hear anything back from Scribe. But the very next day, I got this reply on Twitter:

> Sounds interesting @DomHarvey I'm in London, back in NZ Monday. Could be keen. Email me your lyrics & music track and I'll say yes or no.

Not only was it a reply, it was a tentative yes. This was promising!

I noticed that Scribe didn't use words like 'my man' and 'yo' and 'holla' in his tweet, which made me feel rather foolish. I made a mental note to ease up on the street lingo for future dialogues between Scribe and myself.

I emailed Scribe the lyrics I had written and the backing track—an upbeat, modern take on the traditional 'Jingle Bells'. My song was called 'Christmas Wrapping'. Granted, it was not exactly '99 problems but a bitch ain't one', but I thought it encapsulated the whole feeling of a Kiwi Christmas pretty well.

Christmas in New Zealand and you know
  what that means
Every year we have pretty much the same
  routine
Finish up for work on December 24
By 4 pm everybody's out of the door
The mall is so busy you might as well
  just leave it
You can only get a park if you're a
  paraplegic
When you finally get inside and get what
  you need
You double-check your list because you
  want to exceed
All the expectations so there is no one
  upset
When they finally unwrap the presents
  that they get
It's embarrassing when your sister says
  'lame'
When she sees you gave her your picture
  in a frame
And now it's Christmas Day and the kids
  get up first thing
So damn early they are up before the
  birds sing
Open up their presents—'Thanks Santa—
  too much!'
'Just what I wanted—an iPod touch!'

**Chorus**
Jingle bells, jingle bells, jingle all the way
Santa's in a Skyline coz he traded in his sleigh
Jingle bells, jingle bells, jingle all the way
Sorry for the oil that he left on your driveway

**Rap**
And now it's Boxing Day and we're back to the mall
The big sales on and you want to spend all
Of the vouchers you got the day before
Or exchange the stuff you don't want no more
And if the weather's good we hit the beach for a swim
The shit's so cold that sometimes we don't get in
All the girls are wearing their Daisy Dukes so short
And covering their eyes with the sunglasses they bought
Them Dolce Gabbanas
Probably cost four hundred dollars
But she don't care—probably worth it for the hollas

'Uggh,' she says—'all those guys are so creepy'
But she loves the attention secretly
Dudes driving slow with the 'for sale' sign up
Car's not for sale they're just hoping to hook up
We are New Zealanders and it's a Kiwi thing
So turn the volume up, ma-fucker—let us sing

**Chorus**
Jingle bells, jingle bells, jingle all the way
Santa's in a Skyline coz he traded in his sleigh
Jingle bells, jingle bells, jingle all the way
Sorry for the oil that he left on your driveway

After hitting send on the email to Scribe I nervously anticipated his reply. Would he want to be involved in the collaboration? Would he like the song or think the lyrics were a colossal pile of steaming faecal matter? I cared a lot because the deadline was looming and if Scribe turned me down I had no plan B.

Scribe's reply was good news—he agreed to take part—but he wanted it to be made very clear he'd had nothing to do with the songwriting process. Until that point I never knew it was possible to experience relief, excitement and embarrassment all in one two-line email.

We met in the studio the morning Scribe arrived back from London and exchanged an awkward four-part handshake that ended with our shoulders gently banging together and Scribe's fingers clicking as he pulled away. I always get very nervous when someone goes in for anything other than the traditional handshake. I find it hard enough just to remember all my various computer passwords—how the hell am I supposed to keep up with all the current handshake trends?

We got the song recorded in under an hour. Scribe did two lines, then I rapped the next two lines, until the song was complete.

As established earlier, I am unable to sing. I did think I was fit to rap, though. That assumption was buried when I heard my parts of the song next to Scribe's. His parts sounded awesome: rhythmic and flowing. My bits just sounded dorky. I sounded like a nerdy white guy who was having a crack at rapping. Funnily enough, that is exactly what I am so I probably should not have been so surprised by this.

In the end I adopted the slogan 'Fake it 'til you make it'. I would have to pretend to be a bad-ass rap superstar.

I went back in the recording booth and starting rapping. To get into character, I started clutching my genitals—like 50 Cent and all those guys do when they rap. I was only a couple of lines in when Scribe stopped the session and asked what was up with my voice.

'I'm doing it in an American rapcent! That's when you rap in a different accent.'

When Scribe said he hadn't heard of that before it gave me great pleasure to tell him that 'rapcent' was a word I had invented, just then, on the spot. He was impressed. He didn't say he was, but I could tell by the way he shook his head.

Before leaving, Scribe again made a point of telling me to make sure his name was down on the publishing sheet as a performer but not a writer.

I was starting to get a complex—just how horrible were these lyrics?

The three X-mas Factor songs were all released on the same day. I had done it. I had released an original song. My boyhood dream of being a recording artist had finally come true. And thousands of people really liked it. And when I say thousands, I mean seven.

```
Really catchy love it
Lauren


I love your song Dom! It's got a cool
beat and a good modern Xmas song!
Aarena


This song is the best, lyrics are funny
and the tune is catchy!
Jackie
```

# CHRISTMAS WRAPPING
## DOM HARVEY FEAT SCRIBE

AVAILABLE ON ITUNES MONDAY DEC 13TH
ONLY $1.79 (HEAR IT NOW ON THEEDGE.CO.NZ)

```
Wow! I'm surprised . . . I totally love
this song.
Tania


Dom man u awesome hahaha here I was
doubting  this  song.  U  rocked  it,
rapped it and U didn't even sound that
bad . . . .Scribe  should  be  flattered
that u asked him to do it!
Owen


WOW! I love this one. Go Dom!!! I'm
getting an iPod touch for Xmas so I am
definitely going to buy this to download
onto it.
Ty


Wow Dom that was very funny and catchy.
Scribe is awesome. I vote for you!!!
Mike
```

Jay-Jay Feeney's pop track, Mike Puru's ballad and my rap song were all made available to purchase and, incredibly, all made it into the top 20 of the official New Zealand singles chart. This created a huge amount of envy among real New Zealand musicians with actual talent who do not have their own top-rating radio show as a vehicle to try and sell their music.

But I had no time for this jealousy. I had realised my boyhood dream! With less musical talent than Crazy

Frog, I had not only written and released a song but made it to number six on the charts, sandwiched in between Michael Jackson in seventh place and Katy Perry at number five. A good friend of mine pointed this out in a text message:

```
Enjoy this moment mate. This will be the
only time in your life you have Katy
Perry in front of you and Jacko right
behind you.
```

Now there's a visual that is titillating and terrifying in equal proportions.

# ☑ GO SKINNY-DIPPING WITH MY OLDER SISTER IN BROAD DAYLIGHT

Fortunately I got this one done before things got all, you know, hairy and scary looking. This one got ticked off the list a decade before either of us hit puberty. It was a real family affair, too. While me and my sister frolicked in the shin-deep water, our mum sat on a chair taking photographs. Well, I say 'photographs', but the truth is it was just the one snapshot you see over the page. These were the days when cameras had films that took twenty-four photos and, when finished, those films had to be taken to a specialist shop to get developed. And it wasn't cheap, either. Because of this, Mum would use her camera sparingly. I do recall one particular roll of film Mum used so sparingly that by the time she got the prints back from the Kodak Kiosk at DEKA it included photos of me at the ages of five, six and seven.

In this particular photo, though, I was almost three. Bridget was almost five. Mum and Dad were still both

*Being from a reasonably poor family we could not have everything we wanted. This year the options were togs or a pool.*

in their late twenties. It was the summer of '75 in our backyard in Liverpool Street, Levin.

In this photo I look like I didn't have a care in the world . . . but in hindsight maybe I should have been a little bit concerned about the size of my genitals. Take a good look. The only way you can tell that I'm a boy is that I have short hair. Bridget looks more hung than me. It actually looks like I have two bellybuttons and no penis. I'd like to tell you I have grown considerably since then but nobody likes a bullshitter.

Melanoma was not a word that anybody ever used because nobody knew about skin cancer then. Kids were encouraged to get outside and get some sun on them. A good tan was associated with good health. I don't know if sunscreen even existed. If it did, it was not something we ever had at home. I recall Mum using something which smelt like coconut and worked as a sort of cooking oil for the body. The idea back then was to get as much sun as possible.

If the photo is anything to go by, another thing Kiwis were not big on in the mid 1970s was plants and landscaping—what a barren and sad-looking bunch of sections we all had.

This was also an era where privacy was not a big priority—our ranch slider and patio were at the front of the house looking onto the street, as were most people's outside entertaining areas. And that white picket fence in the photo was the boundary fence at the back of the property. Having a small fence like that, one that lets your neighbours peer right in, would be a negative now days when it came to selling your property. Back then, it was seen as a good thing. There was only one thing better than a small back fence, and that was a small back fence complete with a gate built in. This made it easy to pop over to borrow some emergency supplies—sugar/flour/milk/whatever. A neighbour coming over and asking for half a cup of condensed milk would seem a bit odd now. But in the seventies it was quite normal—people did a lot of baking and shops were shut more often than they were open.

These gates and small fences also made it easy to pop over for a cup of tea and a gossip, because neighbours were not just there to be used and abused for their well-stocked fridge and pantry—Kiwis were actually friends with their neighbours. What a concept.

Smacking was another popular pastime in this era. I remember getting smacked. Lots! Mum was not the primary smacker in the family. That was Dad's role. If we played up during the day while Dad was at work, Mum would pull out the line, 'Wait until your father gets home!' Then, sure enough, when our father got home we would get a smack for something we had done hours earlier. When you're a three-year-old boy, an afternoon can feel like a whole week, so often I would be smacked at 5.30 when Dad got home from work for something that I couldn't even remember doing.

I even recall getting smacked once by Mum's friend Shirley, who lived across the road. I was doing something I shouldn't have. I think she caught me crossing the street without an adult and decided to take matters into her right hand. These days, the law frowns upon neighbours belting the kids next door, but back then it was not something anybody flinched at. Mum probably even made Shirley a batch of pikelets as a way of saying thanks for caring.

Being smacked wasn't the worst of it, though. We also got the belt and, boy, did that hurt. Dad had this brown leather belt that was kept coiled up in a jar in the corner of his top drawer. This belt was never ever used for its intended purpose. It was exclusively for discipline.

When I was bent over the end of Mum and Dad's bed, waiting for him to take his back swing, Dad would always make a point of informing me that what was about to take place was going to hurt him more than it was going to hurt me. I couldn't understand it then and I still don't understand it now. It was bloody painful for me being on the receiving end of it, so if what he was saying was true, my poor old dad must have had a really high pain threshold, because I never once saw him leave the room in tears, rubbing his bottom.

On the odd occasion when Mum was required to administer on-the-spot punishment she would tend to go for the second drawer down in the kitchen and reach for the wooden spoon. This would sting like hell if she held the end of the handle and just flicked the spoon bit at our legs. But often she was so wound up that she would make her arm do the work instead of the spoon. This would usually result in the smack not hurting, the spoon snapping and us kids laughing hysterically.

One day not long after this photo was taken Bridget fell off a stool in the lounge and hurt her arm, which caused her to cry uncontrollably. After a while Mum pulled out the popular seventies line—'Stop crying or I'll really give you something to cry about!' Back then, that line was about as common as threatening to put the kids on the naughty step is now—if the Supernanny was doing her telly show in that era I'm pretty sure she would have used it too.

Bridget didn't stop crying. Mum went to the second drawer down and discovered she was in between wooden spoons, so she gave Bridget a Chinese burn instead . . . on her sore arm. That did little to stem the tears (surprise, surprise). Eventually Mum took Bridget to the doctor and that is when it was discovered that Mum had given Bridget a Chinese burn on a broken arm.

I think Mum felt pretty stink about that one.

This may all sound a bit horrible by today's standards. And maybe time-out or the naughty corner or whatever other methods parents use now are more effective ways of disciplining kids. But I can tell you one thing—we always tried to be on our best behaviour because we didn't want to be hit. And we didn't want to be hit because it was bloody painful! You learned pretty early on where the line was and how far you could push it.

Growing up in New Zealand in the 1970s there was *one* place where you could avoid the belt and that was in the car—the seatbelt, that is. I can't remember when the law changed and it became compulsory for all passengers to be buckled in, but I don't recall ever wearing a seatbelt as a young fella.

On one occasion I fell asleep in the back seat and leaned against the door of Dad's car. When he drove round a corner the door, which had not been properly shut, flung open and I fell out. That woke me up pretty smartly. I remember rolling across the road for ages, my little body being cut, scratched and grazed all over before coming to a halt.

Other family members commented afterwards that it was just good luck that I was not hit by another car. That is wishful thinking, really—this was Levin in the late seventies. There was probably more chance of seeing a man with no arms in a glove shop than there was of seeing another car on the road.

It was years after that incident that the Harvey kids started using these seatbelt things. Not on Mum and Dad's insistence, either. It was actually the great philosopher Ronald McDonald who got us onto the whole seatbelt craze. McDonald's launched a big campaign called 'Make it click' with a catchy jingle. I can still remember most of the lyrics off the top of my head:

```
When you're in the car, make it click
Going near or far, make it click
Front seat, back seat, anywhere you sit,
  make it click
Belt up quick, that's the trick
```

Before that campaign came along I remember going on road trips in Dad's company car, which was a station wagon with a big CNG tank in the back. It was not uncommon for me and Dan, my brother, to sit in the boot area, unrestrained.

Thanks to McDonald's fewer Kiwis are dying in car crashes. But more Kiwis are probably dying of obesity-related illnesses. So, swings and roundabouts really.

I don't recall the particular moment captured in the photo. But I do remember the paddling pool and the toy I am chewing on. I loved that toy. It was a sponge and

I used to love playing with it in the pool and then sucking the pool water out of it—along with skin cancer, nobody knew much about germs or hygiene back in the seventies. But the three-year-old me thought it was the second-best thing ever. The best thing ever would have been my plastic Womble mug with a picture of Tomsk on it. I like this photo. It reminds me of a less complicated New Zealand. When you reflect on how far we have come as a country I reckon there are many things we are doing a lot better. But there's also cool stuff that we've lost along the way. These days it is possible to live right next door to someone for years and not even know their name. Hardly anyone pops next door for a cuppa and a chat anymore. Come to think of it, you can't even knock on someone's door because you were 'just in the neighbourhood' anymore. It's considered polite to text first to check if it's okay to come and visit. That's a bit sad, I think.

# ☑ VISIT A DOMINATRIX

I am a big believer in knocking things before trying them. People say it all the time, 'Don't knock it till ya try it,' but let's be truthful, there are many things in life that you just instinctively know you will not enjoy before you bother going through with them. Visiting a dominatrix was one of those things for me.

I hate the idea of being smacked. I wish I didn't. It would have made my childhood a bit more fun. As I explained in the previous chapter, there was no naughty chair, step or corner in our home when I was growing up. As a kid of the seventies and eighties I was subjected to plenty of discipline, so to me the idea of bondage, discipline and sadomasochism (or BDSM for short) sounds like a nightmare. I struggle to understand why any sane person would want to pay top dollar for someone to humiliate or hurt them. I can come up with a long list of people willing to provide me with those services free of charge and I usually go out of my way to avoid running into those people.

But on my quest to complete my ridiculous bucket list, I discovered there are people who are cut from a very different cloth. People who wake up in the morning and say to themselves, 'Today I think I'll pay a stranger a handsome sum of money to put her fist up my bottom.' Yes, these people who pay for pain and humiliation are a very small minority, but they do exist and there are places they can go where their dark and twisted fantasies can be fulfilled.

I found Mistress Dior through a Google search. Her website was a real eye-opener. It listed the many services she offered and even included a photo gallery that I wish I hadn't clicked through! Damn you, IT department . . . You blocked Facebook at work—how the hell did you miss this site?

```
With the most well-equipped dungeon
in New Zealand, I can make all your
fetishes/fantasies and wicked dreams a
reality. Mistress Dior will cover all
the following and any other special
requests you may have:
```

*Castration fantasy*
*Corporal punishment*
*Caning*
*Cross-dressing*
*Exhibitionism*

*Erotic bondage*
*Fetish*
*Leather*
*Foot/boot worship*
*Flogging*
*Gags, hoods*
*Verbal humiliation*
*Adult baby*
*Medical play*
*Mummification*
*Nipple play*
*School mistress*
*Sensory deprivation*
*Suspension*
*Sissification*
*Slave training*

EDUCATED—EQUIPPED—DISCREET

I did an informal survey among my mates and 100 per cent of us agreed that a 'castration fantasy' is something none of us ever want to experience!

I only saw the scrotum torture and anal stretching photos on the website for a split second but I doubt I will ever be able to forget them. They are definitely not photos you would want to get mixed up with your summer holiday snapshots.

I decided I liked the sound of the verbal humiliation service. I could get the dominatrix experience without any physical pain. That'd be perfect for a wuss like me.

I emailed Mistress Dior and explained I had a bucket list and would like to make an appointment. She replied the next day and told me to call her to talk further. She insisted I call from a phone number that was not blocked.

I called and could hardly hear her when she picked up. In the background there was screaming and a loud echo. After introducing myself three times I gave up and told her I would call her back later. I didn't know what she was up to, but I guessed she was probably in the middle of an appointment with a client.

That made me nervous—imagining some poor bloke in a gimp mask with his nipples being held in clamps while this mistress took time out to answer the phone.

I called back the next day and asked what had been going on during our previous conversation.

'I was at the pool with my kids,' Mistress Dior explained. I laughed. 'Even a mistress needs to teach her children about water safety,' she said. Fair point. It was just hard to picture someone in this profession being a mum. More on Mistress Dior and her home life later.

We chatted for a bit and it didn't take long for Mistress Dior to work out that I was a 'vanilla'. In this context I think it means someone who is a bit conservative or closed minded. I don't think I am either of those things. I reckon I'm just 'normal' . . . I like women to be kind to my genitals.

Our phone call ended with an appointment. I would visit Mistress Dior's dungeon at 3 pm on the following Wednesday.

I didn't know it at the time but I was being screened

during this phone call. Even though I was asking most of the questions, Mistress Dior was treating the chat as a speedy character assessment. She does this with all new clients, and if she doesn't like the sound of someone or gets a bad vibe, she will not take a booking or give out her address. She had nothing to worry about with me—I'm just a boring old vanilla. It's some of the other flavours you need to be wary of—those rum and raisin men are the worst.

Mistress Dior's dungeon is in suburban Auckland, not too far from Mt Smart Stadium, where the Warriors play. Like me, the building that houses the dungeon could be described as vanilla. I had walked past this building many times before and had never given it a double look. It is in a crowded industrial street and looks just like all the other buildings. Made from concrete blocks painted white, the front of the place is windowless and free of any sort of signage.

I parked my car and pressed on Mistress Dior's buzzer. A few seconds later she opened the door. She opened it that way you open the door at home if someone knocks when you have your undies on. I could see the top half of her face but the rest of her was shielded from view.

Before I had the chance to speak Mistress Dior started doing what she does best—bossing men around.

'Quick! Get in so I can shut the door! There are people across the road.'

I turned to see. There was a busy warehouse across the road that had front row seats to the dungeon door. They could see every single client arriving and leaving.

*Mistress Dior's rear entry.
Nowhere near as dirty as it sounds.*

I wondered if they had any idea what was behind this door on the other side of the street.

She shut the door behind us and we both stood in the poky foyer area. This was when I got my first good look at Mistress Dior. She looked forty-something, maybe closer to fifty than forty. She had brownish hair which was teased up. Her earrings and necklace were all miniature handcuffs and her D-cup breasts were bursting their way through the low-cut leather top she was wearing. This top was so low I could see a glimpse of her nipples. She had a matching leather skirt so small I could see her black G-string and the cheeks of her bum when she walked in front of me.

Her outfit was like something from the costume department of *Xena*. She was definitely more intimidating than sexy.

I had seen photos of the dungeon on Mistress Dior's website but nothing could have prepared me for the moment when I saw it with my own eyes. It looked like a gym full of things that will cause you discomfort (or turn you on—depends on how you roll).

The dungeon was a huge rectangular room, like a garage that would be big enough for about ten cars, I reckon. The floor was concrete, painted black. The walls were red and so were the bulbs in the various lamps scattered about the place. Mistress Dior told me she had been a dominatrix for seventeen years, and everything she'd accumulated in that time, all of her tools of the trade, were housed here.

The dungeon was clean and well organised and had no obvious smells. One of the first things I noticed was the sound of the birds chirping outside on this summer's afternoon. If I could hear the birds on the outside, I reasoned, then surely people passing by would be able to hear the screaming from in here during a session?

Dior led me to the only corner of the dungeon that didn't look terrifying—a lounge area with a two-seater sofa. Also in this corner was a small tank with some goldfish in it. Good choice of pet to have living in a dungeon—one that only has a seven-second memory span.

She offered me a coffee, which I declined, and then invited me to take a seat.

She sat down next to me. Close. Giving me less personal space than I would ideally have liked. She intentionally sat so her arm was touching mine.

I asked her if I could tape our session on a voice recorder. She agreed, but on the condition that I never broadcast it or posted it online anywhere. Then she explained why: her kids and her husband have no idea what she does!

I found it impossible to believe her husband didn't know. She has her own dungeon stocked with New Zealand's largest collection of sex toys and torture devices, and the whole set-up was probably worth a couple of hundred thousand dollars. I thought her husband would have to be some sort of a mug not to know.

'He knows I'm into a bit of bondage and some kinky stuff but I only take appointments during the day when the kids are at school and I buy all my gear with money I make from clients. Maybe he chooses not to know what I do.'

It seemed plausible. But what would happen if she was at the mall or the grocery store and she bumped into a client?

'Most of my clients are very wealthy and successful men—pilots, lawyers, CEOs, politicians, that sort of thing. They've got just as much or more to lose than me, so if they saw me in public, they'd stay well away.'

In my mind I ran through a list of all the high-profile Kiwi politicians I could think of. It wasn't all that hard to imagine most of them on all fours wearing women's underwear and licking Mistress Dior's boots.

Dior shared the safety word with me—'Mercy!'

She explained that during a session that is the ONLY word that will get her to stop what she is doing.

'A customer might be screaming and saying, "Please stop, oww, please stop!" but they don't actually mean it.'

I asked if she would consider stopping if someone said, 'I CAN'T REMEMBER THE SAFETY WORD BUT PLEASE STOP!'

She rolled her eyes but didn't answer my question.

'You want verbal humiliation, right?'

I nodded.

'Riiiight,' she replied, in a drawn-out, thinking-out-loud way which suggested that particular option was going to be a problem. 'There's a very thin line between turning someone on and totally turning them off. And it's different for different people. Something that turns one person on can turn another person right off. For example, some people love the thought that what is being done to them is against their religion. Other people, you mention their religion while you're doing something and they're just, "Nup, not into it."'

Dior continued talking and I continued giving her my

full attention. It was already a sort of master-and-slave relationship we had developed in a very short time.

'Some people like the idea of their boss or perhaps their wife finding out. Other people, you mention family and it's, "Nope. Don't like this." So for me to give you a good session, for you to have a good time, we have to talk about things that are a no-go area for you. You need to tell me what you don't want mentioned. For example, some people looooove small cock humiliation, but others really don't.'

I burst into laughter. The nervous and uncomfortable kind.

'Seriously! I've got guys with huge cocks who want to be told that their cocks are useless. I've got guys who want to be told they can't get their cock up. "What's wrong with you? You're not a man, you're a little pussy. You haven't even got a cock worth looking at."

'Other people want to be told they look and act much more like a queer than a man, so I make them dress up. Force them into women's underwear and call their cock a clit and basically treat them like a little sissy bitch. Or I might say you're not a big boy, you're a little baby, and make you wear a nappy and force you to drink so much water that you pee your pants while I've tied you up so you can't move.'

Man, this was some weird shit. Where's the appeal? It wasn't sexy . . . just weird. Or was I just too vanilla for my own good?

'Here you are, laughing out of nervousness. One thing I ask from you? Keep your mind open, cause you never know, you might just enjoy yourself.'

It was unlikely.

'And you do know I'm going to do stuff to you, don't you?' Dior asked. She had been heading in this direction, warming me up, and now the bombshell was about to come—verbal humiliation was not something that could be done as a stand-alone service. Dior lowered her voice so it was only slightly louder than a whisper. 'Yes. You know. You know that, don't you?'

'Oh, well, I . . . No. You know . . .' I stammered.

'I'm not going to do anything you won't like,' Dior said. 'And I'm a professional. So if you say you don't like it, I'm going to stop.'

'Am I going to be your first ever customer to say "mercy" while still sitting on this couch?' I joked (with just a pinch of seriousness).

'I actually had someone who went to get money out of the bank and never came back, which was quite fun.'

My left foot and knee do this uncontrollable bouncing thing whenever I'm real nervous. Once it starts, it's impossible to stop. Not even leaning forward so my elbow is resting on my thigh can suppress it. This leg spasm must have given Dior an inkling that being treated like a 194-centimetre-tall baby and being forced to urinate in a nappy was not an idea I relished.

Dior got to her feet and invited me to do the same. I followed her to another section of her dungeon.

'These are all the medical things,' she announced, waving her hand toward an area well stocked with a wide variety of rubber tubing, forceps, wheelchairs and other hospital paraphernalia. Then she pointed to a rack of big hooks—huge silver steel things that you would find at a freezing works, holding up gutted sheep. These things were massive.

'These are the anal hooks,' she said.

My terror could not be disguised. 'FAAARK!'

Dior carried on. 'Those are cock cages. And these are speculums—doctors put them up your bits to open you up.'

We slowly walked round the dungeon and I looked on in disbelief as she explained the purpose of the different tools.

'Here's a nice little gag that you'll probably be wearing. Collars. All the masks. Strap-ons. Two fuck machines.'

These machines looked hilarious. They were like Black & Decker dustbusters, but the nozzles had been modified and now, rather than sucking up small bits of rubbish, they ended in giant vibrating rubber penises—and, boy, did these things have some grunt!

'Those are all my big boys,' Mistress Dior said, pointing to a cabinet of dildos, including one that was moulded in the shape of a closed human fist. 'And this is the area you probably don't want to know about.' She waved her hand towards a selection of maybe 200 canes, whips, paddles, horseriding crops and other corporal punishment tools.

She was right. I did not want to know about this area. But then again, I wasn't that fussed on any of the items on the menu she had mentioned so far.

Next Dior showed me her rubber suit collection and a thing called the vac-bag. This thing looked like a duvet cover made from black latex with a PVC piping frame inside it.

'The bag has a hole for a snorkel and a hole for a cock. You lie down in it on the floor and I attach the vacuum cleaner to it and suck all the air out. There are hundreds and hundreds of little holes throughout the frame and it vac-packs you so you can't move. And it's an amaaaaazing feeling! It feels like you're being sucked out of an aeroplane.'

Again, maybe this is just me being a boring old vanilla, but I have never been all that curious to know what it would feel like to be sucked from the open door of a Boeing! It sounds like a bloody miserable way to die!

The cross-dressing area of the dungeon was something else—a curtained-off section with racks of women's underwear and clothing, wedding dresses for men who like to dress up as brides, and a whole range of giant baby items.

Then there was the 'Queening chair', quite possibly the sickest thing I've seen in my life. It was a chair with a hole cut out. The client lies underneath it and his head is locked into place. Mistress Dior then sits down and urinates onto the face of the customer. Still, I suppose in any business it is better to piss on rather than piss off your clients.

With the grand tour over, Dior got down to business.

'Right, now you're going to go and have a shower and you're going to clean out your bottom, because I'm going to put something in your bottom so you can feel it. Something very small, though.'

'No. Definitely not. No, no insertions,' I protested.

'Well, okay, I'll do it with your bottom not clean, then! But wouldn't that be an even worse humiliation for you?'

There was a pause in the conversation. I stood speechless, paralysed with fear.

'I'm waiting for your answer! Or are you going to be that person who does a runner?'

'Yeah, I think I'm going to have to be that person. I'll pay you the $250, because I appreciate your time. But I think I may have to give it a miss.'

'Really? Are you really that chicken?' Mistress Dior was shocked that someone could fail to be excited by the prospect of having another person wee on their face.

'Yes, I am that chicken. I'm terrified.' This was no time for bravado. I had to be up-front and honest. I wanted out. And now.

'What are you terrified of? Are you terrified I'll hurt you or are you terrified you'll have a good time?'

'I'm definitely not terrified I'll have a good time. This whole set-up is frightening!'

Dior wasn't giving up, though. 'Okay, how about we do a tie-and-tease humiliation session? I'll tie you up and pretend you're a dirty little bitch. And then I'll force you to do things like suck strap-ons and fuck rubber dolls.'

Cue more of my nervous laughter, before I finally managed to string some words together. 'No, listen, I'm going to have to go.'

Dior finally started to realise there would be no turning this vanilla into any other flavour. Not a chance. We sat back down in the non-threatening lounge corner of the dungeon. She lit up a cigarette and offered me an apple juice, then left the dungeon to fetch the juice from the kitchen.

When she returned, we sat and talked for a while. She offered to show me a Japanese rope technique she practises called *kinbaku*. I agreed to this.

I removed my shirt and placed my hands behind my back and within a minute I was tied up and unable to move, imprisoned within an elaborate labyrinth of knots. And no amount of wriggling would make any difference. The ropes were tight, but not tight enough to strangle or leave marks . . . which I guess is important if you are a white-collar client who would have a hard time explaining to your wife how you ended up with rope burns over your wrists and shoulders after a day in the boardroom.

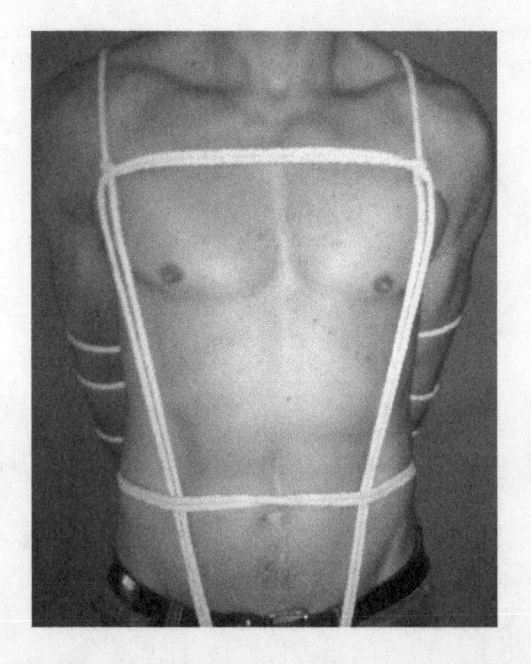

*Moments after Mistress Dior tied me up, my phone started ringing. I had great pleasure in truthfully telling my boss that I couldn't talk because I was tied up.*

Dior untied me and asked me the time. She had another client arriving in twenty-five minutes who she needed to get set up for. I was too nervous to ask what exactly she had to set up.

She saw me out and as the door opened I was stung for a few seconds by the brightness of the natural daylight.

I felt like a different person. I hadn't actually done anything, but I had seen everything. I reckon I can still tick this item off my bucket list, though—I experienced real pain at Mistress Dior's dungeon when I had to hand over $250 for nothing!

# ☑ HIRE A GRANNY STRIPPER FOR MY BOSS

In all my years in radio I've only worked at two different stations and have only had a handful of bosses. Some of them I've got on with better than others. If I had a dollar for every time a boss asked me, 'What the hell were you thinking?' I would have, at a conservative estimate, somewhere between three and four thousand dollars. And you could just about double that sum of money if I was given a dollar every time I answered that stupid question by saying, 'I dunno. I thought it might be funny.'

My boss at The Edge, Leon Wratt, would rate up there as one of my favourites. He lets me get away with a lot of stuff and then brushes it off as 'being creative'. It's funny, back when I was growing up the word they used for it was 'misbehaving'. I now get paid a pretty good wage for the same antics that once earned me the cane, the strap, the belt, the hand, the wooden spoon and occasionally a mouthful of soap.

Leon will tell me off from time to time, and that is never nice. When you have really pissed him off about something his office is a brutal place to be. On occasions I have been sitting there while he is yelling at me, most likely over something I deserved to be yelled at for. On these occasions I try to zone out and transport myself to a happier place—like Baghdad.

Over the years I've become skilled at dealing with management conflict. Here's the secret: *your boss is the BOSS*. In other words, whether you are in the right or the wrong, the boss is always going to win the argument, so you might as well just bend over and take it.

For years before I finally cottoned onto this, I wasted hours of precious golf time sitting in closed-door meetings arguing my case until I had blood pressure higher than an overweight fifty-year-old who's just run to the dairy to buy his pouch of Port Royal. These meetings always had the same outcome—the boss had the final word and I would leave the office feeling beaten up, like I'd lost the battle.

Now, any closed-door telling-off never lasts more than two or three minutes.

This is how it is done. Observe.

**Leon:** Hey mate, there's been a complaint from this woman. She was driving her kids to school at twenty past eight when you said something about rim-jobs and her seven-year-old daughter asked her what that meant.

**Me**: Shit. Sorry, mate. Yeah, that was a bad judgement call on my part. I really dropped the ball.
**Leon**: You sure did drop the ball, all right. She's furious. So am I!
**Me**: She should be. And you have every right to be too. I'm furious at myself. How could I have been so stupid?
**Leon**: You just need to remember the time—between eight and eight-thirty parents and kids are in the car together, so anything to do with sex is off limits.
**Me**: I wholeheartedly agree. In fact, we should just avoid sex talk altogether. There's no need for us to go down that smutty road to try and gain listeners.
**Leon**: Exactly.
**Me**: I'm so embarrassed about this. Would you like me to call her and apologise?
**Leon**: Nah, I can do that. As long as you know this is the sort of thing that could lose us audience share.
**Me**: Yeah, I got it. God, I'm kicking myself. That's Radio 101—I can't believe I let you down so badly.
**Leon**: Don't beat yourself up about it too much, mate. I just wanted to bring it to your attention.

Maybe ninety seconds all up for that hypothetical exchange and not only is the meeting done, but it almost ends with the boss telling me everything is okay. Sure, it doesn't always go as smoothly as that. But it is always faster and less exhausting than standing up for yourself.

In short, Leon and I have a great working relationship. I have a huge amount of respect for him, and if I may speak on his behalf, he not only has a huge amount of respect for me but he even has a crush on me. Bless him. After twelve years of working together we now have an informal agreement in place (which I haven't told him about yet) whereby I just go ahead and do what I want without running it past him and he deals with any fallout afterwards. It's a system that is working very well for one of us.

Leon is New Zealand's most respected radio programmer and he knows his stuff. He has a great sense of what will sound good on the radio and what the listeners will want to hear. What makes him fascinating to me is this contradiction—he loves it when his on-air presenters embarrass each other on air through pranks. He knows how much the audience love it when a well-executed prank is broadcast. BUT if he is the target of one of these potentially humiliating practical jokes, he spews. And the problem is, Leon is ridiculously easy to wind up. It might help to understand that Leon is not very tall. Actually, that last sentence is too politically correct. The man is tiny! Not tiny-tiny like a dwarf or a midget, but he does look like a teenage boy. Because of this he suffers from a severe condition known as 'short man syndrome', and when he's the butt of a joke, his reaction is very predictable. It's the same every time—silent fury. Leon knows the medium of radio so well that he knows just what to do. By not shouting or swearing, and in some cases not even speaking, he is essentially killing the joke—for us and for the listeners. No matter how good the prank is, without any reaction the conclusion is flat and the bit falls over.

There have been occasions when Leon has been unable to disguise his fury, though. When this happens, the payoff is huge. But there is a day or two afterwards where we remain unsure if our employment is still safe!

Here's a few of my favourite Leon jokes that we have executed over the years.

## The famous undie fence of Remuera

This was to be a tribute to the famous old Cardrona Bra Fence. This people-powered tourist attraction is, sadly, no more. The first bra was draped over this fence in 1999. By 2006, when the fence was up to 1000 bras, some mean-spirited locals had complained about it being an eyesore and the council tore the whole thing down.

Leon had taken his whole family to Australia for a week-long holiday. I did some research (well, went through his emails) and found out that his lovely house in the leafy Auckland suburb of Remuera would be empty for that time. For some unexplainable reason he had foolishly gone against his better judgement and decided not to get a house-sitter in.

A mistake he will never repeat!

This gave us a large enough window of opportunity to transform his fence into something that could be considered either an eyesore or a tourist attraction, or perhaps even both!

This joke required as many pairs of old underpants as we could get our hands on, so we had to broadcast our intentions. We were well aware that taking this to the airwaves could cause word of our master plan to filter back to Leon over in Aussie. This was of little concern to us. He was thousands of kilometres away. Even if one of his friends (assuming he had one) texted him to dob us in, there was nothing he could do to stop us. We all agreed that if he called, we would not answer and let it go to voicemail. This would allow us to avoid speaking to him, in case he attempted to intimidate us out of following through with our grand plan. Also it meant any voicemail messages he left could be played back on the air.

So the plan was underway and the response was immediate! Within twenty-four hours courier bags started arriving. After opening a couple of these parcels myself, I delegated the job to one of the station interns. You assume these old underpants had been washed prior to being sent but there was no way of being certain.

A sign-writer came to the party and offered to create a sign for the fence. Remuera was about to get its very first tourist attraction.

The day before Leon was due to fly back we had well in excess of 100 pairs.

Then, it happened.

To save money, Leon had not been checking emails on his phone, trying to avoid costly data charges. But on his second-to-last day on holiday he went to a cafe with free wi-fi to check his inbox, and someone had given him the heads-up about what was going on back home.

The timing was impeccable really—it meant only a day and a half of his holiday was ruined. Had he found out about this on the first day, he'd have spent the whole week in a nervous panic about what was going on back home.

After reading his email he sent me a threatening text. In a nutshell, the text said that he would kill me if I touched his fence. I decided not to reply. If someone sends you a text saying they will kill you, I think sending a reply telling them to 'chillax' will probably just aggravate them.

Anyway, retreat was simply not an option. It was too late for that.

The famous undie fence of Remuera was all set up and immediately became a tourist attraction. Pedestrians were stopping for photos, motorists were slowing down to a crawl to read the sign, some locals even added their own undies to the fence.

Jay-Jay, Mike and I got ourselves in position at 4.30 on the afternoon Leon was due to arrive home. Our hiding place was tucked in between bushes and behind a picket fence directly across the road from Leon's house. From here we would see Leon and his family arrive home and we had a great vantage point to film their reaction.

And yes, we did ask the neighbours' permission first. That was an odd conversation to have with someone you have never met before—'Hello, the man who lives across the road is our boss and we've covered his fence with used underwear. Can we hide in your garden and watch him arrive home?'

Had they been listeners, it would have been fine, because they would have heard what we had been up to. They weren't, but they were still okay about letting three tidily dressed thirty-somethings set up a stake-out on their property.

5.15 pm: Leon pulled into his driveway.

He did not so much as pause for a quick look out his car window as he turned into his drive. He parked up and seconds later his seven-year-old son came running back down the drive and onto the street for a good look. He started shouting at the rest of the family, 'Eww, yuck. Guys, come and see this. There's all these dirty gruts on our fence!'

Moments later, and less than a minute after arriving home, Leon appeared armed with some gardening shears. Then, without hesitation, he started chopping down the display. He was expressionless, too—no laughter, no anger, nothing. Just a calm, calculated determination to get rid of our handiwork in the shortest time possible.

We remained crouching out of sight over the road, unsure when (or even if) we should reveal ourselves.

Another neighbour arrived home from work and

yelled from her car window in a thuck and screechy Kiwi accent, 'Aawwww, din't be such a kulll-joy! Leave it up, ya miserable sod!'

To which Leon, still hacking at the display, replied, 'You can have it over at your place if you want!' as he flung a teal-blue thong (good condition, one lady owner) in the direction of the car.

We sensed a breakthrough in his demeanour. Leon was humiliated but in a good mood due to his week on the beach in Cairns. Come to think of it, his holiday tan combined with his short stature made him look very much like an Oompa-Loompa. All that was missing from his makeover were green hair and white eyebrows.

We jumped out from the neighbours' shrubs armed with video cameras and recording devices and revealed ourselves.

Leon knew exactly why we were there.

'Hey, guys! What are you doing here?' he asked anyway.

He then proceeded to give us NOTHING. All that work for no pay-off.

We went back to the drawing board after that and came up with an alternative plan. IF Leon is brave enough to take annual leave in the future, we plan to create the famous undie fence of Remuera II. This time, instead of using real undies, we'll recruit a sign-writer to paint them on. Granted, it probably won't look as impressive, but it will last longer and irritate Leon a bit more and that's the ultimate goal.

*Not sure what Leon did with the pants once he removed them. But I could swear I saw him in that little black G-string the following Monday.*

## P. D. H. (Public Display of Humiliation)

As a child Leon was a tap-dancing sensation—he took Blenheim by storm. He was a child prodigy in tap-dancing circles, a dancer destined for greatness, and he could have been a world champion, but he threw it all away too soon.

Actually, I made that last bit up. I'm not sure why he stopped dancing. His tap-dancing childhood is not something he is really big on talking about with his staff.

The first time it was ever mentioned on the air was by Jay-Jay. Leon came running into the studio while she was still speaking and just turned the microphones off and cut straight to a song. Then he stormed out. Just quietly, his 'storm out' would have been way more effective if he had those little metal tap-dancing plates on the soles of his shoes.

So, we knew Leon was good at tap dancing. We also knew Leon was embarrassed by it. Perfect! We got hold of a photo of Leon at the age of around eight or nine. In the photo he is wearing a one-piece dancing suit which looks like it is made from some highly flammable fabric. He is holding a rather show-boaty dance pose while standing in front of all his badges, trophies and ribbons. He appears to be wearing a white motorbike helmet, but that was just his well-maintained hairstyle.

As an adult, Leon is modest/embarrassed about his tap-dancing achievements but, evidently, he was pretty chuffed with himself at the time.

We came up with some copy to go along with the photo and booked a quarter-page advertisement in the *New Zealand Herald*.

On the day our ad appeared we spied on Leon from our studio window overlooking the office as he followed his usual morning routine. Once he'd arrived and put his things down, he sat down at a table in the open office area and proceeded to read the newspaper.

This was a nervous time for us. We knew as soon as he got to page A8 that all hell could break loose. He could be in such a rage that he'd stomp through the floor, like a modern-day Rumpelstiltskin.

He turned the page and starred at the ad. His eyes stayed on it for the best part of a minute. Then, even though he still had the sports and business sections left to read, he folded up the paper and walked towards the studio door. WE WERE SHITTING! Leon calmly poked his head in, held up the paper and asked, 'Who gave you the photo?'

**LEON WRATT**

A champion tap dancer and a champion boss.
From all his team at 94.2FM The Edge
www.theedge.co.nz

**Nice pants little guy!**

We had promised Leon's brother we would not reveal our source, but when he was standing there in front of us Jay-Jay got nervous and caved—'Your brother sent it to us.'

At that moment it dawned upon me just what pathetic US Navy Seals we would make. We didn't even put up a fight to protect our source. Nobody needed to torture us. Leon simply asked and Jay-Jay cracked.

Leon walked out and nothing was said about it ever again. I'm not sure what went on between Leon and his brother after that. But his bro has not sent us any embarrassing photos since! Come to think of it, I'm not sure if anyone has seen Leon's brother since then.

### The highly offensive car sticker

Leon's house and garage were connected by an internal access door, which was right by the driver's door of his station wagon. Prior to commencing his thirty-five-minute drive to work in the morning he just had to walk out of his house straight into his car and was off.

If any modifications were made to the passenger side of his car, he would have absolutely no way of knowing.

One morning at 3.30 I went to Leon's house and crept down to his garage. I walked down the back side of the house rather than the drive to avoid setting off any sensor lights. Then I got to work, carefully unpeeling and applying a giant sticker to the passenger panels of Leon's car. This sticker was in a big black bold font and covered most of the vehicle. With the sticker in place, I managed to exit without detection. Now all we had to do was wait.

I was on the air when Leon arrived at work just before 9 am. He waved and smiled at us through the studio window. This was Leon in a good mood, like a man who'd struck every green light on his way to work.

'That was a bizarre reaction,' we all thought. Just moments earlier he would have parked his car and noticed the sticker. We were expecting embarrassment or anger—not a smile and a cheery wave. If we were to use the Seven Dwarves scale, we expected Leon to be Grumpy rather than Happy.

Then it occurred to us—maybe he hadn't even noticed the sticker! This scenario seemed unlikely, though. Surely other motorists would have seen it during his commute and reacted with rude hand signals, toots or abuse.

We put a long song on and ran downstairs to find his parked car. THE STICKER WAS STILL ON THE PASSENGER DOORS. And worse still, all the parking places in the work basement had been taken, so Leon had parked on the street . . . right outside the play centre! There were mums and young kids streaming past and looking at Leon's car. Some laughed and took photos, but most looked repulsed.

A quick team meeting was held on the street. Mike and Jay-Jay voted to take the sticker down and not even tell Leon about the whole prank. I was outnumbered. We peeled the sticker off and the joke was aborted.

Leon has never mentioned it but, in hindsight, I wonder if he did see it there and outplayed us, getting his own back by acting as though he was unaware—even parking right outside the day care on purpose. Maybe it was all part of an elaborate prank within a prank. Like the Leonardo DiCaprio movie *Inception* except with practical jokes instead of dreams.

*The sticker on Leon's car. Made all the more believable since research shows 82 per cent of all sex offenders drive station wagons.*

## Five ideas that never made it past the brainstorm stage

1. Turn Leon's swimming pool into the world's largest drink of Raro.

2. Paint a giant penis and scrotum on the roof of his house then reveal it to him during a hot air balloon ride.

3. Put a classified ad in the paper with his name and cell phone number for a midget men's erotic massage service.

4. Turn a holiday snap I have of Leon working his BBQ topless into a giant billboard warning against the dangers of fat-splashes (in reference to the meat on the barbie, of course).

5. Hire six proper dwarfs and a tall dark-haired woman. They barge into a boardroom meeting Leon is leading and offer him the role of Grumpy.

**The granny stripper at the staff meeting**
This was to be the pinnacle of all Leon jokes. The one that staff would talk about for years to come. Staff meeting at The Edge is 11.30 every Monday morning. The meeting consists of a few staff just reading out notes about what is going on that week. Surely these notes could just be emailed to us all, I have argued, and then the need for a meeting would be eliminated? The response I got was that 'none of you bastards would even read the notes if they were sent'. Touché.

The Edge team is a fairly small and close-knit group of about fifteen people who all get on pretty well and enjoy each other's company, at work and outside of business hours. With this in mind I was pretty confident my idea for Leon's birthday present would be well received by all, even the staunchly religious girl.

From the 'Novelty' section of the website Strippers-R-Us I had booked a granny-gram and arranged for a woman known as Saucy Sandy to meet me outside work at twenty past eleven. I'm not sure if Sandy was her actual name . . . but I can confirm she was anything but saucy!

We would wait outside until I got a text from Jay-Jay, who was in the meeting. The message would say, 'The target is present.' She could have just texted me, 'Leon is here now,' but when you're pulling off one of these jokes that include some heist elements, you suddenly get this uncontrollable urge to pretend you're in a James Bond film.

I was on the street with Saucy Sandy when the text came through. I told her we were ready to go. She was not quite ready, though—'Just give me a minute, would ya love, so I can finish my durry.'

The poor old duck, probably someone's mum and nana, was about to go into a packed boardroom full of strangers and take her clothes off. If she wanted a couple of minutes for a nerve-calming cigarette, who was I to hurry her along?

Waiting on the street was a little awkward and we attracted a lot of double-takes from motorists. Saucy Sandy was a woman in her sixties who looked like she had lived every single day of those years to the fullest. Rolled-up smoke in one hand, black leather whip in the other, she was wearing a black leather corset and underwear with a dog collar round her neck, thigh-high fishnet stockings and black high heels—and without any pants on! She looked like what you would imagine Lady Gaga to look like forty years from now. We also had with us the Strippers-R-Us chaperone and driver who, I suspect, may also dabble in stripping as the fat-o-gram for the company. You couldn't blame people for their curiosity—we did look like a very odd trio standing there on the street.

When Sandy had finished her durry we walked up the stairs and through the bustling reception area, past offices and studios, to the boardroom. I'm not sure who was more nervous at this point, Saucy Sandy or me. Was this going to be taking things too far? Would this be crossing the line? I started to get terrified this could backfire.

I opened the door to the boardroom. Saucy Sandy and her large chaperone remained hidden out of sight. I walked in and discreetly passed Saucy Sandy's CD to Mike Puru, who got it cued up and ready to play in the stereo. As usual, Leon sat at the head of the table, which was conveniently positioned right next to the door.

'Leon, since it's your birthday and we all think you're such a wonderful boss, we got you something that you will never ever forget.' I made a point of using the word 'we' instead of 'I' because that sort of suggested shared blame for what was about to happen. Gutless, I know, but there was no way I wanted to take full credit for this one!

'But first can we all sing happy birthday to our fearless leader?'

All the Edge staff at the meeting joined in for a raucous version of the birthday song. Leon sat there blushing, squirming. He must have known something was up but the question was what!

'Okay, guys, can we please have a big round of applause for Leon's birthday present . . . Saucy Sandy!'

Cue music: Metallica, 'Enter Sandman'.

The song starts slow and builds up. For the first twenty or thirty seconds everybody sat looking toward the open door, just waiting for something to happen, and then she appeared. She locked eyes with Leon as she leaned on the door frame. She then stretched out her right arm and pointed her whip at him. Next she slapped the palm of her left hand with her whip and swung it around softly as she walked towards him.

Everybody was in hysterics, apart from Leon, who just looked mortified. He kept his chair tucked in under the table and would not make eye contact with his living and breathing gift.

As the music built everybody clapped along in time. Saucy Sandy stood right beside Leon. She removed her long leather coat, a bit like that one Keanu Reeves wore in *The Matrix*, and placed her foot up on the arm of his chair, the big tattoo on her thigh—a wolf in the moonlight—only inches away from his face. She danced around his chair, then gently whipped his chest a couple of times. Leon looked bewildered—frightened, actually. But he was laughing, which was an encouraging response.

Then Saucy Sandy put her whip on the table and reached out to take off Leon's shirt. He quickly put a halt to this and refused to remove his top, even when his staff all started an enthusiastic chant: 'Shirt off, shirt off, shirt off!'

And this is where things started to get a little bit weird. Realising she was not going to have her wicked way with the birthday boy, Saucy Sandy brought in her fully clothed plus-size chaperone and bent her over the boardroom table and started whipping her right next to Leon! So close to Leon, in fact, that the chaperone's boobs, each the size of a ripe watermelon, buried his iPhone, which was sitting on the table next to him.

Saucy Sandy then dismissed her helper and turned her attention back to Leon as she started removing what little clothing she actually had on.

She took her corset off to reveal a black bra.

*Unsure where to look, Leon settles for the saggy boobs.*

That is when Leon turned and gave me a throat-slitting motion. Now this could mean one of three things:

1. He wanted me to cut the music and call off his present.
2. He literally wanted to get a knife and slit my throat.
3. All of the above.

I hesitated. Everyone was having such a good time. There were seventeen people in the room and sixteen people were enjoying themselves—that was a pretty good strike rate, I thought.

'HARVEY! KILL IT NOW!' Leon shouted over the Metallica music. He was serious. His eyes were bulging. His eyes only ever bulged when he was in a rage. I was in the shit. Big time.

We stopped the music and everybody gave Sandy the applause she deserved.

I guided Saucy Sandy and her chaperone down to their car and could still hear the laughter and chatter coming from the boardroom upstairs.

When I sheepishly returned, Leon was just wrapping up the most unusual meeting of his career. 'And the best news for the day?' he joked. 'Dom is now suspended tomorrow!'

I was not suspended. But this did make me wonder, what exactly does a guy have to do to get suspended around this place?

# ☑ GET SUSPENDED FROM WORK

Incredibly, in twenty years of radio I have only been suspended on one occasion. I reckon part of the reason for this might be because radio employers know there is nothing a breakfast announcer would like more than a morning or two off work. The true punishment is to keep us working so we have to get up in what is essentially the middle of the night.

I was suspended in February 2010. The suspension was only for one day but it was actually rather enjoyable—I woke up at around 7.30, which may sound early to some people but, believe me, when you are used to getting up at 4.30 am this is a sleep-in of Sunday morning proportions.

After waking up on my day off as a condemned man I enjoyed a leisurely breakfast—the kind I imagine a normal human being would have before they start their nine-to-five workday. This probably sounds like an inane detail but usually my breakfast, which consists of a bowl of cereal, is wolfed down in under three and a half minutes. Over the years I have perfected the art of eating a bowl of Sultana Bran in the space of one pop song. It does not make for pleasant viewing, watching me eat. I actually look more dog than human. But if I don't manage to get it eaten before the song finishes and we go back on the air, it may be soggy by the time the voice break is over. These are the sorts of problems that a music radio DJ faces on a daily basis—she's a hard life!

The suspension came only a week after I had arranged a granny-dominatrix stripper as a present for the boss at a full staff meeting, so I was already skating on thin ice. Still, the suspension came as a surprise and to begin with I thought my boss, Leon, was having a laugh when he said, 'Don't bother coming in tomorrow—you're suspended for a day without pay.'

We push the boundaries a fair bit. You have to in commercial music radio to stand out from the crowd. Every station has access to the same music, so the point of difference has to be the stuff that goes in between those songs. This sort of pressure sometimes means you do stupid things—things you would rather not do but know will probably get you some sort of a reaction.

Leon is usually our biggest cheerleader—he even shields us from a lot of the complaints that come in about stuff we have done. But this particular day, he was furious.

Alison Mau, the attractive TV newsreader, was married to the attractive TV news reader Simon Dallow. Then they broke up and she started a same-sex relationship with a dance teacher, making them the hottest lesbian couple in New Zealand. When I read this in one of the Sunday newspapers it excited me immensely.

The next morning on our radio show, just after 8 am, I sang a little song I had written about it to the tune of the Beyoncé hit 'Single Ladies'.

```
Ali's into ladies (× 7)
She's given guys up
Broke up with Si coz he's a guy
Decided men weren't her thing
Didn't need Dallow
Or any other fella
Wanted to go rug-munchin'
She's into chicks, got sick of dick
Wanted to try some new things
Met a nice girl, gave gay a whirl
And now what I really want to know . . .
When they make love do they have to put
  a strap on it?
When they make love do they have to put
  a strap on it?
Has she thought about making a tape of it?
When they make love do they have to put
  a strap on it?
Oh oh oh oh oh oh ohhh oh oh oh oh oh oh
  ohh (× 2)
```

The lyrics were appalling. And the singing was even more offensive. Nobody else wanted to sing it so I was left with no option but to do it myself. After the show finished, Jay-Jay, Mike and I all went into Leon's office for a meeting. This was nothing out of the ordinary—every day after the show we have a meeting to discuss what worked well and what didn't, then we start planning the following show. We sat down and I was ready for some feedback. Leon is a hard guy to read but I thought he would like the song—he and I have a similar sense of humour. The response from the audience had been mostly good. There were, as you would expect, a couple of complaints from parents who said the car ride to work and school was uncomfortable because they had to explain what the terms 'rug-munching' and 'strap-on' meant.

I brought it up in the meeting.

'So, what about that Alison Mau story? How hot is that, eh?'

'Yeah. About that,' Leon said calmly, before exploding like a bottle of Diet Coke with some Mentos mints dropped in. 'What the FUCK were you thinking?'

'What do you mean?' I replied, even though I knew exactly what he meant.

'That song at eight o'clock in the fucking morning! What were you thinking?'

'Come on, mate. Admit it. It was funny!' I reasoned.

'Not at 8 am it wasn't! How long have you been doing this? I expect way better judgement than that.'

Then he turned his attention to my long-suffering co-hosts Jay-Jay and Mike. 'And as for you two. You guys are in the studio as well, why didn't you stop this from going to air?'

Good one. So Leon was pissed at me. And now Jay-Jay and Mike were too. It is never that much fun having 75 per cent of the room hating your guts. 'Don't bother coming in to work tomorrow!' Leon spat. 'I'm going to have to suspend you for the day, without pay.'

Alison Mau had not complained—I doubt she or her smoking-hot new lady friend had even heard about it. It was Leon who was pissed off—as well as being a radio programmer he is also a parent. And as bad luck would have it he was in his car with his kids at the time doing the school drop-off and was fuming at my poor judgement. 'Fuck, mate! You can't be talking about that sort of shit at 8 am. What were you thinking?'

His argument was the same as the handful of complaints we got from irate parents. 'Come on, mate,' I said, trying to calm him down, 'the lyrics would have gone over the heads of any kids listening. And you must admit the song was a little bit funny!' But the only thing he was prepared to admit was that I was suspended. The Broadcasting Standards Authority agreed with Leon too and fined the company $2000. That's a pretty hefty punishment for singing one terrible song—imagine how much a dreadful band like Nickelback would have to pay if they were stung with a two grand fine every time they sang a bad song?

Some newspapers picked up on my suspension and ran a story about it. They didn't give a rat's arse about some clown on a top 40 radio station being stood down— that wasn't newsworthy. It was just another angle and another excuse for them to write another titillating piece about

Alison Mau. And these follow-up newspaper stories are how Alison Mau heard about the song and that is why she will never invite me around to her house to watch her and her equally hot partner have a pillow-fight in their silk shorty pyjamas while the Cyndi Lauper hit 'Girls Just Want to Have Fun' blasts on the stereo. That's what attractive women do when they get together, isn't it?

**Complaint under section 8(1B)(b)(i) of the Broadcasting Act 1989**
*The Edge Morning Madhouse*—host sang jingle about a public figure being 'into ladies'—included phrases, 'when they make love do they have to put a strap on it', she 'wanted to go rug-munching' and she 'got sick of dicks'—broadcaster upheld complaint under good taste and decency—action taken allegedly insufficient

**Findings**
Standard 1 (good taste and decency)—song lyrics were unacceptable for broadcast at 8.20 am—serious breach of good taste and decency—action taken by broadcaster was insufficient—upheld

**Orders**
Section 16(4)—costs to the Crown $2000

# ☑ BURY THE HATCHET (THE BIG APOLOGY)

It sucks to have people hate you. Essentially, we all want to be liked, don't we? So for the next item on my bucket list I was going to set out to bury the hatchet with an Australian celebrity I had got on the wrong side of. And I'm not just using that as a figure of speech, either. I wanted to bury the hatchet literally. But before we get into that, there are a few other apologies I need to make first that are long overdue.

## Jason and Sam West

Jason and Sam are the two sons of Mike West, my old co-host from my first radio job at 2XS FM in Palmerston North. Mike West and I started working together when Jase was about two or three and Sam was yet to be born.

I owe both these boys an apology. I spent a considerable amount of time around them in the first ten years of their lives, so it is only due to exceptional parenting that these two kids ended up growing up into decent adults.

When Jason started at kindergarten he was overheard by a teacher calling another little boy a name. I would imagine name-calling is a daily occurrence at kindies but this incident was offensive enough for the teacher to call Jase's parents, Mike and Amanda, and ask them to come in for a meeting about their son's behaviour, which they dutifully did.

'I don't quite know how to put this,' the kindy teacher started, 'but earlier today Jason was painting when another boy came and snatched his brush.' So far so good, sounds like poor young Jase is the victim of bullying at this point.

'But . . .' she continued, 'instead of asking one of the staff for help, Jason screamed at the boy to give his brush back and repeatedly called him "penis breath"! He was saying, "Give it back, penis breath! Give it back, penis breath!" It was very loud and everyone could hear.'

Jason's parents were mortified. By now hours had passed since the incident took place, so Jason was just sitting on the floor playing with some toys, blissfully unaware of the trouble he was in and the embarrassment he had caused his parents.

They called him over.

'Jason, did you call another boy a nasty name today?'

Jason shrugged his shoulders and said he couldn't remember, so they tried a different tack.

'Did you call one of your friends . . . penis breath?'

Without a hint of remorse, Jason admitted that he had

indeed done so. His mum continued her line of questioning as the teacher watched on with those judgemental teacher eyes. You know the look. The one that suggests everything the kid does wrong is due to what a shit job the parents are doing.

'Do you know what "penis breath" means, Jason?' Amanda asked.

Of course he had absolutely no idea. He was only three.

'Where did you learn to say that, Jason?'

Jason's innocent eyes lit up. 'Dom told me!'

It was true. I had taught him. But only because a three-year-old saying something so outrageous is actually quite hilarious.

Yes, I was in a world of shit and the next morning the atmosphere in the studio could best be described as icy. I tried to get Mike West to admit it was pretty damn funny. And he agreed with me, eventually . . . about ten years later.

I owe Jason's younger brother, Sam, an apology for the same sort of offence really—low-level child exploitation. I was in my mid twenties and was pursuing a girl called Leanne. Well, I say pursuing, she might say stalking. It's all a bit of a grey area.

On one of our early dates Leanne mentioned that she loved kids and wanted a baby as soon as she met the right guy. Eager to make a good impression, I lied and indicated that I too wanted a baby ASAP. I got the feeling she could see through my lie, though, and I felt the need to do something drastic to back up my words with actions.

We had arranged to meet at her place for lunch the next day, so prior to heading around there I called in at Mike West's house and 'borrowed' Sam, his two-year-old, essentially for the purpose of trying to get Leanne to sleep with me.

Mike gave me a crash course in how to operate the car seat and a bag with some other bits and pieces, and little Sam and I were on our way.

The poor little guy must have been wondering what the hell was going on. I spent a lot of time with him and his family but never really paid him too much attention. Now here I was, alone with him at this strange girl's house, smothering him in kisses and cuddles and telling him how cute he was.

This strategic lunch date for three was cut short after about twenty minutes when little Sam diverted from the script. Suddenly I had a very strong smelling 'code brown' on my hands. It wasn't actually on my hands, thank god! But this toddler I was in possession of had soiled himself and I fully freaked out. There was a fresh nappy in the baby bag Mike West had given me but there was no way I wanted this job. I'm pretty certain my reaction was a dead giveaway that kids were not something I had the slightest interest in. Sam and I left Leanne's place without delay. I carried him out to the car with my arms outstretched to keep the stench as far away from my nose as possible, then drove him home with all four windows down.

Before you say something like 'Awww, that poor kid!' I want to assure you he was fine. I am the one who deserves your sympathy! After that failed experiment I never asked to borrow my mate's toddler as a chick magnet ever again. And because Leanne had an inkling that we weren't on the same page when it came to babies, she was as reluctant to let me take her pants off as I was reluctant to take little Sam's pants off.

## My ex-girlfriend, Kim, and our old flatmate, Mark

Kim was my first true love, my first proper girlfriend. On and off, we lasted for the best part of five years (which during your late teens and early twenties seems like a lifetime). For a while we lived together with a flatmate, Mark, and I owe both of them an apology for what became known as 'the lino incident'.

Kim was dead against pornography, hated it with a passion. Unfortunately, I loved pornography with the same level of enthusiasm. Knowing just how much she despised it I limited my collection to just one magazine at any given time. And, knowing how much trouble I would be in if she ever discovered this one magazine, I had come up with the ultimate hiding place. A hiding place so good that even a full and thorough police search of the property may have failed to find it.

This one fateful day Kim had the vacuum cleaner out and decided to do the bathroom and toilet. Her plan was to suck up the surface dust and dirt, then mop the floors. When she reached the far left corner of the room, the vacuum cleaner nozzle lifted the lino right up off the floor. Kim pulled the nozzle away but the lino was stuck to the end of it. And then she saw it. Right there on the floor, where it had been concealed by the lino—the November 1994 issue of *Playboy*, with Pamela Anderson on the cover.

What I thought was the world's greatest hiding place had been discovered.

Fortunately, I was at work at the time, which gave poor Kim an opportunity to calm down a tad. When I got home later my prized magazine was sitting on the kitchen bench, meaning that I saw it before I saw Kim. This gave me approximately six seconds to think of an excuse. In that limited time, 'It's not mine!' was the very best I could come up with! If I was telling the truth, it meant the magazine must have belonged to our flatmate, Mark.

Finally, after twenty minutes of crying and shouting by Kim and strenuous denials by myself, Mark got home. Instead of giving me the chance to brief Mark about the dilemma and ask him to catch this grenade for me, Kim raced out the front door with my prized *Playboy* in hand and met Mark on the front porch.

'Mark. Is this your magazine?' she demanded.

Mark looked confused. 'Eh? What?'

'Is this your magazine?' Kim repeated. 'I found it under the lino in the toilet.'

I stood next to Kim, looking like a dead man walking.

Going by Kim's tone of voice and the look of fear in my eyes, Mark managed to figure out what was happening and did the honourable thing.

'Ah, yep, that's mine. I put it there ages ago and forgot about it. Sorry.'

What a top bastard. He possibly saved my life. Sure, Kim thought he was a perverted deviant but at least I was off the hook.

**Keisha Castle-Hughes**
At the age of thirteen Keisha Castle-Hughes was nominated for an Academy Award for her incredible performance in *Whale Rider*.

She was eleven when this film was shot. This was her first acting job and the entire country was moved by just how endearing and natural her performance was.

It was widely accepted that Keisha would be bloody lucky to win. She was in the 'Best Actress' category, up against Naomi Watts, Samantha Morton, Diane Keaton and the very attractive Charlize Theron, who had made herself very unattractive for the movie *Monster*. The Academy has a thing for good-looking people who make themselves ugly for their craft.

To let Keisha know she had the support of New Zealand behind her we encouraged listeners to write Keisha a good luck message and send it to us. Our show producer at the time, my old mate Geoff Stagg, was put in charge of hand-picking the best 500 messages and getting them bound together as a book, a little something for Keisha to read on the plane.

The night before Keisha left we met up with her and her mum Desrae Hughes, to hand over this book on behalf of Edge listeners.

Desrae seemed overwhelmed by the generous words from total strangers for her daughter. Keisha seemed grateful but not really fussed by the big book of compliments. I suppose when you're thirteen and you manage to score an Oscar nomination the first time you have a crack at acting you learn to take things in your stride. But since the Academy had judged her to be one of the five best actresses in the world, you'd think she could have at least ACTED as though she was impressed by the gesture.

As Keisha sat with us and randomly flicked through the book, it fell open on a page that made her laugh raucously.

'This is my favourite one!' she said.

We couldn't see the book from where we sat so we asked her to read it out, which she did:

```
Hey Keisha,
Diane Keaton is way better than you.
   You are fucking shit and I hope your
plane crashes on the way to the awards.
And if somehow your plane doesn't crash
I hope you lose when you get there.
```

Keisha was still in hysterics, demonstrating a maturity and thick skin that most people don't develop until much later in life. We were mortified. And because we hadn't bothered to double-check our producer's work, we had no idea if there were any other inappropriate messages in that book. As soon as Keisha and her mum left we all said the same thing at the same time: 'FUCKING GEOFF!'

The anonymous author of that email had three wishes:

1. Dianne Keaton to win.

2. Keisha's plane to crash.

3. Keisha to lose.

Fortunately, only one of their three wishes came true and it was not a midair aviation tragedy!

## Misty, the family pet

Misty was the Harvey family cat, a beautiful black and white Persian who was well loved. Not that you would know it from looking at her. She had some incurable eye condition from birth which meant her eyes were always gunky and weeping. Come to think of it, I hope it was an eye condition. Maybe she was always sad but was unable to wipe away her own tears since she lacked opposable thumbs.

I owe Misty an apology for using her much the same way I used Mark, my old flatmate. She took the rap for me over something I did. Gutlessly, I blamed her because she couldn't defend herself.

I was sixteen and got drunk at a party drinking from a fifty-litre keg of Rheineck. In the late eighties Rheineck was the popular beer to drink. It's probably worth mentioning that this was also about the same time that black slip-on kung-fu shoes and T-shirts with Fido Dido on them were also massively popular. You can still buy Rheineck now, which means some people must still like it. Probably people who want to drink beer but want to spend as little as possible on it!

I was on a super-strict curfew of midnight, so I made

sure I drank as much of this delicious quality brew as I could. I even filled up an empty Coke bottle with Rheineck for the walk home.

I got home with eight minutes to spare and made the appropriate amount of noise—enough to wake Mum and Dad so they knew I got home in time, but not so much noise that they would get out of bed and discover I was trashed.

I hopped into bed and shut my eyes. And that is when the room started spinning. It all happened so quick I didn't have much time to think, all I knew was that I was going to be sick. I sat up and ripped the pillowcase from my pillow and threw up in that two, three, maybe four times in quick succession. I had to do this as quietly and discreetly as possible so Mum and Dad would not be disturbed.

When I was sure it was all out I got the surprisingly heavy sack of spew and put it in the corner of my wardrobe, then chucked some clothes and shoes on top of it, with the intention of disposing of it the following day.

It was probably about a month later when Mum was in my room looking for something (maybe a bad smell?) that she discovered the pillowcase with a foul stench and an unidentifiable hard substance caked to the fabric.

She brought it downstairs to where I was watching the telly.

'Dominic, what the hell is this?'

'Fuck! Fuck! Fuck!' I remember thinking to myself as I inspected the pillowcase with a dumb look on my face. Up until now I had forgotten all about it. How I had lived in that room with that sack of sick is beyond me. It must have smelt like a rotting corpse but I hadn't even noticed it. Now I had to think fast, which has never been one of my strengths. Had I been good at thinking fast I probably wouldn't have vomited into a bloody pillowcase in the first place!

'I dunno,' I said to Mum. Genius, pure genius.

Mum offered her own theory as she put her nose a couple of inches away from the hard mess and sniffed. 'I wonder if Misty has been sick.'

Suddenly, I had a light-bulb moment. Mum had planted the seed and I was going to run with it.

'Oh, yeah. Misty has been sleeping in my wardrobe a bit lately. That's what it will be.'

Logistically, it was impossible. There was no way a cat could have got into my wardrobe, climbed under a pile of clothes and shoes, wriggled into the bottom of a pillowcase and vomited such a large amount of fluid. But Mum seemed comfortable with the story and I was spared being grounded.

For the next few weeks Misty was banned from inside the house. I felt bad about it—not bad enough to own up, though. Owning up would mean being grounded, and being grounded would potentially mean missing out on more keg parties with Rheineck.

## Sprite NZ

Sprite was launched in New Zealand in 1987, when I was fourteen and had a face full of angry red pimples. The sort of pimples that look, and actually were, sore to touch.

Before that there was a similar drink called 'Leed' which you may or may not remember. You probably don't. They tend not to phase out a product on account of it being too popular with customers.

So Leed was taken off the shelves and replaced with Sprite, which tasted the same but was better branded. I remember the year that Sprite came to New Zealand because I was employed by Coca-Cola to help with the launch of the product. Coincidentally, this was the first time I dipped my toes into the pristine waters of white-collar crime.

That's right. I became a small-time fraudster.

I landed the dream job for a fourteen-year-old boy. A team of about ten of us were employed for the two weeks of the school holidays and paid bloody well—$250 a week each! To put that in perspective I had a paper round at that time which paid $16 a week.

The Sprite job brief was simple—knock on people's doors and tell them about this new soft drink on the market, then offer them a free can. If the householder was out, they lucked out on the free drink and got a postcard instead.

The team of door-knockers were driven to the different neighbourhoods in a mini-van by our supervisor, another student who was slightly older and slightly less pimply than the rest of us. His supervising skills were non-existent; I'm pretty sure his only qualification for the job was his driver's licence. He would park up and sit in the van listening to his cassette walkman and play Donkey Kong on his Nintendo Game & Watch while the younger boys went door-knocking.

By the start of week two I devised my scam. Whenever I went to a property where the householder was out, I would just mark on the sheet that they were in and tick my list to indicate they'd received their complimentary can. I bought my not very bossy boss in on my scam and, for a cut, he gladly drove by my house each afternoon, allowing me to drop off the stock gained through my devious plan.

By the time the job finished I had $500 in the bank and enough Sprite to give a man type 2 diabetes. The product is still on the market and is one of New Zealand's bestselling soft drinks. That success has absolutely nothing to do with my role in the launch. If it is any consolation, karma came and got me the following term when I discovered that if you drink four to five cans of Sprite every day for a month you will end up with excruciatingly painful constipation. (Or at least that's what happened to me.)

It's amazing how good an apology can make you feel. That felt quite cathartic, righting all those wrongs. Although, in the process of saying sorry to Keisha Castle-Hughes I have probably now offended my old producer Geoff Stagg. If this is the case, I am very sorry for upsetting you, Geoff . . . but you should have checked those messages before you had the book bound.

Now to the big apology. This one was going to take more than a bunch of words to repair. In order to bury the hatchet I would need to bury an actual hatchet. And the celebrity at the centre of all of this? Rove McManus, the adorable little Aussie. The human equivalent of one of those clip koalas you buy at the airports in Australia. Each week he would end his hugely popular TV show by saying, 'Say hi to your mum for me,' and each week, Mum would appreciate the shout-out. Everybody loves

Rove and Rove loves everybody, right? WRONG! I managed to piss him off.

But to be fair, in hindsight, I do wonder if he was bothered at all or if it was just his people being offended on his behalf. I'll tell you what happened and you can make your own mind up.

TV3 had brought Rove over to New Zealand for a promotional visit. So Rove came in to our studio with his manager and a couple of people from the TV3 publicity department. We had a twenty- or thirty-minute chat with him, broken up with a couple of songs. I can't recall specifics of the interview but I'm pretty sure it would have been fun. Rove is a pro and a naturally funny bloke. The interview wrapped up and we all stepped outside the studio and posed for a photo for the radio station website. Rove then left and we carried on with the show, unaware that anything was wrong.

Less than an hour after that, I got a phone call from my good friend Jana Rangooni, who was the group program director of our company. She was the boss of my boss. She was the boss that you only ever get to see if the news is really good (pay rise) or really bad (you're fired). So in radio it is usually the latter.

'What on earth did you do to Rove this morning?' she asked.

Her choice of words and tone of voice told me we had done something real bad—like held him down and shaved his eyebrow off bad—but I didn't have a clue what she was on about.

Jana continued. 'I've just got off the phone from TV3 publicity and they said he is really upset. He left your building and said he never wants to go back there again.'

I was bewildered. I still had no idea what Jana was going on about. I assumed she must have her wires crossed and one of Rove's other interviews that morning must have gone pear-shaped.

Unfortunately, there were no crossed wires at all. An interview had gone pear-shaped . . . and it was definitely our one. This was late in 2007, and at the time there were magazines out in the shops with paparazzi photos of Rove and the Australian actress Tasma Walton. This was almost a year after the death of his first wife, Belinda Emmett, to cancer. So to ignore these fresh rumours of a friendship or relationship would, I think, have been short-changing the audience. What everyone wanted to know was whether or not he was seeing anyone.

```
Me: Have you been out on any dates? Are
you seeing anyone?
Rove (laughing): Yes—I'm going out with
John Campbell. That's why I'm here, to
hopefully hook up with him.
Mike: So . . . you're not seeing anybody?
Rove: No.
Mike: No? Okay.
```

And that was it. We asked the question. Rove deflected it with a funny answer. Then we moved on. Was it insensitive? I don't know. I don't think it was. That definitely wasn't the intention anyway. I wasn't trying to be edgy or provocative or anything.

And another thing, it was bloody Mike Puru who re-asked the question . . . why wasn't he the one getting any of the blame for this?

The phone call from Jana Rangooni was the first inkling I had that anything was out of order. Jana did that thing where someone suggests you should do something but really they are telling you to do it. She 'suggested' I should write an apology letter on radio station letterhead and drop it off at the reception of the SkyCity Grand Hotel, where Rove was staying. The whole thing felt a little bit over the top, and I really hate saying sorry when I don't actually mean it, but I went along with it anyway.

I sheepishly walked into the foyer of the hotel and hoped like hell I would not happen to bump into Rove. I made it to reception, handed over the envelope and scurried off.

Then . . . nothing!

No word from Rove's camp. No call from TV3 thanking me for doing some damage control. NOTHING. I was left hanging.

I am not up to speed with all the ins and outs of etiquette but I thought the whole point of one of these forced apologies was so the person who had been wronged got the chance to be all smug and say 'apology accepted'.

Over the years Rove kept coming back to New Zealand for these promo visits. The TV3 publicity department would put together his schedule for each visit and we were always blacklisted. Our producer would put in an interview request and TV3 would decline it. We are in a building with a cluster of other radio stations so we would see Rove and his entourage walk past our window. It was all a bit odd—nobody had even given us a date that our Rove-ban would be lifted. As far as we knew we were on the interview circuit equivalent of preventative detention. Maybe there was no chance of a Rove-vival. Sorry. Terrible wordplay joke, punishable by death in some countries. But I couldn't resist.

Then one day out of the blue our opportunity came to put things right with Rove McManus.

Rove was coming to New Zealand to do some stand-up comedy shows. Since this trip was nothing to do with his TV show, his interview schedule was being put together by an independent publicist. This publicist was obviously unaware of our ban because our producer put a request in and it was accepted. It would potentially be awkward but we were okay with that—folks like Ricky Gervais have worked hard to make awkwardness a legitimate form of humour and entertainment. The audience had been filled in on the whole back story and were prepared for whatever might happen next.

```
Rove: I just looked across the table and
there is an axe on the desk!
Dom: Actually if I may correct you, it
is a hatchet.
Rove: Sorry. Yes. That is true. It is the
axe equivalent of me. It's very small.
```

**Dom:** Now the reason we have got the hatchet—we haven't had you in our studio for a number of years now. And the last time we had you in, things were a little weird.

**Rove:** Really? Things got a little awkward? Did we touch? Did we embrace?

**Dom:** No, it wasn't awkward. But then it got awkward after you left. And there were publicists and people running around and I had to write you an apology letter. And since then you haven't been in to see us.

**Rove:** Oh, now I get it. This hatchet here . . . WE CAN BURY IT! We can bury the hatchet! Wow. How long did that take? I was thinking, where is he going with this—is he going to kill me?

**Dom:** No, we don't have murder on the mind. But it has hurt us—every time you've come back to New Zealand we switch on the telly and we see you on *Campbell Live* but you never come to see us anymore.

**Rove:** Well, you have to remember, that doesn't always come to me, that sort of stuff. There are people that go, 'We'll go here or we'll go there,' and I get taken there.

**Dom:** So everything's good? There's no bad blood between us?

> **Rove:** No! I hope not.
> **Dom:** Well, down on the street below there are some road works going on. And there's a big giant hole down there. Could we go outside and bury the hatchet?
> **Rove:** I would love to!

And we did. So now, beneath the asphalt on the corner of St Mary's Road and Jervois Road in Auckland, is a hatchet buried there by Rove McManus and me.

During that interview Rove was either playing dumb or he actually had no recollection of what happened. I suspect it is probably a bit of both. He probably read my apology letter then screwed it up and thought nothing more of it.

Clearing the air felt good. Real good. So did having an actual hatchet-burying ceremony. People often throw round the saying 'Let's bury the hatchet' but I think it has far more impact when you literally go to the effort of burying one. Then again, maybe it's a case-by-case sort of thing. Tiger Woods allegedly cheated on his ex-wife Elin with more than 100 other women. If I was Tiger, and Elin turned up to the gates of my mansion with a shiny new miniature axe in her hand, I don't think my first instinct would be to let her in, assuming that she wanted to forgive me and have a fresh start. In extreme cases, maybe a better idea would be to turn up with a broom and offer to sweep things under the carpet.

*The options were to kiss and make up or bury the hatchet.
Wisely, Rove went for option 2.*

# ☑ KISS A CELEBRITY'S ARSE (LITERALLY)

There are four very common expressions that all have pretty much the same meaning:

- brown noser
- arse-kisser
- to piss in one's pocket
- to blow smoke up someone's arse.

I'd love to know where these terms came from in the first place. Because, let's be honest, none of them actually sound all that pleasant, even for the recipient.

If someone really liked you and wanted to let you know, urinating into the pocket of the trousers you had on would definitely be the wrong way to go about it. Likewise, having someone blow a cloud of smoke into your rectum would probably just seem weird rather than flattering.

Maybe these were all things that people used to do to show their appreciation for one another centuries ago. Thankfully, Hallmark has come along since then and put out a card for just about any occasion, so you can let someone you admire know how you feel without ending up with faecal matter on the tip of your nose. Much cleaner and far less awkward.

There are two groups of people who come into contact with more arse-kissers than anybody else—employers and celebrities. Employers only get it from staff members who have an ulterior motive—they are greasing for a promotion or a raise—whereas the arse-kissing that celebrities get is usually genuine respect from fans. The modern-day arse-kiss from a fan to a celebrity involves a photo on a phone or an autograph on some sort of merchandise.

I was going to change that. I was going to show my appreciation of someone who I admire and respect by kissing his arse . . . literally. The idea was suggested by my work colleagues, Jay-Jay Feeney and Mike Puru, who had accused me on numerous occasions of being more generous with my praise of celebrity guests than they perhaps deserved.

That *lucky* recipient? New Zealand cricketer Martin Guptill.

It was on Monday 12 December 2011 that the New Zealand cricket team had a historic test match win against Australia in Australia. It was the first time in twenty-six years the Black Caps had managed to do this, so these guys became legends overnight.

Martin 'Guppy' Guptill was part of that team.

We arranged for Martin to come into the studio after he got back to New Zealand. We told him the truth, too. This is the text I sent to arrange the interview:

```
Hey mate, any chance you could come in at
8 am on Wednesday? We just want to talk
cricket and kiss your arse a little.
```

When he got to the studio for his interview I had decided to back out of it. It had seemed like a good idea when Martin Guptill was not right in front of me. But now we were face to face, the whole idea just seemed too bizarre.

Then, towards the end of the interview, Jay-Jay brought it up.

**Jay-Jay:** Dom, didn't you have something you wanted to ask Martin?
**Me:** Yeah, I did. But I think I'm going to have to change my mind. I had this idea in a taxi when I was a bit drunk and it seemed like a good idea then. But I don't really want to do it anymore.
**Mike:** Nah, you can't wuss out. You have to ask him.
**Martin:** Now I'm nervous. What the hell is it?
**Me:** I had this item on my bucket list which requires the assistance of a

> famous person. I was going to ask you, but I don't think I can. Now that I'm sober it's just far too embarrassing!
> **Jay-Jay:** Come on, Dom, you have to ask him.
> **Me:** All right, all right. One thing that I wanted to do as one of the items on my bucket list was to LITERALLY kiss a famous person's arse.

Martin nervously laughed, for a long time—around ten seconds, I reckon.

I think he was using his laugh to stall for time while he thought about how to answer this very odd request. Then, his response came:

> **Martin:** Yeah, why not!
> **Jay-Jay:** See, there ya go, Dom! You don't know until you ask. So all you have to do, Martin, is drop your pants and stick your butt cheek out. This is going to be awesome.
> **Me:** Oh god, I'm so embarrassed.
> **Mike:** Yeah, so am I!
> **Martin:** Why are you guys embarrassed? I'm the one who's about to drop my shorts!

I think all four of us in the studio felt embarrassed. This seems to be a recurring theme with our show. We constantly have these 'seemed like a good idea at the time' moments. The ideas come to us when we're off the air or in planning meetings or while we're out drinking, and they seem hilarious. It's not until we're in the studio and about to broadcast it that we start to get a sense of just how messed up the idea actually is.

One of the best (or worst) examples of this is something that got us a slap on the wrist from the Broadcasting Standards Authority. It was an idea that came to us somewhere between 2 and 3 am at a staff party.

Pop star Pink was coming to the country to do some shows and we had tickets to give away. After a good session on the 42Belows we all agreed that 'Pee Your Pants for Pink' was pretty much the funniest idea for a segment ever since the invention of the very first radio.

It wasn't until the following Monday at 8.30 am, when our Wellington reporter was live on the air with us while a woman in her late twenties intentionally soiled herself in order to win these tickets, that we realised just how wrong this was. Hindsight and sobriety are both wonderful things.

Martin Guptill loosened the belt of his cargo shorts and pulled his undies and shorts down to the middle of his thighs and bent over. Much like a home owner apologises to unexpected visitors for the mess, Martin warned us that it could be 'pretty hairy back there'.

For the record, a lack of a tan was probably more of an issue than an abundance of hair—his bum was whiter than his cricket trousers on the first day of a test match.

## KISS A CELEBRITY'S ARSE (LITERALLY)

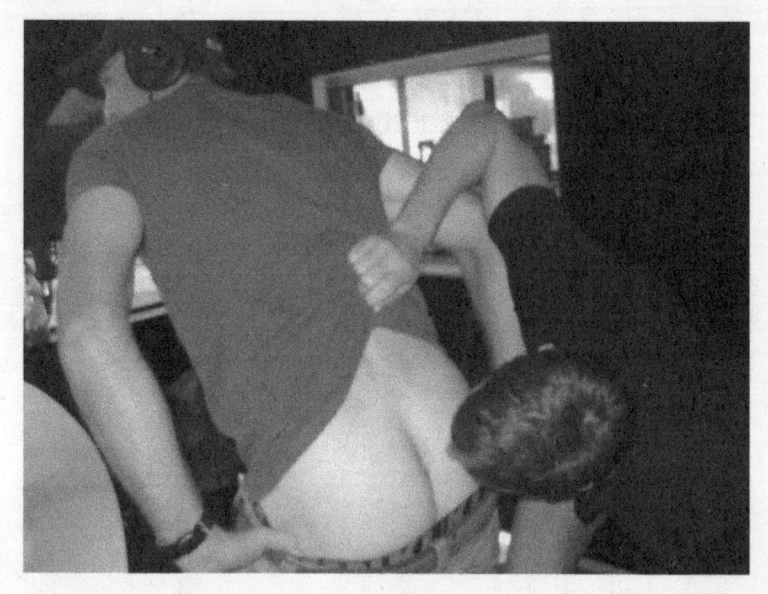

*I took Martin Guptill's advice and stayed reasonably close to the crease.*

I dropped to one knee then went in for a kiss on the right cheek.

I would like to tell you that it tasted like a combination of ingredients that only the rear end of a champion could possess. Things like sweat, determination, raw talent, tenacity and victory. But the truth is it just tasted like . . . well, skin, I suppose. Much like kissing your own wrist only far more humiliating.

After that we shook hands and exchanged a bit of small talk as I walked Martin out of our offices to the car park. It had all the awkwardness of the morning after a one-night stand.

As Martin drove off, he shouted out his window that he would call me sometime . . . but I knew he never would. I'm not sure who felt more violated by the arse-kiss; we may have to call that one a draw. But I was on Twitter later that morning and saw this tweet from Martin and I find it hard to disagree with him:

```
@Martyguptill Having @DomHarvey kissing
my ass is possibly the weirdest thing I
have been involved in.
```

# ☑ EAT AT A BUFFET UNTIL I THROW UP

I have always been intrigued by the idea of the buffet-style restaurant.

Like most people, I suppose I am wired to enjoy the feeling of getting a good deal. If you go to restaurant and spend $30 but eat a quantity of food worth a greater amount, it is a win! Scorecard: you 1, restaurant 0. You have legally robbed the restaurant.

I remember when Valentines Family Restaurant first opened for business in Palmerston North in the early 1990s. This was when they used to have those impressive statues made from margarine. I was in my late teens when Valentines came to town—finally controlling my own life, away from the nagging of my parents. Back then, I used to go out of my way in search of buffets. The Pizza Hut all-you-can-eat Tuesdays in Palmerston North were definitely a highlight of the week for me and my equally famished and frugal friends.

Then something happened which took the gloss off buffets for me. Really it was a culmination of things.

1. I hit twenty-five and my metabolism came screeching to a slowdown. All of a sudden, out of the fifteen slices of pizza I put in every Tuesday, only ten would come back out. The metabolic slowdown is a cruel side effect of ageing, made even crueller by the way it comes on without any sort of warning. The first you know about it is usually an honest aunty you have not seen since last Christmas pointing out just how unkind the year has been to you. Not usually said with that level of diplomacy, though.

2. I started to appreciate quality over quantity. When I first left Mum and Dad's place and started flatting, the idea of going to a restaurant where I could see some exposed white china under my food seemed outrageous. Things like ambience and quality food cooked by a chef who knew what he was up to in the kitchen seemed pretentious to my younger self. These were the days where me and

my mates would go to the fish'n'chip shop and fill up our plastic containers with so much Chinese takeaway that the lid would often crack when we attempted to press it down and take it to the counter.

3. I finally came to the realisation that the sort of girls I wanted to sleep with were not that impressed by my capacity to go back to the buffet for a second and sometimes third bowl of pudding. And if any girl I liked did happen to be on the same page as me when it came to buffets, chances are we would both be too bloated to actually perform after the meal. Instead we would lie in bed while our stomachs provided a soundtrack, a duet of those bizarre little noises your gut makes when your natural acids are forced to work overtime to break down the food you have piled in. Not sexy.

My chequered relationship with food, and in particular the overeating of it, goes all the way back to 1983 and a big family Christmas at Nana and Granddad Williams' house in Levin.

These are the grandparents on my mum's side. Mum

is from a massive Catholic family—she is one of fourteen children. Because of his religious beliefs, Granddad did not believe in contraceptive devices. Evidently, he did believe in sexual intercourse, though.

One perk of this extra-large family was amazing Christmas gatherings. Nana and Granddad's house in Levin had this incredible basement, the ultimate man cave. It had Granddad's bar in the corner, a dartboard on the wall, pool table, table tennis table, spa pool, and a walk-down lounge area where the TV was. For Christmas the net on the table tennis table would be taken down and the table would be covered in paper and loaded up with the various bowls and plates of food that Nana had cooked or other family members had prepared. On a year with a good turnout it would be possible to end up with over fifty family members all in the basement.

Christmas of '83 was a biggie. When you are dealing with a family of that size it is never possible to get absolutely everybody together at Christmas time. But this particular year, there would only be a couple of absentees.

As a ten-year-old, this was exciting, because more people in attendance inevitably meant more presents. It also meant more cousins to play with during the day, and more food on the table tennis table (why this mattered to me I have no idea—it's not like there was ever a shortage of food anyway).

The day got off to a flying start. We woke up very early at home in Palmerston North and opened presents with our immediate family. Then we got dressed in our scratchy and uncomfortable church clothes and made the thirty-minute road trip to Levin, where we went to Christmas Day mass. For a ten-year-old kid, a forty-five to sixty-minute church service on the best day of the year was absolute torture. And it was important to sit quietly the whole time and resist playing or doing kid stuff with my cousins. Any silliness would result in a smack. It was the early eighties and this was a Catholic church—not only was smacking legal, it was almost applauded.

When the church service finally finished the whole huge family would convoy back to Nana and Granddad's for the awesomeness of a huge family Christmas to begin.

Lunch this particular year did not disappoint. I recall there being a hilarious communication breakdown about who was in charge of making the pavlovas, resulting in us having many more than we would ever need. This was not a bad thing. I may have only been ten but I had a pretty accommodating stomach when it came to foods I liked. And because Mum and Dad were in festive moods, the usual pressure to eat vegetables and other unwanted items was non-existent. Left to my own devices I ate nothing but plates of pork crackling, garlic bread and pavlova. Lots of pav. I would have definitely smashed at least a complete pavlova single-handedly.

When 6 pm came around, Grumpy Granddad made it known that Christmas was over for another year. A lot of the family had gone by this time anyway, but for the guests still in Nana and Granddad's basement, the message was clear: it is time for you to leave. Granddad did not make this announcement with words—it was far more obvious than that. He would switch off his cassette player that had been playing the 'Hooked on Christmas Classics' tape all day. Then he would remove the decorations from his artificial Christmas tree and dismantle it for the year.

Not long after that we loaded the car boot up with the presents we had acquired and set off back home to Palmerston North.

It was only a couple of minutes into the journey that my best Christmas ever took a turn for the worse. It came on very suddenly and I felt some of the worst stomach pains I had ever experienced in my ten years of life. By the time we got to the small town of Shannon, twenty kilometres out of Levin, I was in tears in the back seat of the car and Dad had to pull over so I could vomit on the side of the road. The tears and emergency stops continued for the entire trip back to Palmerston North, making the thirty-minute road trip take the best part of an hour.

At home, Mum made me a bed on the sofa and put a sick bowl on the ground. The sick bowl in our household was also the chippie bowl whenever guests came over. We were forbidden from mentioning that family secret in the presence of guests who were eating chips, though. I cannot explain why we only had the one bowl—perhaps bowls were really, really expensive in the eighties.

Mum and Dad then went around the corner for some Christmas drinks with friends, leaving Bridget, my twelve-year-old sister and the eldest, in charge. Before long it became apparent my health was not improving so Bridget called for Mum and Dad to come back home. Since this was pre-internet, Mum went to the bookcase in the hallway and got the *Reader's Digest Medical Dictionary* out. This was a fat book—probably 800 pages—with an index at the back where you could look up your symptoms. You'd then be directed to a number of pages suggesting what you might be suffering from. My symptoms were a high temperature, vomiting and terrible stomach pains. The medical dictionary's diagnosis was that I could have appendicitis which, if left untreated, could cause my appendix to explode inside me with fatal consequences.

```
The very first symptom is abdominal
pain. The pain is not contained to any
particular area; it is spread around the
lower right region of the abdomen. The
intensity of pain may increase as the
infection spreads. Another common symptom
is nausea and/or vomiting as soon as the
pain begins.
```

Naturally, my parents' panic rubbed off on me. So now I was vomiting profusely, in a world of pain and convinced I was probably going to die if I didn't get help in a hurry.

I was raced to hospital on Christmas night, turning my best Christmas ever into one of the worst days of my life.

The accident and emergency doctor checked me out and was not convinced by Mum's theory that it was my appendix, but decided it would be best to keep me overnight for observation anyway.

Not wanting to leave me all alone in hospital on Christmas night, one of my parents slept on a La-Z-Boy chair next to my bed. I can't recall which one had this chore because I was experiencing such discomfort that all I could think about was whether I was going to live or die and what would happen if my appendix exploded overnight.

As the night progressed the vomiting subsided and eventually I drifted off to sleep. The next morning, Boxing Day, I woke up and felt normal again. The unbearable pain from the evening before had completely disappeared. The doctor came in and lifted up my pyjama top and poked and prodded around my abdomen then decided it was safe to discharge me. In his professional opinion, all I had been suffering from was a serious case of overeating.

I felt terribly embarrassed about the whole thing. It was quite humiliating sitting on the side of a hospital bed in the children's ward while the doctor, who looked pissed off at having to work on Boxing Day, was telling my parents off for not paying more attention to my calorie intake.

Unfortunately, overeating was not one of the possibilities raised in Mum's stupid *Reader's Digest Medical Dictionary*! What a kerfuffle.

The worst Christmas Day ever was followed by the worst Christmas holidays ever—not only was I nicknamed Porky by my siblings and parents, but as per the doctor's orders, every single calorie I consumed was closely monitored by Mum. If I went into the kitchen for a drink of water I would hear her in the lounge yelling out, 'You better not be in the bloody fridge, Porky!' I know they had my best interests in mind but it would have been nicer if the olds had resisted using the unflattering nickname.

For my bucket list, I would rediscover my love of overeating. I would go to a buffet and ignore the warning signs my stomach would kindly send to my brain to inform me I had eaten a sufficient amount of food. I would be like the human version of a car being driven with the warning lights on. I would keep going until eventually I would break down. I would eat until I was physically sick. This time, though, the plan was to avoid ending up in the hospital's emergency ward.

The buffet restaurant of choice? Valentines. These places are still in existence, but nowhere near as popular as they were in the early nineties. These days their main clientele seems to be real old people who choose to dine there with their friends and family on their date of birth to take advantage of the 'Dine free on your birthday' offer that Valentines has become famous for.

That is precisely the time of year I selected—my birthday. So not only would I eat more than any sensible human being should ever eat, I would do so for free.

Yeah, I know. It was hardly the crime of the century . . . but it did all feel a little bit naughty.

The day of dining was planned with military precision to maximise my eating potential.

Breakfast? Check.

VALENTINES
DINE FREE*
on your
BIRTHDA
*Dine Free when dining with 3 other full paying guests.
Proof of Birthday required.
Not valid in combination with any other discounted offer.

Small lunch? Check.

Bowel movement? Check.

Nil by mouth for five hours before buffet? Check.

By the time we pulled into the Valentines car park at 1800 hours I was in the perfect frame of mind—hungry but not starving. I was ready to go to battle with the buffet.

Our party of nine got to the 280-capacity restaurant and found that we were one of only three groups there. Granted, it was pretty early on a Friday night but I did wonder if this place ever gets all that busy.

One of the groups already eating was a family. I noticed one of the younger members of this party walking from the food area back to his table clutching a loaf of garlic bread, the sort that is wrapped up in tinfoil, probably a dozen slices' worth. Wondering if he was getting it for himself or for the table to share I kept an eye on him and can confirm that:

```
a) It was not for sharing.
b) He managed to eat the whole lot.
```

He didn't bother breaking the pieces off either; he just shovelled that thing in whole. I don't think he knew he was being watched but he definitely had a secret admirer in me over on table 27.

The centre of attention of one of the other groups was a lady having her seventy-sixth birthday in the company of her children and grandchildren. I know this because the youngest members of this table sang the happy birthday song and then started clapping and counting from one all the way through to seventy-six. It took these kids the best part of a minute to get all the way to their nana's age. Somehow, I don't think they'll bother doing that next year and, if the look on Nana's face was anything to go by, I don't think she'll be too upset if this chanting of the numbers doesn't become a tradition. The poor old thing looked overwhelmed by it all.

The near emptiness of the restaurant was convenient, though; it meant there were no lines for the buffet.

I walked around the food islands trying to formulate some sort of a strategy. In the end I decided to eat the food in appropriate groups, starting with the seafood.

This could potentially have been an unwise place to begin. When I told people my intentions, they were all a bit wary. It seems everybody has a story about someone who got sick from eating dodgy seafood at a buffet.

```
Helping #1
bowl of seafood chowder
smoked hoki
crab-flavoured surimi
shrimp cocktail
2 green-lipped mussels
```

I had survived the seafood leg of the day, phew. I took my empty plate back up to start again. A staff member dumped some fresh French fries into the metal tray under the heat lamp so I went for them.

**Helping #2**
```
chips
battered fish (2)
garlic bread (2)
marinated chicken wings
```

By now I had eaten enough. I felt full. Not full, full. But full enough. Under usual dining circumstances, if I ate anything more beyond this it would just be because I enjoyed the taste. But I had to get back up there. I still had so much more to get through. I drew inspiration from my young mate who had earlier made a loaf of garlic bread disappear.

**Helping #3**
```
pasta
butter chicken
rice
```

It was after the Indian favourite that my body's warning light came on. My arms felt heavy. I was burping. I stood up to stretch and twist my torso from side to side, as if that would somehow allow the food I had consumed to wriggle down further and create some more space, like a food version of that Tetris game. I still didn't feel even close to being sick, though, which was a daunting prospect. I now had the meat section to tackle and, if I made it that far, the puddings to come.

### Helping #4
```
meatballs
roast pork
champagne ham
```

I left the meatballs till last, which turned out to be a blessing. The meatballs were almost the tipping point. I'm unsure if that was because I was full already or if every diner feels that queasy after eating them.

It was during this fourth helping that I started to develop a terrible headache. I can't recall the last time I got a sore head from overeating but I can tell you it was not a nice feeling. Then the meat sweats came on.

I don't know if this is a real condition or just some old wives' tale—it certainly doesn't get a mention in the old *Reader's Digest Medical Dictionary*—but I find when I eat a substantial amount of meat products I start perspiring. Never a good look that, when you're sitting at a restaurant with a glistening forehead and a damp shirt sticking to your back.

Incredibly, I was still not sick. I went to the men's room and splashed a bit of cold water on my face, and while I was leaning over the basin I tried to tighten my stomach muscles in the hope this would bring on the regurgitation. Unfortunately it didn't. Now I was relying on the dessert bar to get me over the line.

### Helping #5
```
raspberry jelly
lemon tart
sliced peaches
```

    fresh cream
    pavlova
    marshmallow
    white chocolate mousse

Fortunately for me, where some people have a sweet tooth I have a mouth full of sweet teeth, which made this fifth (and what would be the final) helping a bit more bearable. I was well over halfway through it when, with very little warning, I suddenly felt the urge to purge. Finally, my body had reached the absolute limit. Hunched over, I scurried back to the toilets and sat down in a cubicle, where I experienced a poo–spew combo. The relief was indescribable.

The vomit was very colourful and seemed to be largely pudding based. Last in first out, I suppose. Pink and red with definite traces of chewed meatballs.

I still felt like absolute crap and had these bizarre shakes. But I had done it. I had conquered the buffet and it had not cost me a cent.

Then something happened after we left the restaurant that was, I think, even more embarrassing than my premeditated overindulgence. When we got back into the car my mum opened her handbag to reveal a plastic click-clack container she had smuggled in with her. It was empty when we arrived; now it was filled to the brim with pasta, broccoli and chicken wings.

'This will do me for my lunch and dinner tomorrow night!' she explained as the rest of the car looked at her with absolute disbelief. 'What? Most people would do this, you know!'

I don't know where Mum conducted her research but I highly doubt anybody apart from the occasional hard-up pensioner would ever do it. I didn't bother to argue, though. I was the one person in the car who had just eaten enough to make myself sick on my thirty-ninth birthday. I didn't feel it was my place to give anyone else a lecture on restaurant etiquette.

# ☑ STICK IT ALL ON BLACK

The plan was simple—get $1000 of my hard-earned money and chuck it all on black. All Black. The Rugby World Cup final. Sunday 23 October 2011.

My little brother Daniel is two years younger than me and is a passionate gambler. Well, a reformed passionate gambler. The day he had to take his golf clubs into Cash Converters to get some money to cover a bad bet was, I think, the last straw, and he gave up his dream of getting rich through being a professional punter. I don't think Dan wanted me to lose money when he came up with this suggestion for my bucket list—I think he saw an opportunity for me to have a pretty good pay day if I was prepared to 'grow some balls' (his words).

Our team were playing well. We were unbeaten in our pool matches, including the game against France, where we beat them by 20 points. And we managed to do all this without our not-so-secret weapon, Dan

Carter, who was taken out of the tournament with a groin injury, sending the nation into a mini-depression. The groin that had given a country so much pleasure was now bringing us utter despair. Add to this the unsettling TV images of our other star player, Captain Richie McCaw, limping through training sessions with a nasty foot injury.

Yet, despite these setbacks, the team still had an air of self-belief, as if winning this tournament was part of their destiny. In the quarterfinals they played Argentina and won well. In the semifinals they met Australia and gave us one of the most intense All Black games ever. So convincing and ferocious was their performance, nobody was in any doubt that after twenty-four years the William Webb Ellis trophy would again, finally, be all ours (insert menacing Dr Evil laugh here).

Now the final was here and the only thing standing between the All Blacks and the record books was a fairly average French side, a side we had beaten a month earlier, a side who were lucky to be in the final after a pretty shitty semifinal against Wales the previous weekend, a side who had a public falling-out with their coach and spent much of the week of the final sightseeing and fine dining instead of worrying about silly old rugby.

Naturally, the TAB had the All Blacks as red-hot favourites. Even though the French are known for their unpredictability and their love of dirty play, it was hard to see how they could stop this Black machine. I was going to prove just how much faith I had in our national team by having the bet of a lifetime.

If I lost, I would be an idiot. If I won, I would still be an idiot . . . but an idiot with a substantial amount of money.

I've never really been a gambler—I'm too much of a tight-arse. I love money. And, like most people, the money I love the most is the stuff that I can get my hands on without actually having to do any work. I also hate losing. This combination makes me a miserable gambler.

On the rare occasions I go to the races, my strategy is to pick the horse that is paying the most money and put $1 for a place on it. My little brother will kill me when he reads this. He is all about studying the form guide and making what he considers to be 'educated investments'. But with my method, the whole day's gambling can be done with one blue Kate Sheppard, allowing me to enjoy myself and participate without parting with a substantial amount of money.

Is this method effective? Well, no, not usually, if I am being perfectly honest. But one of these extreme long shots did come in. Once. It was at the Boxing Day races at Awapuni in Palmerston North. I was there with some mates who took their betting very seriously. They treated it as a science and would spend the morning reading the *Best Bets* form guide, studying the horses' form and taking notes. Their conversation in the back of the maxi taxi on the way to the track sounded like a foreign language to me, as they bantered about quinellas, firm tracks, boxed trifectas and scratchings.

So there we were, race 4, and I chucked a dollar down for a place on the horse that would yield me the greatest return. My friends laughed. Oh, how they laughed. According to their extensive research this horse was so old and slow it would have been faster if the jockey got on all fours, put the saddle on his back and carried the horse round the track. One of my friends even informed me that this horse would finish dead last, right behind Daylight. I looked in the race guide to read up on Daylight. It turns out Daylight is not the name of another slow horse—this is simply the go-to joke for all horsey people when they talk about a horse that finishes in last place a long way behind all the other horses. Good joke, horsey people, good joke!

Somehow, this horse I had a gold coin on found his accelerator on that day and he finished in second place, winning me $87 from my $1 investment. The huge win and the bragging rights I got over my mates made me decide to quit while I was ahead. So I retired a champion and have not bet on a horse that is likely to lose ever since.

I have dabbled in other sports betting but because I'm so frugal it's not really worth the effort. My last win was when I bet on the All Blacks to beat Fiji in a test match a few years back. The Blacks were paying $1.04 to beat Fiji by more than eighteen points. Of course, the All Blacks won convincingly and so did I.

I went back into the TAB to collect my original investment of $10 and my 40 cent profit. I'm pretty sure the fuel for my two trips to the TAB would have been worth more than the winnings.

But on the day of the Rugby World Cup final that was all about to change. Using my credit card, I put $1000 into an old online TAB account in my wife's name. For some, this sum may not be that big a deal. But for a tight-arse like me, it was monumental. It seemed like utter stupidity and went against everything I believe in. This single bet would be more than I had ever gambled in my entire life—even if you took all my previous bets and Lotto tickets and added them up.

When you bet on a rugby game there are hundreds of different ways you can give your money to the TAB. They make it very easy to lose. As their slogan goes: 'You know the odds, now give us your money.' I checked out the various odds and betting options on offer, but decided not to place a bet until just before kick-off.

My gut instinct was just to have this big bet on the All Blacks to win head-to-head. That was paying $1.09, meaning for every dollar you bet you will get your own dollar back plus nine cents of the TAB's money—if your prediction is accurate. So I would risk $1000 of my own money for the chance to get $90 back. It seemed like a big risk for a little reward so I ruled that one out and went for something a bit more daring, something that gave me the opportunity to make some decent cash. I will tell you exactly what that option was and whether or not I was successful at the end of this chapter.

The day had already been tense. The entire country had a strange feeling of nervous excitement about it. We knew the All Blacks would probably win the Rugby World Cup for the first time in twenty-four years. But we also knew the French team had a bad habit of knocking us out of this very tournament, so no one was allowing themselves to pop the corks on the French champagne until we had actually done the business and made the French toast.

*Before the game I got to have my photo taken with the All Blacks coach.*

The atmosphere around Auckland that day was electric. Most people were dressed in black. There were a few very vocal French supporters walking the streets but there was no mistaking which team had the home advantage! Depending on who you spoke to, the game was either going to be real close or a real thrashing by the All Blacks. But nobody was backing the French.

It was 6 pm when we left home and started the three-kilometre walk to Eden Park for the kick-off three hours later. We stopped at a bar on the way for a nerve-calming beer and spoke to some others who were also attempting to relax prior to kick-off.

We bumped into Robbie Magasiva, the famous New Zealand actor and a man who looks like he should have been an All Black. He seemed convinced the game was a done deal—the All Blacks were going to be too strong for France and would win by 30 points. It's funny, maybe it was the sheer size of Robbie or maybe it was the absolute belief he had in what he was saying, but I was with him all the way. By the time I finished my pint I, too, was convinced the only outcome would be an emphatic demolition job by Graham Henry's men in black.

By 7.30 pm we had made it to Eden Park and our category C seats for this (hopefully) historic game. These tickets cost us a fortune—$767 dollars each. But with a successful bet at the TAB I could recoup some of that money. Like Richie McCaw had been saying to the media all week—losing was simply not an option.

Next to us were a couple of men who worked

together. One of them was a South African who picked it to be a real close game. He said the French had played badly right through the tournament and were due for a blinder. But, in his opinion, even if the French played the game of their lives the All Blacks would still be too good for them.

His mate was an Englishman with a big voice and thick accent who was convinced it would be a walkover. Honestly, this guy was so adamant it was as if he had already seen the game played in his mind. 'The All Blacks will win by 25 points. End of story!' he announced. But he was actually just beginning. 'The first twenty minutes will be all about defence. The French are going to come out on fire. The All Blacks will get some points on the board from a try or penalties. Then the French will be rattled and forced to play risky rugby to catch up. And in the second half the All Blacks will just run away with it. You mark my words.'

But there is a big difference between telling a stranger in the seat next to you what the score is going to be and actually putting your money where your mouth is. I had my own ideas about the likely outcome and was ready to make the bet of my life.

It was now just half an hour before the game was due to kick off and I was probably as nervous as the players as I placed the bet on my iPhone. I did it very discreetly. My wife knew about it but I didn't want to tell anyone in the seats around us—mainly from fear of looking like the world's biggest tool if I lost the whole lot. But also I didn't want to be swayed by anyone else's opinions.

The option I selected was paying $3.25. Meaning if my prediction was correct, I would collect $3250 in just over two hours' time. Touch wood.

While it caused me immense pain to put my $1000 on the line, other Kiwis had no such trouble. In total $3.5 million worth of bets were placed on this game, including one losing bet of $50,000 made by someone who was convinced the first points would come from a New Zealand penalty kick.

Fifteen minutes into the game the first points of the match were scored. It was a try by Tony Woodcock. Great news for all New Zealanders . . . apart from the bloke who'd just lost his $50,000. My new English mate leaned forward in his seat. 'See, didn't I tell ya this was going to happen? You mark my words?'

Yes. He had told me. No, I was not marking his words. I didn't pay over $700 to sit at Eden Park and mark a stranger's words. This is the problem when you buy the cheapest tickets possible—you find yourself seated next to other people who have also got the cheap seats! Although in fairness, these were almost certainly the most expensive cheap seats you'll ever get your bum on.

After that things slowed down. Piri Weepu missed the conversion attempt. Then, before the first half ended, he missed another two penalty attempts. It could have been 13–0 to the All Blacks; instead they ran under the stands at half-time leading 5–0. The air in the stadium was humming. The excitement, belief and confidence were still there but nerves were creeping in. Thankfully, annoying old Johnny English next to me was no longer asking anyone to mark his words. I still felt confident about my $1000 bet. But at this point in time I was actually more nervous about the All Blacks losing the World Cup than me losing my money.

The second half was horrible to watch, horrible. I cannot think of a better word to describe it. It was just so intense.

Piri Weepu was relieved of his goal-kicking duties in the second half and Stephen Donald was given that unenviable task.

Stephen Donald. Nickname: Beaver. Possibly the most hated man in New Zealand rugby after a poor performance against Australia a year earlier that cost us the game. He was not even in consideration for the World Cup squad but got the call-up to be the backup for Aaron Cruden. Actually, Aaron Cruden wasn't even in consideration for the World Cup squad either, but he was drafted into the team after Dan Carter's replacement, Colin Slade, got injured.

Cruden was supposed to be in Los Angeles when the World Cup final was being played. He and his girlfriend had booked a trip to Disneyland, which had to be postponed. And an out-of-shape Stephen Donald was actually drinking beer and whitebaiting with friends on the Waikato River when he got a phone call which he must have assumed was one of his mates winding him up.

'Hello? Stephen? Graham Henry here. We need you to come and join the squad in Auckland.'

It was so unexpected I'm surprised Beaver didn't tell the person claiming to be the All Blacks coach to piss off before hanging up and going back to the fishing.

Sports talkback went crazy with outraged rugby fans when it was announced Donald was back in the squad. Poor bloke. Imagine getting that sort of hate for nothing more than playing one bad game of footy.

So there he was. Stephen Donald, in a jersey so tight and small that his midriff was exposed. He had put on a bit of weight over winter, since he wasn't expecting to get the call-up, and the jersey size the All Blacks management had on file for him was no longer the size he required.

He had a shot at goal in the forty-sixth minute, not an easy kick, either.

He struck it and the ball sailed over. Just. 8–0 to our All Blacks.

The most hated man in New Zealand rugby. The bloke who'd had 60,000 people at Eden Park nervously groaning when he came on had redeemed himself. He had gone from zero to hero with the kick of his life. We had a comfortable buffer. France would need to do more than just convert a try. The game was still ours to lose.

Then, only a minute after Stephen Donald's three-pointer, France scored and converted. 8–7 to the All Blacks. Fuck!

You could hear it being murmured around the seats: *'This cannot be happening!'* It felt like a movie we had all seen before . . . and none of us enjoyed it much the last time!

I wonder if any 111 calls were made by rugby fans suffering anxiety attacks. How sixty-five-year-old Graham Henry watched his team play without one of those oxygen hoses strapped beneath his nose is beyond me. The coach's box that he, Wayne Smith and Steve Hansen were sitting in must have smelt of a nasty combination of perspiration and the wee of elderly men. France had a sniff of victory now and began to play that way they only ever seem to play once every four years during knockout matches in World Cups. But the All Blacks were not going to pull their pants down this time.

Both teams played with all the grit, passion and determination that you could hope for in a final. Around Eden Park, thousands of people who had jumped through hoops to get these tickets—registered online, gone into ballots, then paid huge sums of money—had now resorted to watching the game through cracks in their fingers as they covered their faces with their hands.

In our area, a few rows back, one fan stood on his seat during a stoppage in play and made a speech to everyone within earshot. It was the sort of speech you'd expect from a coach at half-time. This spectator wanted more noise from us—this was the time our team needed us the most and we had to show them that we still believed in them. His speech went for all of twenty seconds before someone behind him said what we were all thinking: 'Shut the fuck up!' That caused a ripple of laughter, which was a nice way to briefly break the tension.

After the try to France the score remained unchanged for the remainder of the game. All thirty-three minutes.

The French were playing the game of their lives, but so were the All Blacks. All the beer talk about thrashings we'd heard prior to kick-off had vanished. My new English mate who had broken down the game into twenty-minute blocks was silenced. No longer was anyone concerned with killing the French or beating them by $x$ amount of points. Now the nation just wanted a win. It was irrelevant just how ugly that win was.

Then, with time up on the clock, France conceded a penalty and Andy Ellis kicked the ball out. We had won. Every single person in Eden Park jumped to their feet. Strangers hugged, danced, high-fived and kissed. Yes, it is 'just a game'. But it is our game and this was our moment. We were all New Zealanders and we had all just shared something very special. It had been twenty-four years since the All Blacks had won the very first Rugby World Cup but finally the engraver would be putting us on there for only the second time.

After most big events, people race out, trying to beat the crowds—but not on this day. Not one person. The game had been played and the last forty minutes had been about as difficult to watch as a sex tape starring your mum and dad. Now we had won, the nasty bit was over, and everybody just wanted to enjoy the moment, basking in the success of our team.

The captain and coach spoke. Hayley Westenra sang a depressing song, not that it mattered. Nothing was going to bring the mood of this crowd down. Fireworks went off. Confetti covered the field. And I forgot all about that bet of mine.

*Much like the French, I just about got my hands on the William Webb Ellis trophy.*

We left the ground and slowly walked out onto the streets of the Auckland suburb of Kingsland. Kiwis still hugged and sang, brought together by the lowest scoring game in the history of Rugby World Cup finals.

After walking for fifteen minutes we managed to flag down a taxi. Away from the noise and euphoria of the crowd of strangers and with a moment to myself I had a chance to reflect on what had just taken place.

The All Blacks had won by a point.

This meant my slip of paper that had been worth $1000 when I purchased it was now worth . . .

ABSOLUTELY NOTHING! I had put a grand on the All Blacks to win by between 21 and 30 points. Boy, I could not have been more wrong. What an idiot! I really did believe they would win by that much, though. So did Robbie Magasiva and the loud English bloke. My focus was on just how much I stood to win, not how much I was going to lose. But I suppose that's the trap that gamblers fall into, looking at the reward rather than risk.

Yes, I lost my money. An embarrassingly large amount, too—enough to sponsor one of those dollar-a-day African kids for almost three years.

There are two experiences I will gladly never repeat in my lifetime:

```
1. betting a large sum of money

2. sitting next to a chatty Pom during
   a major sporting event.
```

I actually cannot decide which one of these two things was more painful. Might have to call it a draw . . . don't bet on it, though.

# ☑ GO POOL CRASHING

Admit it, you have probably wanted to do this yourself at some stage.

I do not have my own pool. The people across the road from me do.

Every summer, when the days get hot, I get pool envy. I can hear my neighbours laughing, screaming and splashing in their pool. It always sounds like whatever is happening in that pool behind their big brick fence is the most fun ever.

Every summer I kick myself for not laying down the relationship groundwork and befriending them in winter. And every summer I vow to make friends with them next winter so I can use their pool next summer. But I never get round to doing it.

So for folks like us who like to swim but do not have access to a pool, there are only three options: the beach, a public pool, or pool crashing. Of these three options, pool crashing is the most exhilarating by a country mile.

The premise is very straightforward—find a house with a pool and go for a swim without permission. Ideally, the occupants will be out. Should they arrive home mid-swim, you can just attempt to laugh it off as a hilarious misunderstanding, like this:

> **Angry pool owner**: Hey! What the hell are you doing in my pool?
>
> **You**: You must be Steve's dad. He told us we could jump the fence and use his pool.
>
> **Angry pool owner**: No, I don't have any kids called Steve and you don't have any right to be using my pool, so get out!
>
> **You**: Ha ha, that Steve is such a prankster. He must have given us the wrong address. That is such a Steve thing to do. I'll slap him for you when I see him.

See? Easy! Will the pool owner believe you? Probably not. But they will have to give you the benefit of the doubt.

Is it legal? Well, no. But as far as illegal activity goes, this is hardly the crime of the century. Worst-case scenario would be the pool owner detains you and calls the police. But then, what are they going to do about it? I watch a lot of *Police Ten 7* and I can assure you the cops have far bigger problems to worry about than someone doing their best to stay cool on a warm summer's day.

Best-case scenario? The pool owner will be a good bastard who gives you permission to stay and even provides some liquid refreshments.

'Pool Crashers' is a segment we used to run on our radio show and we got to experience both the best- and worse-case scenarios. We decided to put the idea into radio retirement on the recommendation of our legal department after we experienced the worst-case scenario.

But let's start with a positive. Let me tell you how awesome pool crashing can be when it goes right. This took place in Christchurch on a colder-than-desirable Friday morning in January. We had put the call out over the airwaves for anyone who wished to join us on a pool crashing mission to meet at the radio station at 7 am. Then we would travel in convoy to a selection of pools we had earmarked. With a group of around thirty Cantabrians all dressed down in togs with towels draped over their shoulders, the numbers were higher than we'd anticipated but we turned nobody away—safety in numbers, the more the merrier, etc.

Some of these properties with pools had been suggested to us by neighbours. Others we had located through the fabulously handy Google Earth website.

One property was a house in a leafy suburb that could be best described as a mansion. At the street front were giant steel gates and a keypad for access. The house and pool were positioned well back on the section. The well-manicured front lawn which ran along the side of the driveway was the size of about two tennis courts.

Access through the front gate was not going to be possible so we quietly snuck (well, as quietly as thirty people can sneak) onto the section next door which, as luck would have it, was a building site. And because it was not yet 7.30 there was not a tradesman in sight. From there it was an easy trample through some shrubs and then a short walk to the edge of the pool. When everyone was in position I grabbed the megaphone: 'Pool crashers—are you ready?' All thirty screamed back that they were.

If the wealthy home owner was asleep, he surely would not be now.

Then came the countdown, again through the megaphone: '5 . . . 4 . . . 3 . . . 2 . . . 1 . . . JUMP!'

The morning stillness was broken by what sounded like a pool party in full swing. And this pool was heated! Not just a little bit heated with some pathetic solar panels on a shed somewhere, either. This was a comfortably warm pool. It was like a giant bath that had been run and left to sit for twenty minutes.

I kept my eyes on the house and noticed some curtains moving upstairs. I was braced for the fallout. Any minute now we would be confronted by either a pissed-off rich guy or the police. Moments later a door swung open and a middle-aged man marched out of the house. He had a T-shirt and shorts on; he looked as if he'd thrown on whatever he had next to his bed so that he could come and check out what all the commotion was.

He stood on the side of his pool with his hands on his hips and a look of disbelief on his face. After maintaining this pose for a couple of seconds he surprised everyone by tucking his legs up and bombing into his own pool. Fully clothed! Everyone erupted into applause and cheers. He then got out of the pool and walked back into the house dripping water everywhere and reappeared with cold beers. They were fancy imported beers, too—the sort of beers you have in your fridge if you have a mansion, a heated in-ground swimming pool and a front lawn the size of two tennis courts.

Blown away by his hospitality, we had no problem overstaying our welcome. Thirty minutes later we were still enjoying his heated pool and chilled beers when he reappeared, dressed in dry clothes, to tell us he was going to work. He informed us that he would leave the gate open so we could see ourselves out when we were done.

*The wealthy Christchurch bloke's pool. That's him in the T-shirt, front right.*

He got a hearty round of applause. Most of us left soon after. We did lose a couple of our group so it's possible some of the pool crashers are still in this rich bloke's pool.

Now, the worst-case scenario. This happened in the very fancy Central Auckland suburb of Herne Bay. It was a property I saw on the cover of the *Property Press*. That gives you an idea about the calibre of the property. If it is a shitty three-bedroom brick and tile place with one of those round Para pools sitting above the ground, it ain't going to make it onto the cover of the *Property Press*.

This place was stunning. The sort of house where someone like me would not even bother going to the open home because both the real estate agent and I would know there was no way in hell I could buy it.

Again, we put the call out on the airwaves and on Friday morning at 7 am were joined by about a dozen brave listeners who were keen to have a crack at pool crashing.

The property had a waist-high fence and gate at the front which meant it was going to be easy for everybody to scale and access the pool, which was at the rear of the property.

The house was an old villa that had been completely renovated and was now a stunning modern property. From the street it looked like the front rooms were the bedrooms. The curtains were open and there was furniture inside. Given the time of day, we drew the conclusion that the house was probably not occupied and the furniture was home staging. These assumptions turned out to be accurate. Did that mean we got to enjoy a pleasant early morning swim without interruption? Not exactly.

As soon as we arrived in a convoy of four cars the neighbours across the road came out onto their balcony to look. This was not a good start but, then again, if four cars rolled into your leafy street just after 7 am and a bunch of people gathered on the footpath with togs, towels, old tyre tubes and a giant inflatable banana, you would probably be slightly curious too.

We all clambered over the gate without incident, making our way to the back of the house and then through the glass fence and gate that surrounded the stunning in-ground pool and spa.

On my cell phone, I negotiated the rules of this pool crash with Mike and Jay-Jay, who were talking to me live on air.

```
'How long do you think we should stay
for? Because the couple across the road
were out on their balcony so I'd say
they're probably calling the cops right
now.'
   'It's five minutes' replied Jay-Jay.
   'Really? Do you think that's wise?'
I said.
   'Yep. Definitely. It's five minutes
starting from the splash-in and the
longer you stand there and argue, the
longer you're going to be there!'
```

My courageous co-hosts, from the comfort of their climate-controlled studio, were adamant that the pre-agreed swim time should remain unchanged. I continued to argue.

> `'It's not really prudent for a bank robber to hang around in the bank after he has robbed it.'`

But my pleas for a splash'n'dash fell on deaf ears.

I picked up the megaphone, started the countdown and everybody jumped in.

Then, after no more than twenty seconds in the water, I noticed three more people entering the property. These people did not have their swimming attire on and did not look like they were in the mood for an early morning pool crash.

Unlike us, this trio entered the property the orthodox way, via the automatic gate, and then came marching round the back, where our impromptu pool party was in full swing.

It turned out these three men were builders who had been employed by a property developer to renovate the house. He had purchased it for a cheap price and painstakingly transformed it into the immaculate property that stood in front of us today. We didn't know this at the time but they had arrived, by sheer coincidence, to make sure the property was looking flawless, because a serious buyer had an appointment to view the place later that morning. So when these guys turned up and saw soaking wet tiles and a dozen idiots doing bombs and throwing beachballs around they were unable to see the funny side of it.

This is how the broadcast went live to air:

```
'What the fuck do you think you're doing?
Get out of the pool! Now!'
```

That was one of the three builders, yelling at nobody in particular. I whispered down the phone to Jay-Jay and Mike as the live broadcast continued:

```
'Can you hear this dude? He's furious.'
```

Bear in mind, we had no delay or dump button and no way of censoring any of the swear words, so this all went to air uncensored.

I walked towards him, separated by the chest-high glass fence surrounding the pool, and asked him why he was so mad.

```
'It's a four-million-dollar fucking home,
mate. Who the fuck do you think you
are?'
```

My reply only inflamed the situation further:

```
'We're just here for the pool party.'
```

He pointed his finger at me and spat:

> 'Yeah, well it's not a pool party, mate.
> It's a fucking expensive home. You're in
> the shit! I know who you are, pal!'

As this tirade was taking place, being broadcast to homes and cars around New Zealand, the swimmers got their things and started to scurry down the side of the house towards the front of the property with a real sense of urgency. The way you would leave a building that was on fire.

Our friend wasn't happy about that:

> 'None of you are leaving! You're all
> fucking idiots! You're not even funny.
> We've got an open home today. Is this
> your house?'
>
> 'No. But we might buy it.'

I was lying.

> 'No you fucking won't. Have you got four
> mill?'

Dammit, he'd seen right through my lie about purchasing the property.

> 'You're not leaving until the cops get
> here, mate!'

By this stage we had all evacuated the pool area and were on the driveway. Some of the swimmers had made it to their cars and were almost home free, their escape aided by these angry gentlemen, who had left the electric gate open when they arrived. A schoolboy error on their part.

I was torn. I knew this man's anger was providing us with some compelling radio but I really wasn't so keen on me or any of our listeners who were present being punched in the throat, so I dropped the smart-arse act and tried to defuse the situation.

```
'Come on, mate, chill out. We were just
having a quick swim.'
    'Yeah, well, it's not a swim, mate.
Seriously. And you can turn your fuck-
ing radio station off. You're all just
a bunch of fucking idiots!'
```

Back in the studio my co-host Mike Puru made the decision to cut off the live broadcast. But off the air, the ear-bashing continued. This guy was relentless. If Gordon Ramsay had been there, he probably would have asked him to ease up on the swear words.

Fortunately, the bark of this builder and his two sidekicks was far worse than their bite and we all made it safely away from the property. One of the builders or the nosy neighbours may very well have called the police as threatened, but we did not see any sirens or flashing lights travelling to the scene of the 'crime' as we drove away.

Realistically, can you imagine how stupid it would all sound to the person logging the complaint at the

111 emergency call centre? This builder didn't need the police—what he needed was some sunshine to dry out the tiles and maybe someone who could give him a deep tissue shoulder massage.

I am happy to report that this whole heated incident over a cold dip had a happy ending. After a tense few hours behind the scenes and threats of legal action between the property developer and my employers, the house in question ended up selling. So all of a sudden the anger of the property developer and his foul-mouthed builders was replaced by relief and joy.

To this day I struggle to see how it would have been our fault if the house did not sell. The mess we created that morning was no different to the mess that would be created by a downpour of rain. Surely someone with $4 million to spend on a house would have the common sense to understand that tiles around a pool will get wet and will also eventually dry out.

All the threats of legal action were called off. The builder had to endure a day of friends and acquaintances asking if it was him they'd heard nutting off on the radio. He was embarrassed, but that was fixed with an apology and a delivery of two dozen beers dropped off to his building site that afternoon.

So that is pool crashing: the very-best-case scenario and the very-worst-case scenario. Coincidentally, both incidents had happy endings.

I would recommend pool crashing for the exhilaration of it.

But if it is just a relaxed swim on a hot summer's day you are after?

Maybe the beach is a better option.

*My mate Griff performs a bomb at the rich bloke's place in Christchurch while a skinny white swimmer looks on in terror.*

# ☑ HAVE A MIDLIFE CRISIS (GET BOTOX)

Getting old sucks. The only bonus of ageing is that it's tangible proof that you are still alive, which is better than the alternative, I suppose.

But apart from that small perk, ageing is crap. Physically you are slower and you injure more easily. If you are planning on having a big night, you'd best make it a Friday, so you have two days to recover before work again—and, if you are a man with a similar mindset to me, while you get older the women you like to admire generally stay the same age, which can start to become a tad creepy.

Some mornings I look in the mirror and cannot believe the old bloke staring back at me. I still feel like that twenty-year-old who thinks he can take on the world and kick its arse, except now the reality is I have the face of a middle-aged man looking back at me. I like the outdoors and am pretty slack with applying the old

SPF 30—this has given me a weathered complexion. A face that looks like a cross between a sailor and an old leather belt.

I'd probably be more at peace with my old man face if I had successfully taken on the world and won in my twenties, because immense wealth seems to make people a lot less physically unattractive than they actually are. But sadly that was not the path my pathetic life took, so here I am, thirty-eight, huge mortgage, four weeks' annual leave a year and no parental inheritance on the horizon. FML.

But if there is one tragedy greater than getting old it would have to be people who try to defy it by getting 'work' done. And for men I reckon this is a lot worse than women—society has accepted that women want to take pride in their appearance and hold onto their youthful looks. Us blokes are supposed to age gracefully and be happy about it. The magazines inform us that we get better looking the older we get. Bullshit! It might be the case for George Clooney and Brad Pitt, but it is not the case for most of us.

The funny thing is, when I see a man who has obviously had Botox injections my first thought is never 'Wow, that fresh-faced cool kid has old man hands.' It's always something along the lines of 'Shame! Look at that ridiculous old guy who wants everyone to think he's not a ridiculous old guy.'

Yep, I'm against ageing as much as the next person, but I believe accepting it is a more dignified way to deal with it than putting up a fight you are never going to win.

For my next tick on my bucket list I would have my very own mini midlife crisis—I would go against my better judgement and get Botox (or Brotox, as it should be named to make it sound slightly more masculine). It would potentially make me feel younger and would be a whole lot cheaper and safer than getting a Harley.

Right across the road from my work is a place called 'The Skin Institute'.

Every day from the window of my radio studio I get to see people, mostly women, mostly in their forties, walk through these doors in an effort to make themselves feel better about how they look. All these customers seem to wear very fancy clothes and drive nice cars. This would suggest they are all very materialistic and wealthy (or heavily in debt). Alternatively, they could all be supported by very wealthy older husbands. But if that was the case, why would they be bothered by their fading looks? If you are forty and your husband is seventy, surely it is enough to look thirty years younger?

I called and made an appointment for a 'cosmetic consultation'. That is what they call it. It takes fifteen minutes and is done by a cosmetic nurse.

This would be good. Really, I just wanted some Botox injections so I could see what all the fuss was about and whether or not it actually made a difference.

Plus I had a lot of questions I wanted answered.

How many years could they take off my face?

Would the changes even be noticeable?

If the changes were noticeable, would it be in a good way or a workmates-snigger-behind-my-back way?

Would I still be able to frown and laugh?

Could it end up making me look like one of those celebrities who went too far? Like Michael Jackson, Kenny Rogers or the Duchess of Alba. Next time you're online, do a Google image search on the eighty-six-year-old Duchess. The poor old duck has had so much work done she looks like an alien from a Spielberg film. Still, the work must be good enough to fool her sixty-year-old third husband, who she married in October 2011.

I went for my appointment and was met by Sally, who led me from reception into a consultation room. The place was stylish and sparse and felt like some sort of a cool hospital. Sally was impeccably groomed and in great physical shape. She was maybe in her early forties—hard to tell, though, since there was barely a wrinkle on her face. Obviously she had been making good use of whatever staff discount she was entitled to.

Sally got the ball rolling. 'When you look in the mirror,' she enquired, 'what do you not like?'

'The old guy looking back at me,' I replied and laughed nervously and loudly.

'Are you serious?' Sally replied, clearly trying to make me feel better about myself. She wasn't fooling anybody, though. I knew what she was looking at. I had stared at the same thing many times over the years and watched it deteriorate. Some men my age have what are known as crow's-feet around their eyes. My lines probably resemble the feet of an adult ostrich more than those of a little bird like a crow.

We established that there wasn't really anything in particular I was self-conscious about—I was just keen to try out some cosmetic work to see what the fuss was all about.

'Just looking at you, I definitely don't think you look thirty-eight,' she lied, before getting down to business. 'I would probably say I would treat . . . that,' she announced, pointing towards two crevices that formed what looked like a deep letter 'A' carved right between my eyes.

I nodded in full support of what Sally was saying. She generously responded that most of her guy friends have these lines and they are usually caused by concentration rather than being an angry person. I wondered if she said that just to be nice because she didn't want to make me mad.

I then found out something no one had ever told me before—I frown more with my left corrugator than my right one. How embarrassing for me! Why had no one told me this? It's as if I had been walking around for years with a piece of toilet paper stuck to my shoe.

I had no idea what Sally was on about but she certainly seemed surprised by this whole left corrugator thingy.

She explained that the lines were a result of muscular contraction. Botox would paralyse those muscles, which would stop them from contracting. With repeated courses of Botox the lines could even improve and get better.

She did go on to warn me there was one problem with Botox. I was prepared for her to say it can make your face look funny over time (like some of the vain celebrities we have all seen in magazines who have taken a liking to Botox). That was not her answer, though.

'The only problem with Botox is it can be a bit addictive,' she laughed. 'In the sense that you see really good improvements and you don't ever want to stop using it. It works really nicely. A lot of women find if they can't get their Botox, they don't like it when their frown comes back.'

But what about the pain involved? I hate needles. I avoid them at all costs, so having multiple injections in my face for reasons of vanity seemed absurd.

'It doesn't hurt.' Sally assured me. 'There will be five very superficial injections and then it takes about three or four days to start to work.'

Even worse than my fear of needles was my fear of parting with money, so I asked about the cost involved.

'Every case is individual and it all depends on how many units we have to use, but it is $18.50 a unit, and I would start you off on just a standard dose of about twenty units. Sounds a lot, but it isn't twenty injections— it's just four units into each little injection. So you would be looking at $370,' she announced without flinching. Or maybe she was flinching, but I saw no noticeable movement in that smooth face of hers.

'Cool, all right, let's make an appointment!' I said.

She looked through her diary and the next available slot was an entire week later. Evidentially, this Botox is a booming business.

We ran through a series of health-related questions, then she sent me on my way with an appointment card and an information sheet. As she walked me out I asked out of curiosity how many male customers she had.

Sally told me it was maybe a fifth or a quarter. 'I get a lot of male clients—lots of guys want to look their best. Most of my male clients come in during their forties, but the age of guys ranges from mid thirties to mid sixties.'

That surprised me. Once you're in your sixties why would you waste hundreds or even thousands of dollars on this sort of thing? Even without wrinkles surely the slow walk or smell of urine would be a giveaway to your advanced years.

The following Tuesday was Botox day. I was highly sceptical, but I was prepared (and even secretly hoping) to be proven wrong.

I went to reception and was taken to a waiting area, where I had a few minutes to read the brochures about other services they offered for men including a procedure called 'high definition liposuction'. This is lipo for people who are carrying only a little bit of excess weight and not people who are fat, fat. The before and after photos were of a shirtless guy. Photo 1 showed him with no visible abs (no beer belly either, mind you). Photo 2 showed the same bloke, now with abs and a fake tan.

The funny thing is, in the 'after' photo he had the abs . . . but his arms were still a bit flabby. Perhaps he was going to go back for some of this high definition liposuction on his arms once he had saved up some more money.

Sally came to grab me and took me through to the procedure room. She got me to sign a consent form, which I did without reading it first. It was probably just a promise from me that I wouldn't take legal action against this place if I ended up looking like Shane Warne.

I lay down on the bed and Sally started stretching and moulding the skin on my forehead with her fingers, the way you might flatten out a piece of paper that had been screwed up and then retrieved from a rubbish bin.

'This is a little test that I do. There are two kinds of wrinkles—dynamic lines and static lines. Dynamic lines appear only when you move your face, but static lines are there all the time, even when the face is at rest. Botox helps to relax your muscles, so when you try to frown, you won't be able to. It's all about preventing dynamic lines from getting any deeper,' Sally explained. 'But it's a bit trickier with static lines—like this one here.' She showed me a deep line on my forehead. 'See, even when I pull the skin, it's still there. Now not even Botox can remove that. So after you've had your treatment, don't feel disappointed if the line is still there. At least it will keep you looking natural. In fact it could be quite strange if you came out and there wasn't a line on your face at all.'

'WAIT. A. MINUTE!' I thought to myself but was far too polite (and gutless) to ask out loud. 'So I am about to pay hundreds of dollars for a procedure that is supposed to take the lines off my face and you're telling me it won't take the lines off my face?'

This was a joke!

*Don't feel disappointed if the line is still there!* Are you kidding me? Of course I will feel disappointed.

If I take my car to the mechanic because it is making a strange rattling sound, he is not going to take my money and then tell me, 'Now, don't be disappointed if it still makes the rattling sound. It might be strange if all of a sudden the rattling sound was no longer there.'

Maybe my eyes gave away what I was too chicken to say out loud, because Sally continued with her spiel, trying to sell me on the positives of Botox.

'With repeated Botox treatments, that line will get better and better. If it still bugs you, we can use a little bit of filler. That's a bit like injecting poly-filler into the skin. It lifts the skin, so the line won't seem so deep. But my view is prevention is better than a cure. Start with a course of Botox and we can take it from there.'

Talk time was over. The time for Botox was now. I lay down on the bed and was given one of those rubbery stress balls to squeeze on. Sally placed a small icepack on my forehead to help numb the area between my eyes. Then she cleaned the area and showed me the needle. It looked slightly smaller than the needle a doctor would use for blood tests. But, still, it was a needle and it was about to pierce my skin, right between my eyes. FIVE TIMES!

'All right, close your eyes and remain nice and still. Are you comfy?'

'Comfortable enough, I suppose.'

I inhaled as instructed and could smell nothing but balloons. It was Sally's latex gloves hovering just above my face as she prepared to begin.

'How does that feel? It's just like a little scratch, isn't it?' Sally asked and then answered on my behalf.

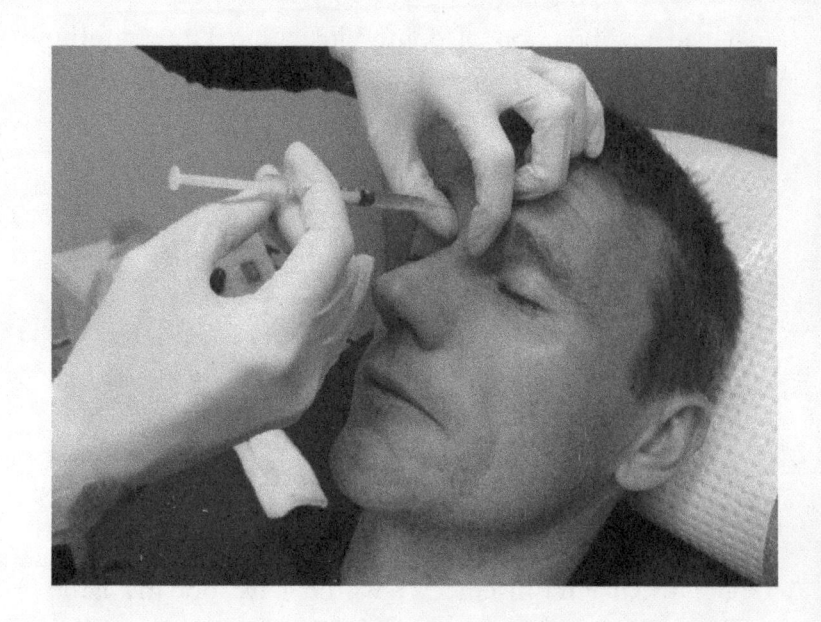

I could feel the needle go in. Her description of it being like a scratch was pretty accurate. It didn't hurt, but I wouldn't describe it as a trip to Rainbow's End either! It was probably more the anticipation than the pain that had put me on edge.

This procedure was repeated another four times: 'Inhale. Eyes shut. Relax. Breathe.'

And then we were done.

'So it's going to look like you've got mozzie bites. That's because you're still going to have fluid settling into the muscle there. Keep your head elevated for the next couple of days—that means no yoga or Pilates where you put your head down into inverted kinds of positions.'

I had no intention of doing either, but I'm assuming they are both popular activities for a lot of the well-heeled Botox customers.

'It won't start to work immediately,' she warned me, again. 'It will take about three days for it to start to work and from there the onset is gradual. In two weeks' time it will be working to its maximum.'

I was led out to reception, where I paid for the treatment: $370, as I'd been warned during the initial consultation.

The receptionist pointed out that I had drops of blood appearing from a couple of the tiny needle holes. She reached over to a box of tissues and pulled a couple out. Under usual circumstances I would have put my hand out to take the tissues and dabbed my own blood. But since I had just been stung $370 for five tiny injections, I just leaned forward and tilted my head down, leaving the poor receptionist with no option but to do the dabbing for me. What an arsehole!

I walked back to the car and did what I imagine every single customer does—checked my face out in the mirror to see if there had been any instant change. As warned, it hadn't kicked in yet.

Over the next few days I kept a watch on my face to see if there were any changes. These were my scribbled diary entries:

**Wednesday:** No change yet. Still look old.

> **Thursday:** Still no change. I actually look two days older than I looked two days ago.
>
> **Friday:** 72 hours now and nothing. No comments from anyone and the line looks as deep as ever.
>
> **Tuesday:** One whole week. Definitely a change. Subtle. The line is still there but nowhere near as deep.
>
> **Tuesday:** Two weeks. Botox at its peak now. I must admit, the change has been quite dramatic. Those deep lines are still there but nowhere near as deep. No comments from other people . . . but I do feel better when I see my reflection.

The changes were pretty subtle but made me feel a bit better about the way I see myself. Friends only commented on the changes once I pointed out I'd had it done.

So, Botox does work and many people seem to swear by it. If you are one of these people, good for you.

Is it for me? No. I am reasonably vain and I hate looking older than I feel . . . but I hated spending $370 on something so meaningless even more. Even if I was super loaded, I think I would still have a problem with this.

So I am sworn off Botox for life now. Botox cost almost $400 and, at best, made me look a year or two younger before it wore off a couple of months later.

Since then I've come up with a way that I can feel young that doesn't involve any sort of surgery and costs next to nothing. Whenever I feel old and need a bit of perspective I just pop down to the RSA round the corner from my house and drink some very reasonably priced beer and eavesdrop on the conversations the other blokes down there have. There is nothing that makes me feel better about my age than listening to proper old people talk about everything from their medical ailments (especially gout), to the heat, the cold, the government, the cost of everything, untrustworthy teenagers riding skateboards, the Asians 'taking over our country' and 'those bloody Maoris'.

These men and these conversations remind me that appearance is actually only a very small part of what makes all of us tick. So whether you are eighty with a face that looks like an old pair of R.M. Williams boots or twenty with a complexion as smooth as Justin Bieber's gooch, if you are a grumpy bastard, it doesn't matter what you look like—nobody will want to be your mate.

# ☑ RUN THE BOSTON MARATHON

I am a marathon runner. A marathon course is just a shade over forty-two kilometres. Some people will run one marathon in their lifetime just to tick it off their bucket list. I, like many others who never seem to learn from our mistakes, run them over and over again. People often ask me why and there are a few good reasons:

```
1. I am an idiot.

2. Running keeps me in shape, which
   means I don't feel as guilty when I
   overindulge in my love of red wine,
   deep-fried food and refined sugar
   products.

3. I don't have the required coordina-
   tion to do any other sport.
```

Growing up, one of my less-generous PE teachers told me I had the coordination of a newborn baby giraffe. This makes me unsuited to (useless at) pretty much every other sporting activity. But I can walk okay and running is basically just extreme walking.

Sadly, I am not fast. If I may follow the lead of my old PE teacher and use more animal kingdom comparisons, I am more a hedgehog than a hare. By the time I eventually make it to the finish line, the skinny African blokes who dominate this event have had ample time to drive home, shower, check out their newsfeed on Facebook, watch an episode of *CSI: Kenya*, then drive back for the prize-giving ceremony.

For my bucket list, I wanted to run the Boston Marathon. Most Kiwis who want to run an overseas marathon go for London or New York. Boston is different from these events for a few reasons. For one, it is a considerably smaller field. Boston is limited to 20,000 runners each year, whereas New York and London both attract double that number.

But the main point of difference between Boston and every other marathon in the world? You have to QUALIFY to take part.

The amount of hoops you have to jump through before you can even get to the start of the Boston Marathon in the small town of Hopkinton is enough to put most people off.

Firstly, you need to run a marathon in under the qualifying time (for your age group) and it can't be any old marathon. It needs to be one that is known as a

'Boston Qualifier'. For New Zealand, the only Boston Qualifiers are the Adidas Auckland Marathon and the SBS Marathon in Christchurch (now known as the Christchurch Airport Marathon). Then, if you manage to run one of these qualifiers in under the appropriate time, you have to get online when Boston registrations open and fight with other mentally deranged runners from around the world to buy one of the limited places.

So, what's the appeal? Why is Boston known as the Holy Grail of marathons? The answer to that probably depends on who you ask. But for me the attraction is the need to qualify and the effort required to get there. Because you have to earn your spot in the field it makes ordinary runners like me feel like a champion just by taking part, as if they've achieved something worthwhile.

This may be hard for non-runners to understand, but some runners end up depressed, insane or divorced in their quest to qualify for Boston. When you talk to other runners from around the world at the race expo the day before the event, you realise just how much it means to some people. One fella I spoke to drove around the US in 2008 to take part in qualifying races until he finally cracked the time he needed, only to be unsuccessful in securing a spot in the field for the following year.

In 2009 he did the same thing again but didn't manage to finish the run in his qualifying time. In one of these qualifier runs he missed the time he needed by eight stupid seconds.

In 2010 he was finally successful. He ran a qualifying time in an approved marathon and was lucky enough to secure a spot in the Boston field. So here he was at the 2011 Boston Marathon. For many, Boston becomes more than just a run—it turns into an obsession.

Fortunately, my road to Boston was nowhere near as intense as Mr Obsessive Compulsive's. In October 2009 I ran the Auckland Marathon in 3 hours and 19 minutes. Before this I had heard of the Boston Marathon but was blissfully unaware of the hype surrounding the race. After I finished, a good mate of mine informed me that my time was only 4 minutes off the Boston qualifying time. He takes his running far more seriously than me—he wears those tiny shorts with the big splits up the side and runs with a little backpack full of water—but the way he spoke about this Boston run made me feel like it was something I should know about, so I went home and hit up Google to find out a bit more.

There were 3,290,000 pages about the event, detailing the rich history of the race. Reading about it gave me a feel for why it is so special—it is a field of like-minded people. No first-timers here, no time-wasters. These were all people who had proven that they were fast enough to run Boston. I wanted in!

The qualifying times seemed challenging, but definitely not impossible. For a thirty-five to thirty-nine-year-old male, the qualifying time was a three-hour, fifteen-minute marathon or quicker. This is the way the qualifying system works: the older you get, the more generous the qualifying times are. If you're eighty or older, your qualifying time is five hours, which would still be a test for a lot of much younger runners—Katie Holmes ran the New York Marathon in 2007 and it took her five and a half hours. Then again, she may have intentionally run slowly to get a good break from her then husband, Tom Cruise!

The seed was planted. I signed up for the 2010 Christchurch Marathon and got training. The Christchurch run was held in June, only four months before a big earthquake struck. Many of the buildings in the central city where the run finishes are no longer standing. At the time, all I was thinking about was qualifying for Boston. With hindsight, I consider myself bloody lucky to have got to do this run through this beautiful old city before the earthquake changed it forever—along with the lives of the people who call it home.

I scraped in by the skin of my teeth. My official time was 3.14.34 meaning I had beaten the Boston qualifying time with a slender twenty-six seconds to spare.

Hoop number 1 jumped through. Now I just had to register. Entries opened at 9 am on 18 October, Boston time. That's a painfully early 2 am New Zealand time, but nothing about the road to Boston is easy, so I set my alarm and sat in the dimly lit office in nothing more than my undies while I filled in the massive number of fields on the page. Honestly, it is probably easier to get a gun licence than to get a spot in the Boston Marathon. By 2.12 am I had typed in all the info they needed, the most important bits being my Christchurch qualifying time and my credit card details. I clicked enter and the irritating little hourglass came up on the screen. Then . . . nothing.

I started again, typing out all the information the Boston Athletics Association required. Once again I clicked enter and once again that annoying little hourglass popped up.

I assumed the page must have been overloaded, so I kept trying. I gave myself until 3 am before I was going to drag myself back to bed, the place I rightfully belonged at that hour, not to mention the only place I was dressed for! It got to 3 am and I still hadn't got in. I went back to bed but was unable to sleep because I was too wired. I was furious, mad, sad, a whole range of emotions. It's not until you can't have something that you find out just how much you wanted it.

Later in the morning, around eightish, I decided to give it just one more try. And this time it worked first pop. I was in! Moments later I got an email confirming my acceptance to the 2011 Boston Marathon. The next day *The Boston Globe* newspaper ran a story about how the 20,000 places were filled in a record-breaking eight hours and three minutes.

I would be one of those lucky (or unlucky, depending on how much you hate running) 20,000. My race number—6320.

Me and my support crew of one, my wife (who was more focused on supporting the local economy through her love of clothes shopping than supporting me), flew to Los Angeles, then got on another plane for the six-hour flight from the west coast of America right over to the east coast. Because it was a direct flight into Boston two days before the run, the plane was full of marathon-looking people—lots of passengers in tracksuits, many with their own bags of fruit for the flight. A lot of serious runners get super-anal in the build-up to a run, to the point where they don't trust food that has been prepared by anyone else. I really wanted to have a good run in Boston but I certainly didn't feel the need to fly with my own bag of apples and bananas—airline pretzels would do me just fine! One guy even did lunges down the length of the aisle every couple of hours, something which made many other passengers (myself included) snigger.

As soon as you land in Boston you can feel the marathon fever. There are posters around the airport welcoming runners to the city. A Boston man, a complete stranger who was waiting at the baggage carousel with me, asked if I was in town for the run and wished me luck, saying he would be out watching. This man was one of the few non-runners on our flight. He had a build more suited to shot-put than running any distance.

Because of the popularity of the run and the amount of visitors it attracts to the city, all the hotels make the most of the influx and hike their prices up accordingly. We had booked one of the cheapest places we could find online, an old hotel called the Lennox. As luck would have it, the Lennox is right next to the finish line, and from our room's window we could see the last 100 metres of the run route. When you're about to run a marathon, the proximity of the finish line to the hotel is fairly important, because after running your arse off for 42 kilometres the last thing you want to be doing is hobbling another couple of kilometres back to a hotel somewhere.

\*

The Boston Marathon is held on the same day every year. It is a holiday called Patriots' Day and falls on the third Monday of April. It has to be on a holiday because every single yellow school bus available is required to transport the runners to the tiny town of Hopkinton, twenty-six miles away, where the run starts.

The sight of maybe sixty or seventy of those big chunky yellow school buses all lined up got me a little excited. I'm not sure why—it's just a stupid bus, after all. I suppose it's because we see them on telly and in movies all the time and they don't look anything like the buses we have back home. Still, pretty lame on my part. I should have edited the confession about the buses out before submitting this manuscript to the publishers.

The bus trip from Boston to the start line seems to take forever and does nothing to calm the nerves—all it does is reinforce just how far you have to run to get back to Boston!

The bus drops you off at the grounds of Hopkinton High School, which is transformed into an athletes' village for the day.

I arrived in the athletes' village and waited. I waited for ages. As you can probably imagine, it is a logistical nightmare shuttling 20,000 people from the finish line out to the start line, so the race organisers get everybody there with plenty of time to spare. I was on the bus by 6.20 am and made it to the athletes' village just after 7 am, even though the race didn't start until 10.

The morning of the run was bloody freezing. Just brutally cold. I'd checked the forecast the day before and knew it was going to be gnarly, so I dressed accordingly (gloves, beanie and a hooded sweatshirt). Even with all these layers on, I was still underdressed and unbelievably cold.

I found a near-empty 44-gallon rubbish drum with one of those plastic bin liners in. Desperate times call for desperate measures, so I hand-picked the half-a-dozen bits of rubbish out and used it as a sort of makeshift sleeping bag. Even that bag did little to stop my relentless shivering. It did, however, mean I could keep my hands warm by putting them down my pants without anyone else seeing I had my hands down my pants. Bonus!

It was easy to spot those who had run Boston before—people had magazines and newspapers to help pass the hours. Others had actual sleeping bags.

Eventually the sun came up, but because the athletes' village was in the grounds of a high school there were two-storey buildings everywhere which did a fantastic job of blocking out the sun's warmth. There was one sunny spot on the field, which was well used by me and thousands of other runners who had not anticipated it would be such a bloody miserable morning.

Half an hour before the race was due to start, an announcement was made telling us to leave the athletes' village and walk to the start line, which was about 600 metres away.

I removed all the extra clothes I was wearing and dumped them on the footpath. This is what you do in the Boston Marathon—all the runners wear old clothes and leave them on the sidewalks in Hopkinton. Then, after the run commences, all the clothes get scooped up and given to the homeless. If you ever happen to be in Boston and spot a homeless person in an Adidas tracksuit, this may explain why.

The gun went off at 10 am and after shuffling along through the crowd for a bit I finally made it to the actual start line. Then enough space cleared to actually start running. I had made it. I was running the Boston Marathon. I had earned my place in this field, and being on this same strip of road with all these other like-minded people was the reward.

Yes, it was a huge pain in the arse to make it here—the hundreds of hours spent training, the qualifying, the arduous process of entering online in the middle of the night, the thousands of dollars it cost to travel here, not to mention the Antarctic conditions I'd had to endure the past three hours. But all of that was forgotten as I heard the stampede sound that 20,000 human beings make when they're all running at once.

And I was part of a community—all these people in front of me and behind me had gone through the same things to be here today.

Most of the 42-kilometre route is lined with spectators. This support is helpful; it makes you forget just how many kilometres you still have left to run before you finish. The most spectator noise comes from a town called Wellesley, which is just before the halfway point in the run. You hit the 20-kilometre mark and start to hear a high-pitched tone. A loud but distant squealing noise. It sounds like the noise a jet engine makes. This noise is made by the girls of Wellesley College and has been nicknamed 'the scream tunnel'.

Wellesley is a posh girls' university with a roll of 2400. It has been a tradition for decades that the girls of Wellesley get on the roadside and scream for the runners while offering up hugs and kisses! No shit! And I'll tell you what—the male runners appreciate this far more than any of the Gatorade stands!

I saw these girls holding signs that said things like:

```
'Kiss me, I'm half Asian'
'Kiss me, I'm single'
'Kiss me, I'm from Lithuania'
'I majored in kissing'
```

And even:

```
'Kiss me, I'm a redhead'
```

I suspect if this last girl really wanted to be kissed she would have dyed her hair a more socially acceptable colour.

I did slow down to a jog to enjoy the atmosphere as I ran through the scream tunnel. It was two minutes of my life where I got to experience what it would be like to be a rock star with groupies. For that brief moment, I was Jon Bon Jovi in leather pants. I didn't stop for any kisses, though. It would have been an act of cruelty to these poor young women. I had been running for an hour and thirty-eight minutes by that stage. I was sweaty, there was a Gatorade stain on my singlet, I had my own saliva on my face from when I spat and the wind caught it and blew it back at me and there was dry snot under my nose. It was very charitable of these young women to offer me their lip-service, but I could not be so mean.

The Wellesley girls make up just part of the Boston support crew. An estimated half a million people hit the streets each year to support the runners. Many even go to the trouble of making signs to motivate the runners (or just give them a laugh). Out of the hundreds of signs I saw these are the best I recall seeing on the 42-kilometre course:

```
You're halfway there. Woo hoo, living on
   a prayer.
Don't stop—take a dump in your pants if
   you need to.
Don't worry—toenails are overrated.
Run like an angry Kenyan.
Chuck Norris never ran a marathon.
Call a cab. It's way faster.
Run, Fat Boy, run!
Bleeding nipples are hot.
You look like crap.
Any slower & you'd be walking.
```

Appropriately, that last sign was being held up at a point 32 kilometres into the marathon, halfway up a hill. There are four hills in a row at this stage of the race. These hills are not too challenging, but after 32 Ks of running, even climbing a flight of stairs can feel like Mount Everest! The final of the four hills was given the nickname 'Heartbreak Hill' in 1936 by *The Boston Globe* and it has stuck ever since—but once you make it to the top of Heartbreak Hill, the run is fairly straightforward (although your legs will probably argue that point).

For the final six or seven kilometres of the run the spectators on the sides of the road are about ten deep. After 35 kilometres, when your body hurts all over and all you feel like doing is having a walk for a little bit, these people cheering you on keep you going. You feel as though you'd be disappointing them by having a walk (not to mention you'd look like a bit of a dick).

The final turn in the run is onto Boylston Street. From here it is a half mile in a straight line to the end. The finish banner gets bigger and bigger with every step you take. The bars and cafes on the side of Boylston Street are packed with cheering customers who got there first thing in the morning to secure their prime positions.

The feeling when that finish line comes into view is incredible, a moment of my life I will never forget. This is where you realise you have done it. You are no longer a Boston qualifier or a Boston entrant. You become a Boston finisher.

My time? 3 hours, 22 minutes, 21 seconds.

Geoffrey Mutai's time? 2 hours, 3 minutes.

Yes, I finished a whopping hour and 20 minutes behind the quick Kenyan but that didn't matter to me. Geoffrey was the winner. But Boston is a place where weekend warriors like me, the plodders of the running community, can feel like a champion regardless of time or placing.

Whatever age you are, I reckon life is a collection of moments, good or bad, that mean something to you. It's the really good or really horrible moments that shape us and make us who we are. They are the moments we remember and hang onto. For me, running the Boston Marathon was one of those good moments. Something I won't forget, ever.

Finishing Boston cost me thousands of dollars, hundreds of training hours, and three toenails. But as the marketing team at MasterCard would say: the memories and the finisher's medal? Priceless.

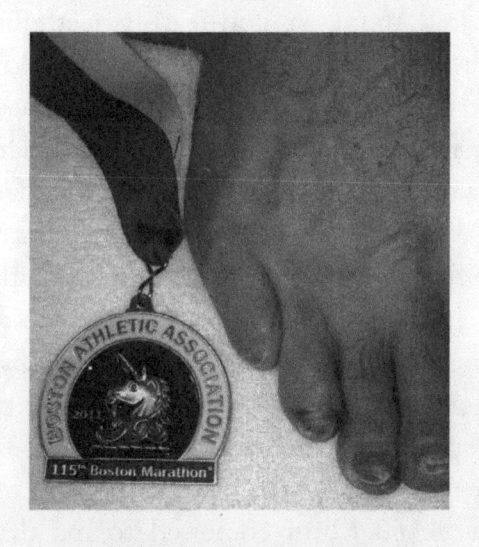

*The medal and the dead toenails.*
*Both badges of honour for any marathon runner.*

# ☑ PRANK MY MUM

My poor old mum. A god-fearing Catholic woman, four children, ten grandchildren. Sixty years old with no criminal record. I suspect she has been snapped speeding once or twice but otherwise she has lived a blameless life.

This woman has not done anything to deserve such an arsehole son. Well, nothing apart from once dragging me home from school and washing my mouth out with a cake of Palmolive Gold after I was overheard swearing. In my defence, the offensive word in question was 'blimmin', which I thought was a lite version of 'bloody'. Mum disagreed with my reasoning so my mouth paid the ultimate penalty.

One weekend Mum confessed to me that she had done something naughty and felt really bad about it. She had been given a blender from Farmers as a present. She couldn't work out how to use all the various attachments because there was no instruction booklet inside the box.

Mum owns a laptop and has a basic grasp of how to work a PC but I think the internet frightens her a bit, so she uses it for what she knows and nothing else—she goes on Skype and Facebook to stay in touch with her grandkids dotted all around the place. But it would never occur to my old mum that she could probably Google the make and model of her blender and print out a copy of the missing manual.

Instead, Mum did potentially the worst thing she had ever done in her six full decades of life—she went into a Farmers store and found the blender she had been given as a gift, then opened the box and stole a manual.

Granted, this is hardly a heist that would make a decent movie plot. A great crime thriller like *Usual Suspects* would not have been the blockbuster that it was if Keyser Söze's crime had been to pinch an instruction booklet for a Kambrook blender. But it was still shoplifting and still something that was playing heavily on Mum's fragile conscience.

I had wanted to do something evil to my mum for my bucket list, so when she told me her secret I saw this as the perfect opportunity. This was going to be easy to pull off. Convincing Mum that Farmers would be on her tail for this would be about as difficult as convincing a six-year-old that a tiny lady with wings flies into children's bedrooms collecting dirty old teeth and replacing them with coins.

So I planted the seed. I told Mum it was lucky she hadn't been stopped by a store security guard, because they have security TV cameras everywhere that are being monitored all the time.

This whipped poor old Mum into even more of a panic. She asked me if she should go back to the store and sneak the manual back into the box.

I told her not to worry about it, because if she made it out of the store she'd probably got away with it. Yeah, I felt a little bit bad . . . but I knew the pay-off would be worth the stress I was causing Mum. Plus, she did wash my mouth out with soap for saying 'blimmin' thirty years earlier, so I kind of owed her some payback!

A few days after Mum and I had this chat, I got my mate Kally at work to give her a call. We recorded it, with the intention of playing it back on the air further down the track. The conversation was short and ended abruptly.

```
Mum: Hello, Sue speaking.
Kally: Hello, is that Susan Harvey?
Mum: Yes, speaking.
Kally: Susan, this is Kerry from Farm-
ers security . . .
[Sound of Mum fumbling round with her
phone before hanging up]
```

I immediately tried to call Mum back but her phone went straight to voicemail. She had intentionally terminated the call and switched her phone off to avoid facing the music. Later that day I drove over to Mum's place for a visit. This phone call was one of the first things she brought up.

'I just went to a brand-new doctors for my foot because it's swollen but it was so embarrassing. I think I might be in trouble. When I was with the doctor my phone went and I said, "That will be my daughter," so I answered it and it went straight onto the loudspeaker.'

As I mentioned earlier, Mum is terrible with any sort of new technology. And when I say 'new technology' I mean anything that is more advanced than a cassette deck or VHS recorder. How a cell phone manages to automatically go onto speaker when answered is beyond me but if it was going to do it for anyone, it would be my mum.

She didn't stop for a second to question how a Farmers security guard could have obtained the number of her prepaid cell phone to call her about taking some paper from a box. Nor did she stop to question why a huge corporation that loses hundreds of thousands of dollars of stock each year to shoplifters would bother wasting their time on something so petty.

'It was a man—he said his name was Kerry and he was from Farmers security and I had to quickly try and turn my phone off. They caught me on their video stealing my book. So I quickly hung up and said to the doctor, "I don't know who that was." Brand-new doctor, first time I have ever seen them and now they probably think I'm some sort of a criminal. I felt so embarrassed. If I knew the doctor better I could have made a joke about it, but since they don't know me they probably think I'm a thief.'

I pointed out to Mum that she was, in fact, a thief. She took something that wasn't even hers. Then I told her that she shouldn't be scared and if he happened to call back she should just do the right thing—admit it, apologise, offer to return it—and that would probably be the end of the matter.

'Yeah, that's what I'll do. But surely they wouldn't go around ringing every person that stole a brochure. Oh, I'm so embarrassed. I'm a sixty-year-old woman. Mum would die of shock if she heard about this.'

She was talking about her own mum, my nana, a healthy eighty-five-year-old woman who probably spends more time in church than the average priest. Seriously, she goes to a Catholic mass most days. Some days she even goes twice.

It must be a difficult task staying awake for any priest who has to sit through my nana's visits to the confessional booth to clear her conscience of her sins. Apart from going through the express lane with more than twelve items from time to time, I cannot imagine what sins my nan would have to get off her chest.

Mum agreed that she would face the music if the Farmers security guard happened to phone back. I left her and went back to work and got Kally to make the follow-up call. I had planned to leave it another day, but as funny as I found all of this we really needed to get this over and done with so I could reveal it was a joke and Mum could stop living like a fugitive. But sadly for my mum, before she got relief she would have to endure a wee bit of pain. Here is a transcript of the phone call that ensued.

**Kally:** Hi, is that Susan Harvey?
**Mum:** Yes, it is.

**Kally:** Hi, Susan—I spoke to you before. My name is Kerry Thompson from Farmers security.

**Mum:** Yeah.

**Kally:** Sorry, I must have had a bad line before. I got cut off.

**Mum:** Oh, okay.

**Kally:** Just calling in regard to a small issue. Last week we had you in our St Lukes store and we have you on camera going into a box that appears to be for a blender and pulling out what we think is the instruction manual. Would that be correct?

**Mum (nervously):** Oooh, yeah.

**Kally:** Okay. Well, can you explain what was happening there?

**Mum:** Well, I was given a blender and it never . . . [Mum pauses and takes a deep breath] it never had any instructions with it.

**Kally:** Right.

**Mum:** It was bought from Farmers. And it was given to me and it never had any instructions and I just assumed I would know how to use it.

**Kally:** Right.

**Mum:** And anyway, I couldn't work the thing out. I'd been in a couple of times to try and have a look to see

how it would work and then on Sunday I went in and . . . [Four seconds of silence follows before my poor old mum lowers her voice and completes her sentence] . . . I took it.
**Kally:** Okay.
**Mum:** I've got it, so I can return it.
**Kally:** Right. Did you think to just come in and speak to someone from staff to get a bit of help there?
**Mum:** Well, I thought about that but . . . no disrespect, but Farmers staff are quite slow. You know what I mean? I can stand there for ages waiting to be served.

Good one, Mum! So first you steal from them and now you shit on the staff who work there! Well played.

**Mum:** I know what I SHOULD have done.
**Kally:** But you found it easier just to shoplift?
**Mum:** Well, I wouldn't really consider it stealing.
**Kally:** How do you think the next person would feel, though, if we sold those goods on without an operational booklet?
**Mum:** Absolutely. I totally agree. I most definitely apologise. I am certainly in the wrong.

**Kally:** Okay, well, we take these issues fairly seriously because we don't like dealing with complaints from customers, as we pride ourselves on our customer service. So what do you think we should do about this situation?
**Mum:** Well . . . [another long, deep breath] . . . I can return it.
**Kally:** Okay, do you think that is sufficient?
**Mum:** I don't know. No, probably not.

For crying out loud, Mum—don't roll over and give up so easily. It's sixteen bits of paper you took, not a giant plasma telly!

**Kally:** Okay.
**Mum:** I mean, I'm sixty years old, for goodness sake!
**Kally:** Yeah, and I guess that was one of the questions we asked ourselves—what is a lady of this age doing stealing goods?
**Mum (pausing, then laughing nervously):** I'm sorry for laughing—it's actually not funny, it's very scary. Especially when you put it like that.
**Kally:** Yeah, we don't find it funny either.
**Mum:** No.

**Kally:** So I guess what we suggest is that you come in and we will sit down with management and have a discussion about this and decide whether or not we need to take this further with the police and so forth. Generally we don't like to do so because obviously there could be some fairly serious consequences. So how about we arrange a time for you to come in and we can have a talk about this and see if we can come to a mutually beneficial agreement.

**Mum (sounding totally beaten and deflated):** Sure.

**Kally:** What's a good time that suits you?

**Mum:** Perhaps, I don't know, what about Saturday?

**Kally:** Saturday? Yes, we can work with that. What time?

**Mum:** Umm, god, I don't know. Maybe half past ten?

**Kally:** Righto, we can make ten-thirty work. I would recommend you bring in a support person or potentially a lawyer.

**Mum (after pausing again, for about two seconds this time):** YOU'RE KIDDING ME?

**Kally:** Well, it's just a recommendation. We don't want you to feel like you're in a situation where you are being bullied.

We want to make sure we manage this as best we can, legally.
**Mum:** That's ridiculous, though!
**Kally:** Well, it's just in your best interest.
**Mum:** Yeah, but it's a brochure!
**Kally:** As I said, Susan, we do take these matters seriously.
**Mum (after another pause):** Well, you obviously do. Okay.
**Kally:** Do you have someone you can bring in?
**Mum:** Yep. Yep, I've got a son who's probably quite happy to help me there.

My only brother lives in Brisbane, so it was me she was talking about. Here she was, on the verge of tears, more nervous than she has ever been, and I was the first person she thought to call . . . even though I was the arsehole who was putting her under this terrible stress. The joke had gone far enough. My dormant conscience came to life and I jumped into the phone call.

**Me:** Yeah, Mum. I'm free on Saturday. I'll help you out.
**Mum:** Oh no! Dominic, how could you? I'm nearly crying. That is nasty! Oh, Jesus.
**Me:** Sorry, Mum.
**Mum:** Ooooh, I don't believe this. Why did I give up smoking? I could have one

right now! Phew, I won't be going to jail after all.
**Me:** And you can happily blend things now that you know you can keep the stupid manual!
**Mum:** Okay. Anything else? I've got things to do.
**Me:** Nah, that's all.
**Mum:** All right. Talk to you later. Bye.
[Click.]

And with that, Mum hung up.

She sounded mad at me. Maybe she was. Or maybe she was just busy. She did have an old SodaStream that she never could figure out how to work. Maybe she was off to Briscoes to hunt out another instruction guide.

# ☑ GO TO A GAY SAUNA

I'm not homophobic or anything. I would never discriminate against someone based on their sexuality. But I must confess, I do have a reasonably large fear of gay sex involving me. I'm fine with everybody doing whatever the hell they please. No problem with that whatsoever. But it just isn't my cuppa tea.

I was talking to my mate Mike, who happens to be gay, and I mentioned that I never use the change rooms at the gym. There are two reasons for this.

1. I have an irrational fear of getting athlete's foot, a skin condition where the skin flakes away in between your toes. For some odd reason it was drummed into me by my parents as a kid that I must be careful if I'm using communal showers because

> I could end up catching athlete's foot. I didn't really know what it was but it made me scared shitless of communal showers.
>
> 2. The gym I go to has change rooms complete with a spa pool and a sauna. It also has a reputation as a meeting place for gay men. I don't like the idea that men who are into men could possibly be checking me out. To me this seems like an unfair perk that the gay community enjoy. I know I would be as happy as Larry (whoever the hell Larry is) if I was allowed to change and shower in an area full of naked or partially dressed women. So surely for the gay community, the best part of the whole workout is getting to hit the change rooms post-workout where you get to see a smorgasbord of sausage.

In my thirty-nine years of life I have never been even the slightest bit curious about the same sex. I have a penis and I'm still not bored of it despite decades of using and, sometimes, abusing it. But I have no need, want or desire for another one.

The closest I had ever come to a gay experience was probably a urine-stream lightsaber fight at the urinals of

Riverdale Primary School in Palmerston North with my friend Aaron while we were humming the *Star Wars* theme music. Given we were only seven at the time this is far less homoerotic than it sounds. So, for the next tick on my bucket list, I was going to pop along to a gay sauna.

It was my gay mate Mike who suggested it. So I was more than a bit surprised when he told me he had never been to one himself. Then I suggested he could tag along with me, be my wingman for this mission. He replied by making a shuddering motion, accompanied by the words: 'Ewww, god no!' That made me nervous. Imagine if I ended up getting athlete's foot?

A NZ Google search of 'gay sauna' took me to the Centurian Sauna for Men. Instead of making me a bit curious or intrigued, though, the website and the services this place offered made my sphincter muscles twitch with fear:

```
Our spacious facility includes 14 private
rooms, a 3-level theatre, maze, Sky TV, a
sun bed, spa pool, steam room, dry sauna,
internet and much more. We also provide
our guests with free lubricant, condoms,
shampoo and mouthwash and also free tea
and coffee. A selection of food and
drinks are also available.
```

I feel uneasy having my coffee made at the service station by the same bloke who just filled up my BBQ gas bottle.

I was definitely not too stoked at the idea of having my coffee made for me by the guy who is also dishing out free lubricant and condoms.

> We are constantly upgrading our facilities and services so make sure you visit our sauna regularly to keep up with our improvements. Stay for an hour or all day!

And you actually CAN stay all day if you can handle that much fun. The sauna is open from 11 am till 2 am seven days a week. That's fifteen hours a day. It is open more than it is shut. You could literally spend more time here than home. You could make this place your second home . . . you could even make your own home your second home. All you would need to do is get your postage redirected to the sauna.

I then clicked through to the 'features' section of the website. Sometimes ignorance is bliss; this was one of those occasions. It would have been far easier to go in not knowing what was behind the doors. Here were some of the many features on offer:

> Internet room—surf the net or watch the local news in privacy and comfort
>
> Spa pool—a spacious spa pool is available within our facility

> Steam room—our steam room is one of many forms of hot entertainment at Centurian (very popular!)
>
> Maze—Centurian features a unique maze that is changed from time to time
>
> Sling room, for those interested in something a bit on the wild side—continuous porn is also played in this room
>
> Douche toilets—a unique feature of Centurian Gay Sauna is the douche toilets—the water is warm and the units are always kept clean
>
> Sun bed—a sun bed in a private room for working on that perfect tan
>
> Gay movie cinema—watch gay porno movies on our big screen projector

After reading that, the thought of going to this place just seemed too terrifying, too far out of my comfort zone. For this mission, I would need a wingman. And since my buddy Mike had already turned me down, I knew just the person to ask next.

Robert John Scott. My best mate. He was my best man. I was his best man. We have known each other for twenty years. We used to be in a gang together, too. The numbers in our gang increased and decreased over the years and peaked at about seven or eight but there were three core members—me, Robert, and his girlfriend at the time, Jeanette (who later went on to be the *Target* lady who said pretty much everything was 'entirely inappropriate'.) The gang was called 'The Cunty Club' and there was just one rule—when you spotted another member somewhere you had to yell the C word out as loud as you could, and the other member/s present would have to do the same back. The game was very juvenile and offensive, but bloody funny. We discovered that if you shouted that word out loud enough you could actually make it sound just like an odd noise instead of the most offensive word in the world. It was a private joke and anyone else in whatever room it happened to be must have wondered what the hell we were doing, making these strange noises that sounded like some sort of wounded animal.

Robert and I have travelled to Fiji and Bali together. We are probably about as close as two guys can be. And he has already seen my genitals, on numerous occasions, so that would be one less mental hurdle to worry about.

One of these occasions was the catalyst for one of the most embarrassing moments of my life to date. We went to Beachcomber Island in Fiji for a holiday. This was my first trip overseas—I was still in my teens.

That trip was booked for us by a good friend who was working as a travel agent in Palmerston North at the time, Shane Cortese. He is now a popular TV actor who has been in *Shortland Street, Outrageous Fortune, Burying Brian, Nothing Trivial, Dancing with the Stars* and *The Almighty Johnsons*. It is such a waste. He really was a very good travel agent.

Beachcomber is a favourite for backpackers travelling on a budget. We slept in a big dorm, the bar on the island has sand for a floor and nobody wears shoes.

On our second night on Beachcomber we were drinking at the bar. We had been there all afternoon. It was now late into the night and we were still at the bar in our togs. I was standing there talking to these two girls from Australia who had arrived on the island that day. I was really quite drunk, but so were the girls, so we were all on the same wavelength.

Then from out of nowhere the Australian girls starting screaming and laughing. Everyone else in the bar looked over and joined in the chorus of laughter.

I was standing with my togs down around the middle of my thighs with my erect penis boinging up and down.

Robert had down-trou'd me at a time when, evidently, I was enjoying talking to the Aussie girls, and the elastic band of my togs had caught the end of my penis, causing it to move up and down like a diving board at the pool.

My reaction times were dulled by the copious amounts of Fiji Bitter I had consumed, to the point where I didn't actually realise what he had done until the laughter from the other holiday-makers alerted me that not all was normal. My togs were probably only down for four to five seconds but that was long enough for enough other people to see it to ensure the story would be passed around the island and would follow me around for my entire stay. Suddenly I was the Beachcomber Pervert—the guy who got sexually excited just from talking to girls at the bar. Good one, Robert!

*Robert and I at the bar on Beachcomber Island. Wearing matching 'Bobby' hats sent to our radio station to promote the new Bobby Brown cassette.*

The two of us were lifelong friends. No falling-outs in that time either. But it was going to be a big task to get him to go to a gay sauna with me. These days he is a married man with two kids—including a teenage son. He also does a breakfast radio show on The Breeze, a station for conservative middle-aged women.

My prediction was that Robert would turn me down, citing reputation reasons. I sent him a text message to get the ball rolling. We texted back and forth and within two hours Robert had given me his answer:

```
Okay . . . maybe I could help out.
```

Wow, that was easier than I had expected. Maybe he was even a bit too eager. We made a date—the following Tuesday at midday.

On the Monday afternoon Robert texted me to confirm and asked what he needed to bring. This was a good question and not something that had even crossed my mind yet—would we wear togs? Did we have to BYO towels or did they provide them? I called up the sauna to ask.

'If you're coming tomorrow, all you need to bring is yourself—it's Towels-off Tuesday, so you get to run around naked.'

With no word of a lie, that is what he said—we would get to run around naked. Fortunately for me, Robert is not as fast a runner as I am, so in the unlikely event it came to a naked foot race, the survival of the fittest would ensure the hungry pack would capture Robert before me.

I texted Robert back and lied, 'Bring your togs and a towel, mate.'

I could not tell him the truth. Not yet. The whole

'Towels-off Tuesday' gimmick was a detail that he really didn't need to know about until we got to the sauna reception. By then, it would be the point of no return. Tell him by text right now and I could risk losing my wingman—and this was not a mission that could be done solo. Not by me anyway.

I picked Robert up from his work at midday and he threw his bag full of redundant gear (towel and togs) in the back of my car. We got a park just over the road and went into the fairly unassuming building. I had walked and driven past this building before and had never really noticed it, let alone wondered what lurked beyond the doors.

We both nervously walked up the two flights of stairs. The walls were plastered with posters promoting safe sex, with slogans like: 'My ass, my rules. Always insist on a condom for anal sex.'

We got to the unattended counter at the top of the stairs, hit the buzzer and waited for service. In the few seconds we were waiting, Robert noticed a blackboard sign: 'Towels-off Tuesday. Cum and have a good time.'

In an angry whisper, the sort a dad would use if he was telling his kids off in public, Robert fired out two questions in quick succession: 'Did you know it was Towels-off Tuesday? Do you think they spelt cum like that intentionally?'

Before I had the chance to respond with yes and yes, a petite, fully clothed man in his twenties appeared at the counter.

'Heeeey, boooys! How can I heeeellllp you?' he asked in a voice that left little mystery about his sexual orientation. Each word sounded like he was about to break into a song.

'How much is it to get in?' I enquired.

'How much is it to get in? Usually two or three drinks for me!' He broke into hysterical laughter, but I had a sneaking suspicion he may not have been joking.

The cover charge was $23 each; I handed over my EFTPOS card and paid for both of us. As the transaction was being processed, Robert cleared his throat and anxiously spoke up from behind me. 'So what does it mean when it's a Towels-off Tuesday?'

It seemed like a question that did not need to be asked or answered but Robert went there anyway. The reply did absolutely nothing to put his mind at ease.

'It means no towels and no clothes. COM. PULSE. REE!' The desk attendant stretched that word out so each syllable sounded like its very own sentence. 'You boys can run around naked until you can't take it anymore.'

Wow, what a sales pitch, I thought to myself.

He then handed me back my card and receipt. The receipt would suggest we had spent $46 at a place called the Centurian Café. I didn't notice that cafe thing on the EFTPOS slip until long after we had left and it made me laugh—they do serve tea and coffee here so I guess technically you could call it a cafe. But I can't say I've ever been to a Starbucks that runs a Towels-off Tuesday promotion!

'Have fun in there, booooys!' the assistant instructed

us as he handed us two small white towels, not much bigger than a face cloth, and two locker keys. He then pushed a button under his counter and the door to our right unlocked.

We walked through and were immediately in a room that looked like a gym changing room. There was a bench seat in the middle surrounded by walls of lockers. Unlike a gym, though, this locker room also had a locked cabinet of sex toys. These things had names like 'Darrin's Dick' and 'Liam's Wang'.

I thought this was a bit odd—this was a place full of penises, so why on earth would anyone feel the need to pay money to buy a pretend one?

Robert and I both removed our clothes and as we did so a huge naked man walked in. He was bald (on his head), probably in his mid forties, and well built—not fat, muscular. I immediately turned and started up a fake conversation with Robert—the sort of conversation you start up if you're in the middle of talking about someone and that person happens to walk into the room. I was petrified that anything I said or did could be misread as some sort of an invitation or come-on by other sauna customers.

Robert and I left the locker area and had a look around. The layout of the place was confusing and complex—there were doors and turns everywhere. The first thing I noticed was the darkness. The lights were so dim it took a little while to adjust—like when you are outside in the summer and then go inside. There was loud thumpy music playing too—dance music by David Guetta. And everywhere you walked the place had a strong smell of men's deodorant. I'm guessing the staff spray this around on a regular basis to mask other, far less appealing smells.

Given the day and time—Tuesday lunchtime—the place seemed quite busy. Everywhere we went we seemed to bump into and walk past naked men. All sorts of naked men too—fit, fat, skinny, Asian, Caucasian, hairy, shaven, pierced, tattooed.

The young man at reception was right. We truly could run around naked until we were unable to take it anymore.

We walked down a hallway past a whole row of tiny rooms with locks on the doors. At a guess, these rooms were about two and a half metres long and two metres wide. All these rooms had in them were a container full of condoms stuck to the wall and a waist-high wooden platform with a black vinyl mattress on it—a very basic sort of double bed.

It was in this area of the sauna that we found what is known as 'the sling room'. It was about the same size as the other little rooms—only this one had a small leather hammock, about the size of a beach towel, suspended in midair at about waist height from chains on each corner.

We kept walking and stumbled upon the cinema, where a projector played an adult movie against the wall. Robert and I stood at the door and watched for a couple of seconds, just long enough to see what was going on. I'm not sure of the movie title or storyline but one of the lead actors was lying on his back holding his legs up so his knees were touching his chest while the other movie star was licking his bottom. From what I saw it looked like the man lying on his back was having a far more enjoyable time than the guy who was doing the licking.

We then heard a sound and turned around to see a skinny old man, probably in his late sixties, sitting on the grandstand-style seats playing with himself. He didn't stop just because he had company. He waved hello with his free left hand. Instinctively, we turned and briskly walked away without exchanging pleasantries. Yes, this was incredibly rude on our part, but in our defence neither of us have ever walked in on anyone doing this to themselves before, so we were unsure what to say or do. What the hell is the protocol in situations like this? Even now, I still don't know what we could have said.

'Hey, mate . . . you enjoying the movie?'

'Hi there, how's it hanging?'

'So, do you come here often?'

'Have you been paying attention to the movie or have you lost the plot?'

Obviously, this behaviour which would be frowned upon and considered inappropriate at any other movie theatre anywhere in the world was perfectly acceptable and even encouraged at a gay sauna.

We were both by far the fastest walkers out of all the men we saw. We moved briskly from room to room, and every time we encountered a naked man or couple we were off again. We were the only people here not having a great time, though. Everybody else seemed quite relaxed and comfortable on this particular 'Towels-off Tuesday'.

'Can we go now?' Robert asked in a tone that suggested he had seen more than enough.

I did not need my arm twisted.

Through the confusion of dim lights and booming dance music we eventually made our way back to the locker area. On the way we passed a well-lit area that looked just like the lounge of someone's flat. The telly was turned on (much like the man we had just run away from in the theatre room) and it was playing Channel 1—*Emmerdale Farm*. The La-Z-Boy chairs and sofas were all unused. Either sauna customers are not that interested in *Emmerdale Farm* or they just don't feel comfortable hanging out, watching the telly on Towels-off Tuesdays. If they introduced a new themed day like 'Wear Something Wednesday', maybe all the seats in this area would be taken.

Back at the lockers I got dressed very quickly. I had arrived at the sauna well prepared, wearing jeans, T-shirt and jandals—a handy outfit for a fast dress or undress. Robert, on the other hand, had lace-up shoes and socks, a button-up shirt and jeans. I was fully dressed and ready to leave before my poor old mate had even started to do up his shirt.

Awkwardly, a dripping wet nude man stood behind Robert. His locker was just below Robert's, so he had to stand and wait patiently for my mate to get dressed before he could get his items out.

We walked back out through reception.

'Whaaaaat? You boys leaving already?' asked the man at reception who had served us only a few minutes earlier.

'Yep. Not really our scene,' we replied.

'Fair enough. Lots of people come and go pretty fast,' he said, putting particular emphasis on the C-word so the intentional innuendo would not be lost on us. He followed it up with a laugh that suggested, incorrectly, he knew what we had been up to.

We walked down the stairs and back to the car in silence. As we crossed the road Robert stopped in his tracks.

'Oh no! No! No! No!' Robert seemed fully gutted about something.

'What is it, mate?' I asked him.

'I was in such a rush to get dressed I left my hoody up in the locker.'

Being such a great mate, I offered a solution. 'I'll wait in the car. You go and grab it.'

Robert turned around and started walking back to the sauna as I continued towards the car.

A couple of seconds after I got in, the front passenger door opened.

It was Robert: 'Fuck it. I'm not going to worry about it. It's only a hoody.'

# ☑ BE A LIFE DRAWING MODEL

So there I was, 6.30 on a Saturday night standing in the lobby of a place called The Art Station wearing nothing but a bathrobe. In front of me was the closed door of an art studio. On the other side of the door were a group of eight fully dressed women, all aged around thirty, who were about to sketch me naked. It is a struggle to put into words just how nervous I felt. I was shit scared. A similar feeling to the time I went skydiving, only with the skydiving there was an actual chance, albeit a tiny one, I could be killed by a parachute malfunction. Today, embarrassment was the only thing that I could possibly die of.

I think we are all a bit self-conscious about how we look naked. We all have parts that we think are unusual, abnormal or just not quite what they should be.

I have read enough *Cleo* magazines over the years to know that girls like a man with a good firm bottom, for some reason I struggle to explain. Experts say it has something to do with how women are wired subconsciously—they reckon a tight muscular bottom means a guy will be a better thruster and therefore more likely to help the women reproduce. This sounds like a bunch of arse to me, pun most definitely intended.

Unfortunately the sort of bum the ladies like is pretty much the opposite of my white, saggy, dimple-ridden little thing that resembles an inflated white balloon that has been sitting in the corner of a sunny room for a week. Sadly, my gym and weight regimens over the years have generally involved lifting weights that will benefit parts of the body I will get to see in the mirror. Therefore, the backyard has been neglected.

Being naked in front of another person for the very first time is, I think, quite a nervous occasion for most of us. But this is precisely the cauldron I had decided to throw myself into to earn another tick on my bucket list. I would be a model for a life drawing class.

My initial plan was to volunteer my body at an art class at a polytech or some sort of a night art class. But before I got round to making the necessary phone calls I came across a flyer for a business called 'Strike a Pose'.

The brochure had a picture of the famous statue of David and the following blurb:

```
For a hens' party, birthday or girls'
night out to remember, experience Strike
a Pose—New Zealand's most original
life drawing class. Your Strike a Pose
```

> experience will include a lesson in life drawing with a nude male model, music, frivolity and games—the ultimate arty party for any occasion.

I couldn't decide if this life drawing class would be easier or harder than a serious life drawing class at a polytech. You know, the sort of class where aspiring artists of both sexes with a set of those very expensive-looking pencils that come in one of those posh-looking little tins look closely at every aspect of your body—but not in a pervy way—then draw what they see. They would be sober and no doubt mature and refined enough not to laugh at any oddities they noticed. They would also be so absorbed in their own art piece that they would potentially see my arse-dimples as an artistic challenge instead of a mild deformity.

A hens' party put on by the Strike a Pose people would have a completely different vibe to it—all girls, all in a good mood, all under the influence of a Vodka Cruiser or two—and it was unlikely any of them would actually harbour aspirations of being the next Vincent Van Gogh. All of these factors might make it a less awkward and more relaxed experience. But on the flipside, intoxicated girls would probably have no problem pointing out and sniggering at my many flaws.

I should have gone with the polytech option. I think that would have caused me the least embarrassment.

Courageously, foolishly, or both, I emailed Strike a Pose and volunteered my body for one of their parties, and by the end of the day, they replied.

```
Hi Dom,
That's fantastic and yes we would be
happy for you to come and model in one
of our classes. Why don't you give me
your number and I'll give you a call to
discuss? Classic!
    Look forward to hearing from you soon.
    Kind regards
    Amanda
    www.strikeapose.co.nz
```

I replied and after emailing back and forth we settled on a date: Saturday 5 November 2011. It was a hens' party of eight women starting at 6.30 pm.

I was committed now, but the date was still a couple of months away. I told myself I would hit the gym a couple of times a week and cut out the junk food in order to get myself in good shape. I'd also do lots of squats and butt clenches to try and revive my bum, which looked like it had died from neglect years earlier.

I had to do all of this. Strike a Pose usually hires their models by putting notices on boards at gyms, so most of the models are either personal trainers or just guys who are in incredible shape. Guys who probably enjoy standing naked on a stage while others admire their well-chiselled physiques.

Sadly, I failed to follow through with any of my good intentions. Why do the dates for things like this always seem to creep up on you so fast?

*

The day before, Amanda called to give me a briefing.

She told me I had to be at the venue at 6.15 on Saturday evening. There, I would be ushered into a private room well clear of the hens' party. I would wait here to be brought in and presented to the partially drunk aspiring art students at 6.30. Amanda then described how the whole arrival and 'unwrapping' would take place.

'Before you come in we do a brief tutorial, like a still life, so we do some warm-up exercises with apples and a banana. Then we do a tutorial of the human figure. At that point we will have you come in with a robe on, your grand entrance. And we'll get the girl who's having her hens' party to come up and take your robe off and that's always a bit exciting for the girls.'

I laughed nervously at the prospect.

'Then we get into the first drawing. And from then on we just get into lots of drawing games—we do musical easels, a blindfold draw, a left-hand draw and stuff like that.' Amanda paused, waiting for some kind of response, but I had nothing to say. The thought of being totally naked for two hours in this environment had left me speechless.

'Other than the initial shock of being nude it will be easy,' she said. 'We had a guy who modelled for the first time last weekend and for the first pose he was pretty nervous but by the second he was already sort of relaxed and stuff, so I'm sure you will be fine.'

I was not so convinced. I was not a model. I was just an idiot with a bucket list. I am very well aware of my physical flaws so the prospect of standing under bright lights without any clothes was about as exciting as Christmas Day for a Jewish kid.

I arrived at the Art Station and was met by the Strike a Pose girls. They took me upstairs and gave me a tour of the studio where, in under an hour, I would be the most vulnerable a human being could be.

If the tour was designed to put me at ease it failed miserably. It only made me more anxious. There were two big bright, warm lights shining down onto a raised stage in the centre of the room. Around the stage eight easels were set up with clean sheets of paper all ready to go.

I was taken downstairs to a kitchen area where I was instructed to get undressed and put a bathrobe on. Amanda left me alone for a couple of minutes so I could have some privacy to get changed, which I found funny. What was the point of that?

I very quickly knocked back a couple of fairly substantial glasses of wine which I had hoped would calm my nerves. They didn't.

One of my biggest fears was of getting aroused. My genitals are like a disobedient dog and I have almost zero control over what they do. And just like the owner of a disobedient dog, I am the one who looks bad when 'it' acts up. It's so unfair. I'm unsure if other men have this same lack of control but my penis thinks about rude stuff all the time. So even if I'm thinking about something important, such as 'I hope this prostate check I am getting right now comes back negative' or 'How am I going to execute the perfect dive from this diving board into the pool six metres below?' my renegade rod will show total disregard for the situation and completely let me down.

Out of necessity, so I can live my life day to day without being arrested, I have become a bit of a ninja when it comes to concealing my excitement. The easiest and most effective way to do this is to utilise the belt area of your clothing to do the tuck-up. Then eventually it goes away and falls back down into the proper place. I should throw a warning out there, though: the tuck-up manoeuvre cannot be done if you are wearing togs without a top at the beach. Do the tuck-up in this scenario and suddenly you have what looks like some sort of an offensive periscope poking from the top of your board shorts. In this beach situation the alternatives are limited but in the past I have taken to lying face down on the sand until things go back to normal or kept my hands strategically placed in front of me until I could get in the ocean. A dose of cold water is as effective at putting out erections as it is fires.

I first became aware of this handicap at the age of twelve when I was at St Peters Intermediate in Palmerston North. It was class speech time and after two weeks of preparation everybody had to stand in the front of the class and deliver a two- to three-minute speech on a subject of their choice. I wish I could tell you what I spoke about but the topic was overshadowed by something else that happened. I knew what was developing but could do nothing to stop it. All I could hope was that nobody else would notice. Sadly, that was not the outcome. I kept on reading my speech from the cue cards in front of me even when I could hear the whispering and suppressed giggling from my classmates. Then one of my best mates in the class, someone who I should have been able to count on to have my back, burst into laughter so loud that the teacher, Mrs O'Connell, stopped me so she could deal with this disruptive pupil who was being inconsiderate during my speech. Good on her, she had my best interests at heart, but I knew the reason for the outburst of laughter and I had a feeling this situation could end badly.

'Dean, this is incredibly rude of you!' Mrs O'Connell said sternly. 'Dominic is making his speech and I expect you to be polite enough to sit and listen quietly. Whatever made you laugh must be hilarious. Would you care to share it with everyone else?'

Now, as I mentioned earlier, Dean was a good mate. He had let me down with the interruption. Surely he would make it up to me now by either refusing to answer the question or making something up on the spot. Surely.

'Miss! Dom's got a stiffy!' Dean shouted and pointed simultaneously. Now the entire class lost it. Miss O'Connell could do nothing. Her repeated pleas for silence were drowned out by the laughter that could probably be heard from as far away as the office block on the other side of the school grounds. Fortunately by then the evidence had shrunk, allowing me to strenuously deny the allegations and blame it on the fabric of my shorts gathering in a bunch at the front. But the damage had been done and there was no way any of my classmates were going to give me the benefit of the doubt.

Luckily this was towards the end of the year. After that I left St Peters to start at Palmerston North Boys High School. Had this not been my parents' plan, I reckon they would have had to move me to a different school anyway—one little incident like this can ruin a student's entire school career!

Since that day I have been aware of this incurable problem and have just done my best to manage it. If it happened today in the life drawing class it would be an unmanageable situation, a catastrophic embarrassment with nowhere to hide.

From my waiting place (holding cell) I could hear the girls arrive, then heard them all walk up the wooden stairs in their heels. This distinct sound just served as another reminder that they all had footwear on and I did not.

The first twenty minutes of the class were, as Amanda had explained to me on the phone, a crash-course in sketching, where the girls would be taught the basics about drawing the human body. Then the girls would draw some intentionally phallic-looking fruit—a banana and two apples. Boy, after drawing these the girls were going to be let down by what was supposed to be the main event. I should have asked Amanda to swap the fruit with a courgette and a pair of mandarins.

As I waited I could hear muffled laughter from time to time coming from the studio upstairs. The girls were all in good spirits which was encouraging. They were not afraid to laugh, though, which was expected but still concerning.

Amanda knocked on the door and asked if I was ready. I took in a big deep lungful of air then exhaled in a feeble attempt to lower my heart rate. Sadly, I don't think anything would have been effective right then.

We walked up the stairs and waited in the lobby just outside the closed door to the art studio. The stereo came on and the music kicked in. *Dum. Dum dum dum. Dum dum dum. Dum dum dummmm.* 'Eye of the Tiger'. The *Rocky* theme music. That played for what felt like an eternity, but it was probably only thirty or forty seconds. The door was opened and I walked in to generous applause and cheers from the aspiring artists. I quickly looked around the room and glanced at the girls, in position at their respective easels with aprons on. They were all attractive, which immediately made me stress out about my little problem with those spontaneous erections.

I took my place on the stage, still robed. Jen, the bride-to-be, was invited to join me on stage to remove the robe. It is hard to explain the awkward vulnerability I experienced at this point. Many men would probably think this sounds like a dream come true—being the only bloke in a room full of women who are looking at your penis. But the reality is definitely more embarrassing than sexy (at least, that's the case when I am the model in question).

Jen untied my robe and removed it. I stood completely naked on stage, unsure what to do with my hands. The urge to use them as a penis shield was overwhelming! It is your natural human instinct. I had to resist doing so as Amanda gave the girls their instructions.

The first assignment was a straight drawing. I just had to pose with my arms folded for approximately ten minutes while the girls drew. Amanda had suggested to me that after the initial shock of being naked I would become comfortable. This was not the case. From my spot on the stage I could see a few of the works in progress and became incredibly self-conscious when I could see the girls drawing my penis—there was no doubt what body part they were studying at that moment!

After holding this pose for ten minutes I was told I could step down from the stage. There would now be a ten-minute recess while the girls got to sip their drinks and have a look at all the other drawings.

'Do you want the robe?' Amanda asked.

'Hell yes!' I replied without hesitation. I know there was nothing left to the imagination anymore but there was no way I could have a casual conversation with a fully clothed person if I was fully naked. It just was not doable.

Next up a chair was placed on the stage for a tandem pose. This involved me being seated on the chair while the mother of the bride sat on my lap. This would provide some coverage to key areas of flesh, for which I was grateful, but it also increased the chance of arousal. Fortunately, this worst-case scenario did not occur with this sweet lady in her late fifties perched on my lap.

For the final pose, Amanda from Strike a Pose gave me my instructions in advance. I just had to stand with my robe on and my arms by my side. The bride-to-be would take care of the rest.

Holding up a picture of the famous statue of David, Amanda then called Jen up onto the podium and issued her instructions. 'Okay, what I need you to do is take off Dom's robe and move his arms and legs into this pose. Maybe a bit of a tilt of the hips and the head to get it as close to David as possible.'

Maybe it was the warm lights and the wines from earlier catching up with me. Perhaps it was just the touch of the bride's soft skin and warm hands on my body. Whatever it was, I could feel myself expanding. My genitals had let me down, but I maintained my professionalism. I held my pose and did not look down or flinch. All I could do was hope the problem would not get any bigger.

Fortunately, it did not get any worse and I assumed I'd got away without any of the budding artists noticing.

Unfortunately, I had been busted, but everyone present was too polite to say anything about the elephant trunk in the room. I found out the next afternoon when Amanda texted me:

```
Just a quick text to say u were amazing
last night. The girls loved you. Really
nice to meet you. Hope u enjoyed
it . . . u looked like u did ha ha!
```

Gutted! If there was ever a time in my life where I wished to suffer from the common problem of erectile dysfunction, this Saturday night was that moment.

Prior to the class, Amanda had told me that none of her male models had ever been aroused while posing. I had warned her that there was a first time for everything. In any case, surely the bride-to-be would have been flattered if she had noticed, wouldn't she? I have no clue as to how the female mind works but I would imagine it is good for a girl's ego to discover she has the ability to get a man aroused just by touching his arm!

After the class had finished Amanda from Strike a Pose told me I had done great for a first-timer. She said she would call me up if she ever had a model fall through at the last minute and needed a ring-in. Whether that was the truth or not, I appreciate her letting me know! If her name and number pop up on my phone screen on a Saturday afternoon I will know to ignore it. This is an experience I will happily never repeat!

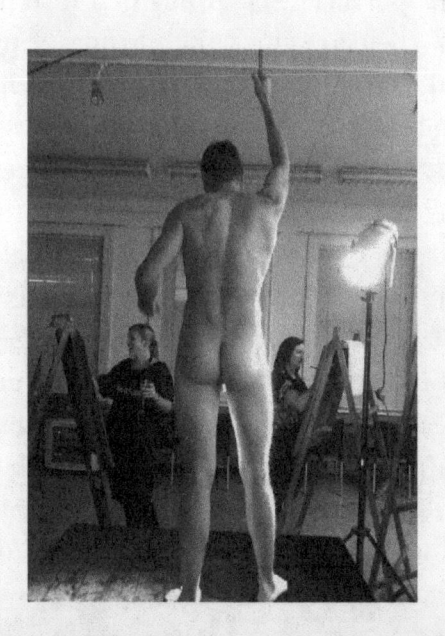

# ☑ CROSS-DRESS

This is a pretty big admission from a Kiwi bloke but I am very much in touch with my feminine side. I love bubble baths. I can appreciate the aroma of a nice pear-scented candle. A well-made chick flick is one of my favourite genres of film. And when I sit down, if I'm not thinking about, I tend to cross my legs like a lady.

And, yes, there have been occasions when I have been really, really hung-over and have sat down to pee (it just makes more sense when you don't have total confidence in your aim).

In the past when friends have been engaged, I have sometimes found the plan for the hens' night (facials and massages) more appealing than the agenda for the stag party (paintball and fishing). I can't help this! It's not my fault I'd rather be massaged with nice oils in a dim room while listening to pan-flute music than run around a muddy paddock while my friends try to shoot me with exploding balls of paint at close range. Those things fucking hurt—where's the enjoyment in that?

But that's about where my feminine side ends—otherwise I am all male.

I hardly ever cry. I shed a tear about as often as Graham Henry smiles.

I believe flatulence can be used effectively for comic purposes.

I never go to the toilet without taking in some reading material.

And sometimes I blow my nose on my towel before throwing it into the laundry.

So what? I'm a disgusting pig who just happens to enjoy massages, facials and Katherine Heigl movies. Big deal, get over it.

But even with these reasonably strong links to my feminine side, I have never ever contemplated wearing clothes or underwear that were designed for women.

It just makes no sense to me. I don't see the benefit. Nighties are a different story, though—they are very comfortable. I have a fabulous collection of them.

Men who dress as women have always amused me, mainly because they don't fool anybody. The crossdressers I have seen never look all that feminine. They just look like a bloke in women's clothing, apart from this one time in Phuket when I got fooled by a ladyboy, but that is not a story I really wish to revisit in this book.

I wonder what goes through the mind of a crossdresser. When he gets dressed and puts make-up on and prepares to go out and mix with other people, does he actually THINK he looks like a lady? Or does he KNOW he looks like a man dressed as a lady but still feels good about that compromise?

The worst cross-dresser of all time must be the wolf in the kids' story 'Little Red Riding Hood'. He dressed up as an elderly lady. Although he did manage to convince a girl that he was her nana, so maybe he didn't do such a bad job after all.

If you wander around Auckland's famous red-light district Karangahape Road, you can sometimes see these guys and, quite frankly, a lot of them look terrifying. Whether it's the stance, the walk, the jaw, the bulging Adam's apple, the stubble or the comical falsetto voice, there are always a number of obvious giveaways. I've seen a few Polynesian guys dressed up and these lads were huge. Bigger than any woman you will ever see. These guys never look convincing at all. They just look like club rugby players who are entering into one of those wacky 'dads in drag' fundraising evenings for their team.

Cross-dressing is not something I had ever wanted to do. Even when I've had the house to myself I've never been tempted to try on the wife's panties and take a look at myself in the mirror . . . okay, maybe I have thought about it once or twice but just thinking about it does not make you a weirdo (cough, cough).

But this is exactly what I would do for my bucket list. I would transform myself into an attractive lady. I would be a brother undercover as a mother.

The event? A six-kilometre fun run . . . for women

only. I would be the only male runner taking part alongside 3000 females.

Running is an activity that involves very little conversation, so this would be ideal—because no matter how much time a cross-dresser spends getting ready, any doubt is removed as soon as he opens his mouth. I'd have to avoid spitting as well. You hardly ever see women joggers spitting so doing so would potentially reveal my shocking secret.

First stop: the fancy Auckland shops of Newmarket. I went into the Trelise Cooper store. I only know the bare minimum about men's fashion and even less about clothes for women. But I had heard of the name Trelise Cooper.

I flicked through a few dresses hanging on racks then played a hide-and-seek game where I searched furiously for the well-obscured price tag. When eventually I did locate the tag I realised why it had been so well hidden—$829 for one dress.

I think I'm the same as most guys in this respect—I always check the price before I even bother trying anything on. In fact, when it comes to clothes shopping I would say this is one of the main points of difference between the sexes.

When men shop, we do so like this:

```
1. Find something we like.
2. Check the price.
3. If the price is acceptable, we will
   try it on.
```

4. If it fits, we will buy it. (Sometimes we don't even need to try it on).

When women shop, it seems to be more like this:

1. Find something you like.
2. Take three different sizes of the same thing to the fitting room.
3. Stand in front of the mirror in the garment while you think about it.
4. Listen to the sales assistant when she tells you how much it suits you.
5. Decide to buy the garment.
6. Purchase the clothes without even asking the price, because dresses like this don't come along every day.
7. Take the tag off and hide it in your wardrobe, because if your partner finds out he will be furious.

I am convinced this is why women's clothes cost more than men's—women fall in love with the clothes before they bother finding out the price. So it becomes an emotional purchase and the price becomes irrelevant.

And another problem is this—the more the dress costs, the more it stands out, meaning the lady owner can only wear it once or twice before other bitchy girls start talking behind her back, saying things like, 'OMG. Is that

Trelise Cooper dress the only thing she owns? Laaaame! She wears it, like, all the time! It's sooooo tragic.'

So you have an insanely overpriced item that you can only wear out in public a couple of times before it gets given a permanent spot in the wardrobe where it remains for a couple of years until you accept you will never wear it again and you put it in a clothing bin or sell it on Trade Me for $30. And that, ladies and gentlemen, is the sad and lonely life of an expensive designer dress.

Next stop: The Haus of G, Glassons. Having two snobby sisters and a wife, I had caught snippets of conversations about this popular chain store before. From what I picked up it seemed there was only one real problem with Glassons . . . it was just too damn affordable, which meant lots of women shopped there and ended up wearing the exact same clothes.

Walking through the front doors the first thing that struck me was the loud music—Taylor Swift or some similar female singer drizzled in generous amounts of oestrogen.

I'd imagine if you were a girl you would find the store design and set-up quite aesthetically pleasing. It's like a *Cleo* or *Dolly* magazine brought to life—the funky wallpaper, chandeliers, the smell, the ambience. Words in big fonts designed to inspire the customers and make them feel good about themselves are printed across the walls. Words like 'Dream', 'Believe' and 'Sale'.

The store was busy and I was the only man as far as the eye could see. I scanned the shop floor looking for other lads who had tagged along on their partners' shopping trip but there were none present. I was alone, outnumbered, vulnerable, afraid.

Okay, that's bullshit. But I definitely felt like I was in a place that I had no business being in. I was on a mission. Like Brad Pitt and George Clooney in *Ocean's Eleven*, I had a job to do: I had to get in, get the merchandise and get out of there in the shortest time possible.

I found a rack of yellow summer dresses close to the doors and checked the price on the first one. The tags were much easier to find here than at the Trelise Cooper shop and this one was a far more reasonable $79. I found one with an XL tag and felt my heart rate lifting and my throat getting that horrible nervous dry feeling as I played through in my mind just how awkward it was going to be asking to use a fitting room. The best story I could think of was that I was buying it as a present for my sister who was 'about the same size as me . . . so can I try it on as a size guide?'

In the end I just faced the wall on the shop floor and discreetly and quickly held the XL dress up against my clothes. It looked about right so I took it to the counter. As I waited in line for the cashier I found a straw sunhat on the rack to my right that I thought would go well with my pretty summer dress. Reluctant to draw attention to myself I just grabbed one and hoped it was a one size fits all.

All in all I reckon I was in Glassons for three or four minutes. This may be some sort of record for someone making a purchase in a women's clothing store. But I was not there to set any world records; my mission was to turn myself into an attractive lady and participate in a sports event for women only.

I would not be trying to win. Going fast would draw too much attention to myself. Then my sex and the legalities of me being in the run would be questioned. I would be scrutinised like that South African runner who people thought was a bloke just because she was heaps faster than everyone else—Caster Semenya. Remember her? She won the gold medal for the 800 metres at the 2009 World Champs. And she was totally wasting all the other girls in her races. Combine this blistering speed with the fact she has a masculine face and giant shoulders and suddenly people start talking. After that win at the World Champs she was subjected to gender testing and didn't run again until the IAAF cleared her to return to competition the following year. And that is one thing that puzzles me about Caster Semenya and this gender test the IAAF do. How did it take them months to do the test and confirm the results? Surely there are a couple of simple and far less time consuming ways to prove someone is a man or a lady?

Even a reasonably non-invasive Genital Squeeze Test, or GST, would have surely solved the secret of Semenya's sex. It's a common procedure, the GST, but its catchy acronym never really took off after the government launched their Goods and Services Tax.

A GST requires just a gentle squeeze and pat down there on the outside of a person's clothing, the way you check the freshness of bread in the supermarket.

The World Champs where Caster Semenya's sexuality

was questioned were light years away from this six-kilometre Sunday morning fun run that I was participating in. But my sexuality could also be questioned. Sceptical female runners might try to give me a GST. Is it wrong that I found this possibly-could-happen-but-probably-won't-happen scenario quite exhilarating?

Race day arrived and Jay-Jay and I got up early. I showered and, instead of using the cake of Imperial Gold soap to rigorously wash myself down, I used a delicious lavender-scented body-wash and slowly caressed my body as I rubbed it on. Then I draped a big soft bathrobe around me and wrapped my towel up around my wet hair like a turban. This small change in my morning routine immediately made me feel a good 10 per cent more feminine. I was ready to get my girl on.

I struggled into the yellow dress. I hadn't tried it on in the store the day before but it looked pretty damn big, so I was confident it'd fit okay. With the help of my wife and a wee bit of force, we got it on. Then came the long blonde wig, a thin black belt for decoration and the gorgeous sunhat, and I was good to go.

I would wear my regular size 12 Adidas running shoes—everyone else would have their trainers on so my choice of footwear would not be brought into question. For the same reason I would resist the urge to wear make-up—the majority of runners would not be made up so neither should I.

When I looked in the mirror prior to leaving the house I liked what I saw. A very handsome lady stared back at me. She was gorgeous, mysterious, intriguing. I thought the female me looked very European—not in a Bulgarian weightlifter way, either, but in an international model fresh from the beaches in the South of France way. I looked good. I was actually convincing. I was now ready to go public as a lady.

Some early morning road workers on the back of a truck laying down orange road cones were the first to comment. This was just moments after we got out of the car. After staring at me from the moving truck, one of the young blokes shouted out something like: 'Hey Big Bird! Can you tell me how to get to Sesame Street?' This was followed by laughter and applause from his colleagues. What if I did just happen to be a tall and muscular woman? A comment such as that would be soul-destroying. Luckily I could take it on the chin—my big square masculine one!

None of the women who approached me for a chat did so thinking I was part of the sisterhood. Not one woman came to me asking if I had an emergency tampon they could borrow. (Girls do ask each other to borrow these things, don't they?) A couple of them wanted to know where I got the dress, but most of them wanted to know what the hell I was doing dressed as a woman.

'Is it that obvious?' I wondered.

It seemed the answer was yes. It must have been the lack of make-up, I reckon. A bit of eyeliner and some lippy and I think the outcome would have been quite different.

Yes, I felt pretty. But to everybody else I just looked

like one of those guys I took the piss out of earlier in the chapter, one of those terrifying blokes on K Road who dress in drag and smugly believe they have duped everyone.

Even during the run I went past some young children on the footpath who were there cheering on their mum. Their dad pointed me out to them and they laughed. Their laughter, combined with the finger pointing, made it very obvious they were laughing at me and not with me.

So I made a dick of myself. I did not manage to trick any person of any age. And, apart from me, nobody seemed to think I looked like a sexy chick. But the one positive from this whole experience?

This is a bit embarrassing to admit but I have never felt so free and liberated on a run. The summer dress was so light it felt like I was running naked. It was so much less restrictive than my regular men's running shorts. Unfortunately, this fun run left me emotionally scarred and a bit fragile, so I will never dress as a woman in broad daylight ever again. But if you happen to see a very tall lady with a rectangular jaw in a yellow dress going for a jog very late at night, you should do a double take. It might just be this sexy man-bitch!

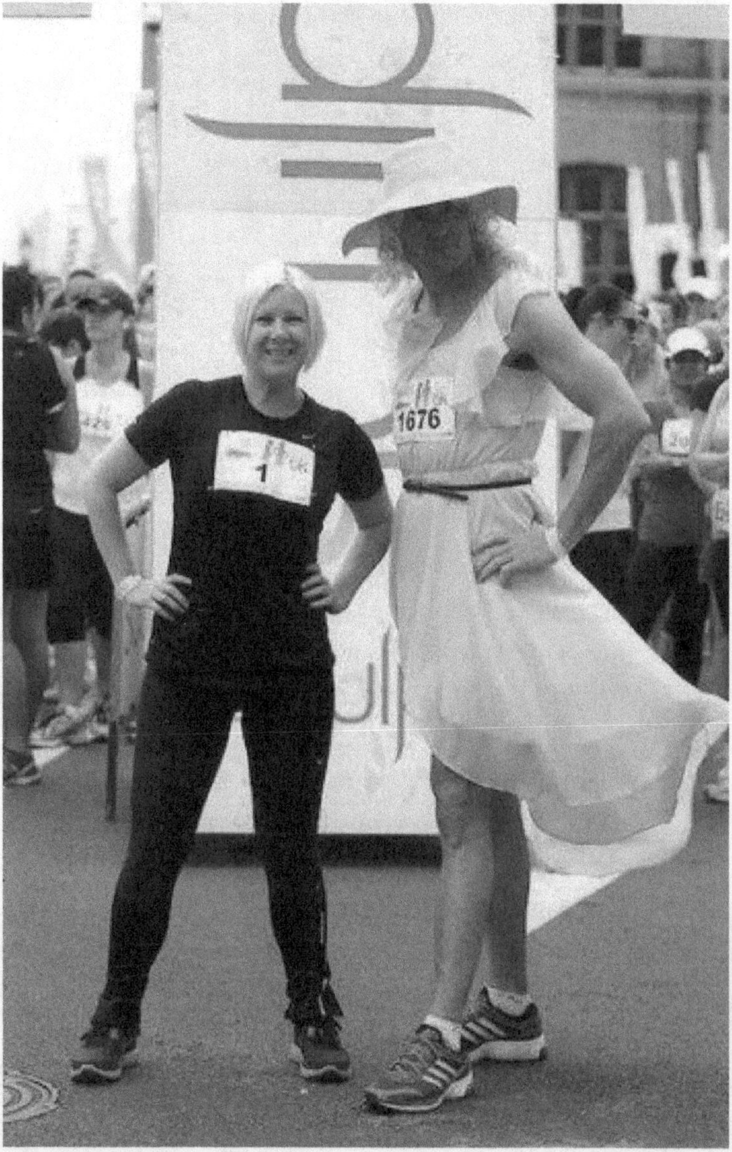
1
1676

# ☑ GET A BAD TATTOO

I don't have any tattoos. It's not because my body is a temple or anything, far from it. It's not because the pain makes me nervous (okay, maybe that's not entirely true). I think the big reason I've never been inked is that I'm a commitment-phobe.

I often notice tattoos on other people and wonder if they are still happy with the work they have had done. Like the two guys I saw at the Wet'n'Wild theme park on the Gold Coast—probably best mates, possibly brothers. These blokes were in their early twenties and each had a tattoo of a dumbbell weight on their left boob . . . or pectoral muscles, as they probably call them. I find it hard to see how this could have ever seemed like a good idea. These guys were in good shape, so I'm guessing they train together at the gym and that's very nice for the both of them. But surely it would be enough to have the matching triceps, deltoids, trapeziums and bicep muscles?

But each to their own. Beauty is in the eye of the beholder and all that. Some people may be happy with tattoo work they've had done even though others think it is absolutely shithouse. Like the lady I met at the swimming pool at Aggie Grey's resort in Samoa a few years ago. She had her back painted with a slogan in a very generous font size. Her tattoo read: 'The older the WOOD, the hotter the fire.' I asked her about it and she explained that Wood was her family name. Maybe it needed an explanation in a small font at the bottom of her back, like a footnote. Because without explanation, I assumed she must have married an old bloke and the slogan was something to do with the age of his genitals and an appraisal of his performance in bed. That theory would also explain why she choose such a big font—so her elderly lover with his ageing wood and fading eyesight could still read the tattoo when they were making love in a particular position. She told me she still loved her tattoo. But then again, she never had to see it, did she?

I wonder if tattoo artists ever feel bad about what they are doing. It would not be good for business, but surely an artist with a conscience would speak up and say something to a customer who is about to make a bad mistake, just to act as one final voice of reason, since the warnings, if any, from friends and family did not get through. I mean, all it would take is the artist to say something like: 'Are you sure you want to do this? What if you and Angus break up? That's not a very common name and I cannot imagine other non-Anguses would be too pleased at seeing your unclothed breast for the first time and discovering they are trespassing on some skin that is clearly the property of another man.'

A lot of people who get the name of a lover tattooed and then regret it down the track often opt to get it covered over with more tattoos or get it changed or tweaked so it takes on a new meaning. During the height of his romance with Winona Ryder, back when they both thought they would buck the celebrity trend and be together forever, Johnny Depp decided to show his love for her by getting 'Winona Forever' on his right shoulder. Then, the unimaginable happened—they broke up! Johnny got his tattoo touched up, and now it says 'Wino Forever', suggesting that he has gone from having bad taste in women to having a drinking problem.

If you did get the name Angus, like in the hypothetical situation above, I suppose you could go back to the artist who did it and add the words 'burgers are delicious' next to it.

I have had some close calls over the years, moments in my life when peer pressure or poor decision-making almost got the better of me. These are the THREE BEST TATTOOS I NEVER GOT (BUT ALMOST DID).

## Celtic knot armband

Celtic knot armband tattoos were very popular in the early nineties. Four of my mates at the time got them and I came very close. Lack of money was the only thing that held me back. Thank god I was broke. I have never been to Scotland, Wales or Ireland and I have no ancestral links to those countries. My strongest link to that neck of the woods is probably that I own a couple of U2 CDs.

## Your name

A good mate of mine in Palmerston North endured the unimaginable discomfort of having the shaft of his penis tattooed and maintained it was the best decision he ever made. Immortalised in dark green ink forever were the words: 'Your name'.

His tattoo became the basis of a party trick and a sure-fire way to break the ice with members of the opposite sex. I definitely toyed with the idea of getting one exactly the same. I had sufficient funds to get the work done this time; it was only the thought of the pain involved that stopped me following through.

But it worked a treat for my mate Dan. His conversations with girls at bars usually followed this path:

```
'Hi, my name's Dan, what's your name?'
   'Angela.'
   'Angela? Oh wow. You won't believe
this. I have "Your Name" tattooed on my
penis.'
   'Ha ha, is that right?'
   'Yeah, it is. I'll show you later.'
```

It was possibly the world's most profitable dick joke, and it served Dan very well in the 1990s. I haven't caught up with Dan for a while so I'm not sure what he's up to these days. For all I know, he could have ended up being imprisoned for exposing himself. It wouldn't surprise me if that occurred. There can be a very fine line between a risqué visual gag and indecent exposure. I doubt this particular tattoo would make prison time easy, either. If I was in a prison with hundreds of other men I would make it a priority on the very first day of my sentence to find the tattooist in my cell block and get the word 'NOT' tagged onto the front of that short phrase.

## The Confederate flag

Okay, so this one could be considered a bit of a stretch. I was eight years old and it was to be a temporary tattoo, a homemade one at that. It was 1981 and the must-watch TV show (well, it was for this little kid) was *The Dukes of Hazzard*. I loved Bo and Luke Duke, I loved Daisy and Uncle Jesse, Rosco P. Coltrane and Boss Hogg. But the star of the show for me was the General Lee. That was going to be the first car I ever owned. Before I eventually did get my first car I would change my mind another couple of times and dream of owning a car like KITT from *Knight Rider* and the A-Team van. In the unlikely event anyone actually cares, for my first car I ended up buying a Holden Gemini sedan. It was maroon, cost me $5995 and would have been totally useless in a high-speed chase to avoid the county sheriff after I was caught making my own moonshine.

The flag from the roof of the General Lee was my go-to doodle. It was all over my exercise books at school and was even etched onto my cricket bat.

One morning before going to school I came up with

the brilliant idea of creating my own temporary tattoo. Instead of just drawing the flag straight onto my arm, for some reason that only an eight-year-old could explain, I drew the blue and white flag with an orange background onto a piece of paper. Then I got a damp flannel, moistened my shoulder, pressed down the piece of paper and held it in place. The end result was blurry and smudged but you could still tell what it was. I could not have been more pleased with myself.

Once my handiwork dried I pulled my T-shirt sleeve down and grabbed my backpack. My friends at school would be so jealous when they saw I had a tattoo. Sadly, they never got to see it. As I went to leave the house Mum approached. Bo and Luke Duke had Boss Hogg always trying to bring them down. I had my mum.

'What have you been doing in the bathroom?' she enquired.

'Umm, nothing really,' I answered with sheepish look of guilt all over my face. She lifted up the sleeve of my shirt.

'WHAT. THE. HELL. IS. THAT?' she shouted. I should have been offended she couldn't tell it was a tattoo of the flag from the roof of the General Lee.

'It's a tattoo, Mum. It's not a real one, though. I made it myself with felt tips,' I explained, in case she somehow mistook it for an actual tattoo.

'There is no way you are going to school like that!' she exclaimed, then dragged me by my inked bicep with a grip a little tighter than it needed to be and marched me into the bathroom. What happened next would probably be considered child abuse these days. But in 1981, this was possibly considered textbook parenting.

Mum started running the hot tap, then went to the laundry and got a scrubbing brush. One of those real bristly ones, the sort you would use to get an oil spill off concrete. Then, using the brush, the water and brute force, she removed the tattoo and two to three layers of skin.

In my personal opinion, my homemade Confederate flag looked far more appealing than the scab that replaced it. But being eight years old, my opinion in this situation mattered little. The tough love appeared to work, though—never again did I attempt to give myself a temporary tattoo! Maybe subconsciously that incident played a part in putting me off getting a real tattoo later in life.

It's not just regular people who make bad choices when it comes to tattoos, either. Johnny Depp is far from being the only celebrity who has made a big ink mistake over the years. Some of these beautiful people may regret it. Most have them have egos so big that admitting a monumental cock-up is not something they would ever be likely to do.

Pop singer Pink has a barcode on the back of her neck. And it looks like a crap job has been done on it too. Still, at least shoulder-length hair will cover it up.

Nicole Richie has the word 'virgin' on her left wrist. She explained in an interview that this is because her star sign is Virgo. What an idiot! How dumb is this girl? Who the hell sees the word 'virgin' and thinks of the zodiac signs? And it looks even more ridiculous now when she is pushing around her stroller with her children, Harlow and Sparrow. Maybe she should go and get the word 'former' tattooed on her right wrist.

Kimberly Stewart has a tattoo that reads 'Daddy's Girl' in honour of her dad, Rod Stewart. That's very nice. The problem is the location Kim selected—it's less than six inches from her genitals. Partners of Kimberly are probably thinking about Rod when they are that close to her vagina . . . but I suspect her daddy is the last thing on their minds.

Mike Tyson for some reason thought it would be a good idea to get a traditional Maori design around his left eye. Then again, after biting Evander Holyfield's ear, getting addicted to drugs, making a reality TV series about pigeon racing and being imprisoned for rape, this tattoo could possibly be one of the least-stupid decisions he has made!

To earn another tick on my bucket list, I needed to follow in the footsteps of these beautiful people (well, Mike Tyson excluded) and get inked.

The big point of difference would be that I would not regret my tattoo in time. No, my tattoo would cause immediate remorse. From the time I left the tattoo parlour, the reaction from mates and family who saw my work would be along the lines of 'Tell me the name of the guy who did this—I want to call the police and have him arrested for vandalism!'

For ideas, I posted a status update on Facebook asking if anyone had a tattoo they regretted getting done, and how long it was before the remorse kicked in.

```
My ex made a tattoo gun out of a teaspoon,
needle, old phone charger & some Indian
ink & since he had some alright tats
said 'Trust me babe I'll give you a mean
tat!' so I did . . . Then checked the
mirror & he'd put his initials on my ass.
I dumped him not long after but still
have the reminder of him . . . Now I'm
married & my man has different initials.
Awkward.
Kirti


My friend got a tattoo saying SWAGGER
down her stomach and she regrets it lots!
Helaina


I got a gang tat when I was 14 now I'm
19 and regret it big time! I'm not even
in a gang anymore, I'm a changed man.
Jayden


I got my kids names on my back on a
Saturday morning. He did a shit job as
they were all crooked so I rang on the
Monday about getting removal done!
Gillian
```

I got a paw print tattooed on my back when I was 15 just so I could piss my dad off. I started regretting it when my mate's 6-year-old son started telling me there was a blues clues clue on my back. Lol
Melissa

I got 'yours' on the lower part of my back (above my crack). I was 14 and it was a home done job haha. 8 years on I'm still mocked for it.
Leilisha

I have the jackass logo (the skull and crutches) on my back and the reason I regret it is because it looks like shit and it's the bloody jackass logo. Whenever someone points it out it reminds me of how stupid I was. I got it when I was 15 I am now 21. Time to cover up, I think.
Danille

I was at the bus stop on my way to school and accidentally jumped on the bus going the opposite way to town, I was 16 and got a rose on my boob. I'm now in my 30s and I hate it SOOOO much!
Natasha

```
Just saw a woman on Queen st who
had a Pikachu tat behind her right
ear . . . Regret that much babe?
Tara

Tweety bird on my stomach! When I was
17!!! DUMB IDEA!! Looks like big bird
when I'm pregnant.
Lucie
```

I made my mind up on a Tuesday and walked in off the street on the Thursday morning to a tattoo place just down the road from my work, Dermagraphics tattoo studio, in Auckland.

Working on the front desk was the heavily tattooed Mel, an attractive girl with an impish, pixyish look. Both her wrists were covered in tattoos of buttons. I mentioned I liked them and she thanked me and explained that 'Buttons' was her nickname. Then it occurred to me that people with tattoos must get this all the time—strangers commenting on their work. This sounds like a nuisance to me but I suppose if you get work done on a body part that other people are going to see, suddenly it becomes a bit more public and a bit less personal.

Buttons flicked through the booking diary and said her afternoon was blank. We agreed I'd come back to get the work done at 1.30.

I typed my tattoo subject into Google and ran an image search. I printed off a couple of pages and took them back with me. I thought Buttons would have a good idea of what image would look best permanently dug into human skin.

Mel showed me a photo and told me a story about a lady she had worked on in the morning. 'She's fifty-five years old and has wanted a tattoo her whole life but her husband told her she wasn't allowed. They broke up and her new man is a biker, he's covered in tats, so he helped her design it.'

It was a big skull on her left bicep with the slogan 'Born to be Baaad' and, yes, there were two additional vowels! Seems like this old girl had a fair bit of catching up to do—because apart from the tattoo informing the reader that she was baaad, you would never have guessed.

We went into the studio where my work would be done. I took my shirt off and perched myself on the white leather bed, my legs dangling over the side and my back facing Mel.

I had no idea what to expect. The week had been busy, so I hadn't really given any thought to it. I knew it would be painful, everyone says it is, but because so many people have them these days I reasoned that it couldn't be *that* painful. Lots of real weedy-looking little guys have them—my pain tolerance has gotta be higher than those guys!

Boy, was I wrong about that. More on the pain soon.

As Mel was stencilling my lower back and getting her needle and colours sorted, we got talking. She told me she was an artist who had stumbled into this line of work three years earlier. She was always into art and claims she could draw before she could even talk. She got her first tattoo when she was nineteen, 'and it was all downhill from there'.

I asked her about the very first tattoo she gave. As far as first day on the job nerves go, this would have to be right up there with being a surgeon, I reckon.

I don't know about you but there is NO WAY I would want the honour of being the first-ever client of a tattoo artist. Inexperience plus nerves are a dangerous combo for something so permanent.

Her first piece was a pair of wings on the feet of a young man.

'He was an exchange student who lived at my parent's house. He didn't have any tattoos and I hadn't tattooed anyone so we were both freaking out a bit. It was real funny, too, because I started and it wasn't leaving much of a mark and he was like, "Oh wow, this doesn't hurt a bit," and he was a real wimp. And the guy who I apprenticed under, he went, "Okay, I need to show you something," so he sat down and did one little line and the kid was like, "Holy shit! That hurts! That hurts," then my mentor handed me the gear back and said, "Don't be afraid to get right in there."'

What a story to hear just minutes before the work on my back was to commence. I don't know which quote made me more nervous—the 'Don't be afraid to get right in there,' or the 'Holy shit, that hurts, that hurts.'

Her tutor essentially told her that if it doesn't hurt you ain't doing it right.

I asked Buttons if she makes many stuff-ups these days.

'I don't think I've ever made a big enough mistake for

anyone but me to notice, you know? Every mistake I've ever made has always been fixable.'

This was a reassuring answer.

'What are the most common tattoos people get in this spot?' I asked her. I was getting my tattoo right at the bottom of my back, just an inch or two up from my bum. Tattoos in this location are commonly referred to as 'tramp stamps'.

'Not many guys get that area done,' Buttons said, telling me what I already knew. 'It's usually women and the most common things are butterflies or tribal designs.'

I was surprised I didn't even get a chance to back out, just a casual 'Now, are you SURE you want to do this?' I would have thought something like this would be covered by some sort of code of conduct or rulebook. Maybe it is just something tattooists with a conscience say to younger clients. Buttons probably thought, and rightly so, that this client was old enough and ugly enough to get a tattoo without a lecture.

I asked her if she had ever talked anyone out of getting something done.

'Yeah, I always try to talk people out of getting their significant others' names on them,' she confessed. She seemed quite proud of this sensible stance of hers.

I was quite pleased to hear that, too. If you must get a name on your body, get your kids' names. They will be part of your life forever, even if they grow up and only call twice a year (sorry, Dad). But your lover's name? I have always thought that was a really bad relationship jinx.

When I was still at school I had a part-time job packing groceries at Foodtown. This was back when there were two people on each checkout—an operator and a packer. There was an older woman who I would work with some days who had her husband's name tattooed on her right bosom. His name was Eugene. I know this because during a quiet spell one day she told me this titbit about her, well, tit bit. Then she unzipped the front of her smock and showed me, right there at aisle 13. I warned her that if they ever split up she would have a hard time replacing him, because there are not too many men by that name in the Eugene pool. She didn't laugh. I explained the wordplay to her. She still didn't laugh. After that she went out of her way to avoid working with me. Bit rude—she was the one who flashed me in the workplace.

I asked Buttons if she had ever been successful in talking someone out of getting a name done.

'Yes. And I felt really bad about it too, because he was a younger guy. He was like twenty-two or twenty-three or something. He came in and he wanted to get his girlfriend's name on his ring finger.' I liked this story already. Tommy Lee and Pamela Anderson exchanged ring-tattoos when they got married. The tattoos survived. Their marriage? Not so successful.

'He set the appointment without discussing what he wanted and he came in and I started talking to him and he's like, "Yeah, I'm proposing to her this weekend," and I was like, listen, she's your girlfriend and she hasn't said yes yet? Maybe wait ten years or fifteen years down the line then look at doing that. At least wait until after she says yes! And he laughed and was like, "Yeah, you're right. She hasn't said yes yet," and when he left he was like, "Wow, what if she doesn't even say yes?" And I felt bad because I made him question his relationship.'

She did the right thing. Some of us guys often confuse really romantic gestures with really stalkerish gestures. We mean well but just miss hitting the target sometimes.

**Romantic gestures:**
```
Picnics in secluded spots
Hot air balloon rides
A boat ride on a lagoon (like in The
   Notebook)
```

**Romantic gestures (that can seem a bit stalky):**
```
Getting her name tattooed as a surprise
Breaking into her apartment and
   sprinkling rose petals everywhere the
   day after your first date
Buying her a big bunch of sunflowers on a
   first date because you checked out her
   Facebook page and found out that was
   her favourite flower
```

It can be a fine line, but most girls will let you know if they really want something. So it's a brave man who makes assumptions as bold as getting her name inked.

*

Button was ready. She started and so did the pain. IT WAS INTENSE!

She warned me that the outline would be pretty uncomfortable but the colouring-in bit would be a bit more manageable. All up it should take about forty minutes or so, she estimated. Fortunately we were done and dusted in exactly thirty-two minutes.

I am a self-confessed wuss and my pain threshold is ultra-low, so this was a gruelling half-hour. I mean, I wasn't crying or begging Buttons to stop, but it did hurt like hell. I am not a particularly sweaty person but beads of the salty stuff were dripping down my arms and onto my jeans from my armpits.

*Tattoo face. The face of a man in extreme discomfort.*

To describe the pain I would say it probably feels like someone getting a ballpoint and digging the nib deep into your skin then slowly slicing down and around. I've never done that with a pen but I can't imagine it'd be much fun.

My whole body felt like it was about to combust, especially the area that was being tattooed—that was throbbing.

Courageously, I got through it and made a promise to myself that I would have a new-found respect for any person who has a tattoo.

The respect would be limited only to their pain tolerance though. I couldn't promise myself that I would refrain from taking the piss out of their design.

Buttons covered up her artwork with glad wrap, charged me $160 for my very first tattoo—a tramp stamp—and sent me on my way.

Mum came over that evening. I showed her and her response was not all that favourable. She was laughing but she didn't really seem amused: 'For goodness sake. Yuck. At least it's in a place where you can cover it.'

Here I was thirty-eight, practically a middle-aged man, and I felt Mum's disapproval. I half expected her to get the scrubbing brush from the laundry and attempt to scrub it off, like she did with the Dukes of Hazzard tattoo I'd given myself thirty years earlier.

'Do you get the joke?' I asked her. She shook her head.

I explained the joke to her.

The comedy value of a joke is always diminished by at least 50 per cent if it needs to be explained by the teller.

Even then I didn't get the desired reaction. Nope. Even when the old lady had been told the thinking behind the work, there was still no laugh. Fuck me. The visual joke which I was now committed to for life might not even be a good one. Maybe I should have sounded out a few trusted friends first, like trying material out on a test audience.

I showed a few workmates. The reactions were mixed. It seemed the joke was way more subtle than I had thought.

Fortunately, my real friends—people on Facebook who I have never met—they seemed to like it:

```
So freaking awesome. How can you regret
that?
Alana

O for awesome!
Fran

So funny and such a random thing to get!
haha
Hope

There is nothing to regret about that
that's so funny and SO kiwi.
Belinda

Too funny and Dom I bet that thing hurt,
looking at the pictures with your spine
bone poking out. Bugger that
Jess
```

```
LMAO! That's some funny shit
Suzanne


Love it Dom. I have one in the same area
and proud of it, I don't care if it is
called a tramp stamp. Mine has special
meaning as most people's do.
Kerrie
```

So, was the goal achieved? Did I get a tattoo that I would immediately regret?

I have to say, mission well and truly accomplished.

If I am at a restaurant leaning forward and my shirt lifts up, I feel self-conscious.

When I take my nephew to the swimming pool, I feel self-conscious.

On a hot day if I run without my top on, I feel self-conscious.

Occasionally I forget it is even there, like when I was in line for a Mr Whippy at the beach over summer, shirt off of course. Then you can hear sniggering or whispers from those behind you and it serves as a reminder: 'That's right! I have a tattoo on the small of my back, a tramp stamp.'

Will I get it removed? No way. I've heard the removal is twice as painful as getting the work done in the first place so that is not an option.

My mum's big concern was how I would feel about it when I am a seventy-year-old man. I suspect that if I am lucky enough to make it to that number I will probably have far more things to get embarrassed about than a faded old joke tattoo I got in my thirties. While I am in a nursing home having some poor nurse clean me up after I shit my pants during a tense game of housie, it definitely won't be the tattoo that is the cause of my humiliation!

I present to you . . . (drum roll) . . . the world's first ever LITERAL TRAMP STAMP!

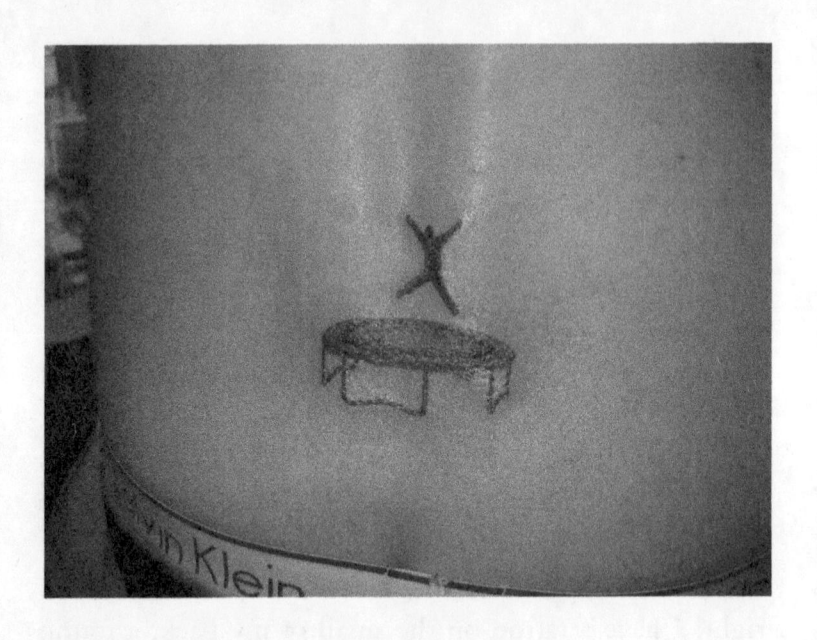

# ☑ JUMP OFF THE TALLEST BUILDING IN NEW ZEALAND

I've always hated scary theme park rides and all those thrillseeker activities that all New Zealanders are supposed to be right in to. You know, that adventurer spirit of guys like Sir Edmund Hillary and AJ Hackett.

I have parachuted, twice. The jumps were five years apart. I can safely say there will never be a third time.

The first time was in my early thirties. Up to that point there had been numerous opportunities to skydive but I always avoided it because I was absolutely petrified at the thought. But there I was, in Fiji for the filming of a reality TV show, *Treasure Island: Couples at War*, with my wife, Jay-Jay Feeney, who is even less daring than I am, and we were told by the show's host, Jon Stevens, that to start the series all contestants would have to parachute onto the deserted island where the show would be filmed. This was bullshit for the telly, of course. Yes, the island was uninhabited but the crew had no trouble getting there by boat. If any of the contestants refused to jump, the team they ended up being on would lose half their rations of rice before the game had even properly started. I really did not want to be 'that guy', the dick on a reality TV show who refused to jump, let his team down, then got sent packing in the very first episode and ended up looking like a pathetic loser in front of the entire country.

So Jay-Jay and I both faced one of our greatest fears and went up 10,000 feet in a helicopter and did a tandem skydive, landing on a sandbar on a deserted island. I had done it. I could not believe it. This was something I had been avoiding my whole life and it was nowhere near as frightening as I'd built it up to be—only a tiny bit of wee came out. I would almost go as far to say I enjoyed the experience. I made a pact with myself that day that if I ever had the opportunity to jump again, so long as it was in a place as pretty as Fiji, then I would do so without hesitation, my illogical logic being that if I was going to plummet to a gruesome death I would want the ground I was racing towards to be scenic, something that was easy on the eye.

After that first jump I think I went through the same thing women go through with childbirth (only on a far greater scale than silly old childbirth), where the experience is harrowing, traumatic and excruciatingly painful . . . but afterwards the relief and rush of endorphins is so great that you somehow block out the memory of how horrible it truly was.

And that is how, five years later, I again found myself inside a rickety old jump plane in the gorgeous South

Island resort town of Wanaka, circling up to a height of 10,000 feet (that's about three kilometres in the sky).

As the plane got higher and the ground got further away from us, I remembered just how much this sort of stuff gives me the absolute shits and decided that if I managed to survive this jump, I would drop the promise I made myself and never ever do it again!

We reached our desired height and then I jumped out with a big Yugoslavian man, my tandem master, strapped behind me, as if we were attempting to join the mile-high-spoon club.

I reckon on both these occasions the only reason I jumped out of the aircraft in the first place was due to the bloke attached to me, breathing onto the back of my head. Abort the jump and I'd be letting someone else down.

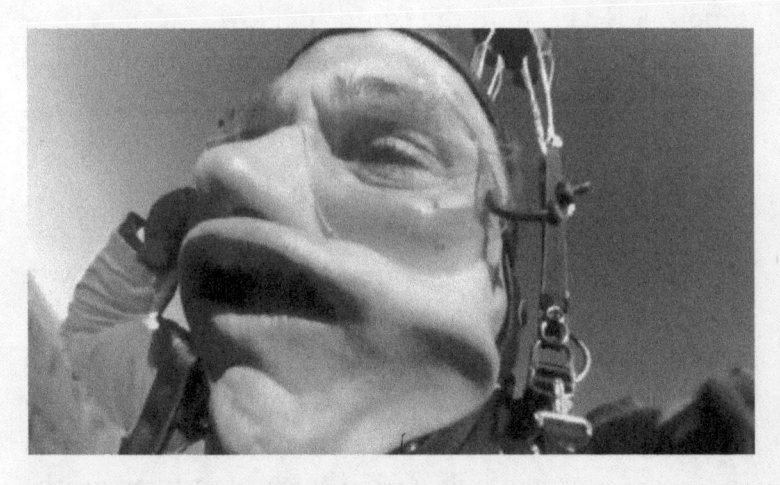

*As I was falling out of a plane three kilometres up in the air, having an ugly skydive face was the least of my concerns.*

The big Yugoslavian fella informed me he had jumped 9000 times before so my odds of survival seemed pretty good, I reasoned. But for the forty seconds that I plummeted through the air at terminal velocity, with the ground rushing up towards me, I was convinced a gruesome death was imminent. The enjoyment I got from the skydive jump was all relief-based and only came when the chute popped open and jolted me and my Yugoslavian daddy to a glide. That's the moment you realise you have cheated death.

So, as a general rule of thumb, I avoid all these sorts of activities. I CAN do them—I have proven that to myself—I would just rather not. This seemed to be a good reason to put a new extreme thrillseeking activity on my bucket list —the Sky Jump from the Auckland Sky Tower.

It's an imposing structure, the Sky Tower. Plain and simply, it is a beast. In the skyline of New Zealand's largest city it is twice as tall as any other building and looks like a giant syringe. It is probably just good luck that it has not become some sort of a statue of worship for intravenous drug users from around the world.

At 192 metres, the view from the top on a clear day is breathtaking. I have been up there many a time with friends and family from out of town (who somehow mistook me for a tour guide) and even though the option to do so is there, I have never had any interest at all in jumping off it. Riding the high speed lift up and down the tower and standing on the thick glass floor on the viewing level is about as daring as it gets for me these

# JUMP OFF THE TALLEST BUILDING IN NEW ZEALAND

days. And if anybody ever tries to call me out and accuse me of being scared, I politely remind them that I have skydived. Twice. From a height far greater than this silly little tower. That is usually enough of an argument to get someone off my case.

But the truth is, jumping from a lesser height like this actually scares me far more than jumping from a plane three kilometres up in the sky. I can't explain why, it just does. Either way I suppose you are rooted if something goes wrong. But at least from up at a greater height there is a little bit more time to ask yourself, WWMD? What Would MacGyver Do?

Some people have the nerve and courage to do these things in their childhood and then lose their nerve as they get older and more sensible. Sadly that is not me. As a young fella I was too afraid to even go on the rides on offer at the A&P show. So even though the option had been available for many years to jump from the Sky Tower, it was not something I had any desire to do. I am not scared of heights but I am scared beyond belief of falling from heights.

I know this falling from heights is a stupid thing to be scared of. And yes, I'm well aware that I have a better chance of being killed by choking on a chicken bone, but that does not reassure me—they both sound like unpleasant ways to die.

I thought the best way to manage this would be to make a booking, so I would have time to mentally prepare myself, psyche myself up and talk myself into this. It worked, too! In the days leading up to the jump I managed to keep calm.

A good mate suggested I try a thing called positive reinforcement and visualisation. It all sounded a bit airy-fairy, like advice a sports psychologist would give the Black Caps when all they really need to do is stop being so crap at cricket, but I gave it a go and it appeared to work. I reminded myself of some useful facts:

```
Nobody has ever died jumping off Sky
Tower.
   The speed of the fall is only eighty-
five kilometres per hour—slower than
driving a car.
   The fall is only eleven seconds.
   The oldest jumper so far was an eighty-
six-year-old woman, blah blah blah.
```

It would be a filthy lie to say I was looking forward to it, but I wasn't dreading it and never for one minute did I consider backing out. That is, until I pulled into the car park on jump day. This probably all sounds a bit melodramatic and over the top but the walk from the car park to the Sky Jump front desk felt like what I imagine the walk from your cell to the electric chair might feel like for inmates on death row. I was that big black dude in *The Green Mile*!

I got to the payment and assembly area at the base of the giant tower; they call this area Mission Control.

There is something quite absurd about going to a cashier and paying $225 of your own hard-earned dosh to do something you don't really want to do. It defies all logic.

I got handed a blue and yellow jumpsuit to put on. The suit looked ridiculous but I didn't care. My mind was occupied by far more important thoughts.

But somehow the simple act of putting this suit on transformed me from a spectator into a participant. I remember being surrounded by other jumpers who were beaming huge grins and laughing giddily in anticipation. There was even a family of four who had paid $700 for the opportunity.

We were corralled to the lifts and escorted to level 53! For emphasis I will write that number again in word form, and in caps—FLOOR FIFTY-THREE!

As the lift raced up my mouth went dry in the corners (usually a warning sign that vomit is in the departure lounge of the human body . . . and pretty keen to get out). Most jumpers were calm, relaxed and chatty. Seeing the young kids bouncing around in excited anticipation reminded me just how irrational my fear was. But this brief moment of common sense faded as soon as the lift doors opened and the view presented itself. Earlier in the chapter I described this view as 'breathtaking', but now it was an opponent, an enemy. Now any trace of bravery evaporated and all that was left was terror.

We were given a full safety briefing. I paid close attention and hung off every word the supervisor said. I stepped into a safety harness which went on the outside of the jumpsuit. Since I had my bulky jeans on under the bright-coloured jumpsuit, the harness gathered up, causing mild discomfort around the genitals and making me look like I was wearing some sort of an adult nappy. It just added to the all-round embarrassment and feeling of total loss of control I was feeling right now.

As soon as you step outside the tower the first thing that hits you is the change in temperature and just how bloody windy it is up at this height. On a clear day a gentle breeze at ground level can feel like a gale up there.

They close the tower and cancel jumps on real windy days, so, in one final desperate attempt to avoid jumping, I enquired about the knots swirling around today.

'This wind is nothing, bud,' the sky jump experts informed me. 'The tower has to be pretty much swaying before we stop doing jumps.'

'Good to know. That's great news,' I lied.

Before I was guided anywhere near the jump pad my harness was clipped onto the wires and equipment that would spare me a certain death. As I was being locked into place with the winches and buckles I ran a quick but thorough assessment of the two staff. Were they to be trusted? One of them was a good-looking girl in her twenties, and my brain asked and answered hundreds of questions about her in the span of a few seconds. Is she emotionally stable? Did her boyfriend dump her last night? What if Aunty Flo happens to be in town? Is she hung over from last night? In other words, if she is having a particularly bad day . . . will that mean that I am about to have a particularly bad day?

Clips in. Safety check done. The staff, who I had determined were emotionally stable, sober, happy and reliable, were finished with me.

'You're good to go, mate!' they told me with a thumbs up.

I motioned back with the thumbs up. The problem was, I sure as hell did not feel good to go.

The metal platform you stand on is about the size of an average apartment balcony and at that height it seems bloody tiny. There are handrails on both sides to guide your four-metre walk out to the edge.

I shuffled out slowly. About a metre from where the platform ended and the abyss began, I dared to glance over the edge. What a dick move that was—the view sickened me and caused adrenaline to pulsate through my limbs, which were already partially paralysed by fear.

'All right, mate, whenever you're ready . . .' the jump master informed me, which I think was a nice way of letting me know there were other customers behind me waiting to jump, so could I please stop procrastinating and just jump without mucking around.

Outwardly I probably looked fine, maybe a bit nervous and pale but otherwise normal. The staff would have had no indication of my internal turmoil as I took the final couple of steps towards the edge. I was determined to jump on my first 3–2–1–jump countdown because I knew that with every countdown I failed to jump, the chance of me going through with it would diminish and I knew how much I would loathe myself if I had to make the walk of shame off the platform back into the tower to ride the elevator down to the ground floor.

A few minutes earlier I had watched another man jump while I waited my turn and he had done it with vigour, grace and poise. It was as if he had picked out a cloud and aimed for it as he dived off the tower.

I would love to tell you I followed his lead, but sadly, my exit was way less impressive. In fact, it was downright awkward.

I got myself into position and waited for the green light: '3–2–1–JUMP!'

I obeyed, kind of. It was not exactly what you would classify as a jump. It looked more like the way someone might jump from a van roof to the ground below. I squatted down and placed one hand on the platform for support as I lightly tipped myself over. This move probably spared me one metre of height, which is not going to make any difference when you are 192 metres up, but my petrified brain was not to know that. The tower staff must have been wondering what on earth I was doing when I knelt down but I was actually unable to bring myself to jump while standing upright. What an idiot.

After leaving the safety of the platform I fell for no more than a second before I came to a halt and started bouncing around, suspended 185 metres in the air. I had studied other jumpers and I knew this bit was coming. They do this so they can take a photo of each jumper but the six- to seven-second midair pause seems like a bloody long time when it is you bouncing on the wire!

The bouncing around, the height and the knowledge that all that was keeping me alive was a not very impressive-looking wire was too much for me to stomach. I shut my eyes and just waited to start moving again.

'For fuck sake, hurry up and take the fucking photo!' I said under my breath as the time dragged on.

I started moving again and as the giant 'X' on the landing pad got closer I actually started to enjoy myself. Or maybe it was just relief, like with my skydive experiences. Sometimes it can be hard to tell the difference between those two emotions, relief and enjoyment.

The feeling of falling through the air parallel to this giant tower was incredible. But even more incredible was the sensation of coming to a halt at the bottom. I had dodged a bullet, I had survived. I had ventured out of my comfort zone and made it back unscathed. What a feeling. The next few hours I felt invincible. I had killed the beast, tamed the tower. I now fully get the beer coaster slogan that says: 'Do something every day that scares you.'

The more scared you are of doing something, the better it feels when you do that something and come out the other end alive. I had just done something I would never forget. Every time I see that tower, and as an Auckland resident it is hard to go through the day without seeing it, I remember the moment I conquered it.

I also remember that feeling of relief after days of anguish. I've been asked if I will do it again and the answer is easy. No bloody way—not a chance!

# ☑ LEARN TO MEDITATE

I'm a sceptical type. Not a full-blown sceptic like those people who think the moon landing was done on a film set and the 9/11 terrorist attacks were an inside job by the US government, but I do often mistrust people and ideas unless I can see some concrete proof. This is part of the reason I stopped going to church the day I left home. I was born and raised in a strict Catholic household but as soon as I became old enough to form my own ideas and opinions, I just found a lot of the stories that were shared in church too hard to believe—like the whole turning water into wine thing . . . not even a topnotch magician with a Vegas residency like David Copperfield can do that. I remember one Sunday in church leaning over to Mum and saying something like, 'It would have been impossible for Noah to build a ship big enough to hold two of *every* animal in the world, wouldn't it?' Instead of giving thought to my reasonable question,

Mum just gave me a discreet but incredibly painful pinch and warned me not to be naughty because God was watching. After that I didn't dare ask her why Noah decided to take a pair of termites on his ark. Surely that was a silly move given the materials at the disposal of boat builders at that time.

So when I left home I cut ties with my religious past, and since then I've tended to be a bit suspicious of anything to do with religion and spirituality. To earn the next tick on my bucket list, I decided to put my scepticism and preconceived ideas on the shelf and get a bit spiritual. I wasn't sure exactly what this meant, where I was going to start or what I was going to do. I was hoping all that stuff would come to me, or as people who are into this stuff say, I would 'ask the universe for the answer'.

Funnily enough, even though I feel a bit sheepish writing this, I think that is what happened. By chance, an old mate of mine, Richie, came round to visit me. I hadn't seen him for a while, a good few months, and he seemed different. Physically he looked just the same but his demeanour was more relaxed, calmer. Like a guy who had just had a good shoulder massage from one of those Chinese men at the mall with very nimble fingers. Richie was one of these blokes who was always wound up and stressed, so the change was obvious. I had to ask the question, 'What's got into you, bro?'

'What do you mean?' he replied.

I wasn't sure how to elaborate. Something was definitely different but it was hard to explain exactly what it was. He just seemed less . . . angry, I suppose.

'I dunno, mate,' I said. 'You just seem more chilled out than usual.'

He seemed pleasantly surprised that I noticed a change in him and told me he had started a thing called TM—transcendental meditation.

I laughed loudly. It was an instinctive reaction. Richie was cut from the same cloth as me. This is a guy who loves his Xbox so much he took it away on his honeymoon to Italy. This is not a guy you could imagine sitting on a mountain top with his legs crossed while wearing those comfy but ridiculous-looking drawstring meditation pants while thinking about being at one with the universe.

Richie joined in my laughter with a courteous laugh of his own. That was when it became apparent my friend was serious.

It all seemed a little bit kooky to me, this talk of transcend-something-or-other meditation. But the results were undeniable. My mate had changed and changed for the better. I pushed him for more details.

'Real easy, bro' he explained. 'It costs $1800. It takes a few afternoons to learn. Then you mediate for twenty minutes twice a day. You should Google it.'

Richie knows me pretty well, so I suspect he wanted to keep his answer brief for fear of being ridiculed.

'Yeah, but what do you *DO*?' I probed.

'That's the thing! You don't do anything. Twice a day, you sit down in a chair and shut your eyes for twenty minutes.'

'That sounds fucked up, mate.' This is a bad habit I

have—when I don't understand something, I just write it off as being 'fucked up'. This is an easier way to get through life than actually taking the time to understand stuff.

I quizzed Richie some more, partly because I thought this could be the spirituality thing covered off for my list, but mainly because I could tell he was excited. I thought it was important to act like I was interested—it's what a friend does.

'But what do you do when you're sitting with your eyes closed?'

He told me he had his own personal mantra that was given to him in a ceremony by his teacher. When I asked, he refused to tell me what his mantra was, because sharing the mantra was forbidden.

A secret mantra you are forbidden to share, a special ceremony? This was all starting to sound very much like some sort of cult or Hogwarts spell.

'I'll text you my teacher's contact details,' Richie said. 'You should go to an introductory seminar.'

'I might do that,' I replied, and thought nothing more about it. I wanted to try something spiritual but this all sounded like a bit too much of a commitment, more effort and money than I really wanted to put in just to get another thing ticked off my bucket list.

Then something started to happen. You know when you get a new car how you start to notice that same sort of car on the road all the time? These cars have always been on the road—the only difference is you are more aware of them now.

This happened with me and transcendental meditation; I started hearing about it all the time. Evidently, it is popular with a lot of celebrities. But then again, so are scientology and heroin. I wasn't going to try it just because Jerry Seinfeld, Russell Brand, The Beatles, Oprah and Hugh Jackman all swear by it—but my interest had been tweaked enough that I decided to attend the free introductory session.

Martin Jelley was the TM teacher Richie put me on to. I had expected to be taught by a man whose name was a bit less pudding and a bit more spiritual-sounding but Martin was impossible to dislike. He sounded friendly on the phone, warm and softly spoken. We chatted for a bit and he invited me along in a very non-threatening, no-pressure kind of way. I'm a hater of the hard sell so this approach was perfect.

I assumed Martin would have a certain look. Like an unkempt grey beard and fingers that smelt like stale incense. Boy, was I wrong—Martin looked more accountant than spiritual teacher—clean-cut with grey hair that matched his trousers and shoes and a white short-sleeved shirt with all but one button done up. Even though he did not have one in his breast pocket, he looked like a man who would always have a ballpoint pen on stand-by somewhere.

Then there was the meditation centre, which I imagined would be some sort of a hall with a wooden floor and no furniture, maybe some Persian rugs and cushions for comfort. In actual fact it was the lounge of a nice townhouse in the up-market Auckland suburb of Remuera.

My snarky first thought was 'Ahhh. So this is what that $1800 fee pays for!'

My second thought was how I really must stop making sweeping generalisations about stuff I actually have no idea about.

Maybe this meditation thing would be the cure.

Martin sat in the lounge with his back facing the wall in a chair from a dining room set. Set around the room in a semicircle were a selection of armchairs and two-seater couches, enough seating for seven or eight people.

There for the free introduction to TM were myself and five other people. Everyone seemed normal enough. There was a guy in his twenties who had been put onto TM by a mate at his work who promised him it would make him less stressed, a mother and daughter who were learning together hoping it might help the teenager's insomnia, and a married couple who ran their own business and had decided to learn more about TM after reading about it in a book by celebrity jeweller Michael Hill.

I know all this because everyone had to briefly introduce themselves. I hated this part. I hate these sorts of things. Don't know why—maybe because it all seems a little bit too touchy-feely for me.

When my turn came I resisted telling the truth. I didn't think it would go down all that well if I explained I was there because I was completing a bucket list of silly things. Instead, I talked about my friend Richie, whose life had been changed by TM, then I copied everyone else and said I wanted to be happier and less stressed.

Fortunately the room seem satisfied with my reasons. Well, how could the room not approve? Essentially I'd just repeated what they had all just said!

This free ninety-minute introductory lecture was mandatory for everyone who wanted to learn the technique and was pretty much just a sales pitch that went through the benefits of TM. Martin showed graphs and figures from some 600 studies that had been conducted over the past thirty years by 400 researchers at 215 universities. These were some big numbers—but still considerably smaller than the $1800 fee!

The claims were vast and many—TM will make you stop drinking, quit smoking, stop taking drugs, cure depression, make you nicer, stop criminals reoffending, reduce your blood pressure, and make you more creative and more alert. It had the feel of a TV infomercial. By the end of the session I was half expecting to be given a free set of steak knives. The other attendees in the room seemed convinced and if they did share any of my scepticism, they sure as hell didn't show it. I stuck around despite my reservations. There was no denying TM had changed my mate Richie in a good way (plus I had a chapter of a certain book that I needed to write!).

The course fee seemed a bit less outrageous when it was pointed out that it was a one-off fee that meant you were a paid-up transcendental meditator for life, able to visit any TM centre anywhere in the world at any time and retrain or meditate in a group for free.

With the introductory seminar out of the way, I handed over a cheque for $1800. Now I had six more steps to complete before I could officially sit down and close my eyes.

Each of these steps is two to three hours in duration and only one of these is where you are actually taught the meditation technique—that is the step where you get the mantra in your own personal ceremony. All the other sessions involve a lot of talking—mainly about how awesome TM is. Every student has a one-on-one interview with the instructor to establish what they want to get out of TM. I confirmed that I would like it if all that stuff they promised from all those studies actually came true . . . apart from the bit about stopping drinking. I happen to be quite fond of alcohol so I would be really gutted if I learned this new thing then suddenly lost all desire to drink.

The day I was given my mantra and learned the technique was one of excitement and nerves. What if this did end up being a personality-changing experience? I sheepishly turned up to the TM centre mid-afternoon carrying a Pak'nSave bag with three very specific items—an apple, a hanky and some fresh flowers. These three things are used in the ceremony before you are taught how to meditate and given your very own mantra.

Don't ask me what they do with the stuff after the client leaves. It's supposed to be an offering to the Maharishi Yogi, the man who introduced TM to the Western world, but I suspect it is probably a gift to the meditation teacher's wife. Not an overly romantic gesture, giving your wife re-gifted supermarket flowers. But probably better than nothing if you are from the 'thought that counts' school.

The curtains were pulled today, blocking out a bit of the daylight, and the room smelt of incense.

There was a makeshift altar in the room, a coffee table with a white tablecloth covering it. For the first time in this whole process I was seeing glimpses of my preconceived ideas about meditation—that whole mystical Ancient India vibe.

An obvious if not very convincing attempt had been made to make this room in an Auckland townhouse seem a little bit Eastern, a little bit more meditatey. It wasn't really likely to fool anyone, though—the noisy construction going on three houses down was a constant reminder we were in suburbia. It did cross my mind that my induction ceremony could be less effective with a bandsaw sound going off in the background but Martin didn't mention it or seem bothered by it so we proceeded.

On the altar there was a tray and a framed photo of a very wise and happy-looking old man in a robe. He was sporting grey facial hair as long as any you would have seen—a bit like Gandalf but nowhere near as well maintained as Sir Ian McKellen's character was.

Next to the photo of the man with the grey beard a candle burned. In front of the picture was a tray. Martin instructed me to put my three Pak'nSave purchases on the side of the altar.

We both stood for the ceremony. Martin started to chant. I think it was chanting, it could have been a song. Hard to say, since I didn't recognise the words or the language.

Whatever it was, it sounded very soothing and calming. I'm sure it would have had a greater impact without the offensive 'NNNNNNNNNNNNEEEEEEEEEENNNNN' sound from the bandsaw at the building site in the background.

Martin then took a few grains of rice out of another cup and sprinkled them on the tray. A couple of the flowers and my apple were also placed on the tray.

The whole ceremony was all very surreal—the flowers, the rice toss, the chanty song thing, the old bloke in the photo—but I was totally into it. I suspect this was probably because I felt like I was in a bit of a calm daze brought on by the surroundings—the incense, the lack of light and that peaceful chanty song thing again.

Martin sat in a chair and motioned for me to do the same. He told me what my mantra is. It is a two-syllable sound. I don't think it is even a word in any language. Everyone who trains in TM gets allocated their own personal mantra and signs an agreement promising not to share it with anyone. I am not sure why there is such secrecy placed around the mantra. You can find the sixteen different TM mantras online with a quick search, but without the training to go with it they don't really mean much. I'm not sure how the teacher decides what mantra to give a student but I quite liked the feel of my mantra, or more specifically the feeling it gave me when I said it. From the moment my mantra was given to me I had no trouble saying it or remembering it.

Martin then started saying my mantra out loud, slowly and thoughtfully, in a nice relaxed tone, the sort of tone you would use if you were trying to shut up a crying baby. The mantra had a nice rhythm to it. After Martin said it a few times he told me to join in. So there we were, two grown men, practically strangers, sitting in a darkened dining room in the middle of a summer's afternoon just making a sound in unison. I had my eyes shut; I assume Martin did too. I didn't want to open my eyes to check if his were shut in case they weren't. That would have been awkward.

Then Martin stopped chanting my mantra and, in a whisper, told me to slowly dial the volume of my mantra right back to a whisper, which I did.

My next instruction was to continue chanting it more and more quietly, until I was saying it to myself.

This was to go on for twenty minutes. This is TM and followers of it are encouraged to do this twice daily.

Usually I battle to sit still for more than a minute or two. This inability to concentrate even had me tested for ADHD as a young fella. But on this day I did not move, twitch, itch or scratch for a whole twenty minutes, and the time flew! It felt like only a quarter of that time. But before I knew it I heard Martin instructing me to stop chanting my mantra and then just sit silently for a minute.

I felt good. Actually, I felt really good. The whole time I was meditating it felt like I was in a deep sleep while still being wide awake. That sounds like a contradiction but there is really no other way I can put it. My body and mind were in a complete state of pure relaxation and stillness, but my mind was still aware of sounds and surroundings. I could hear cicadas in the trees outside and the sound of power tools going down the road. I was also aware of one or two flies buzzing round the room, but was not bothered by any of it.

I still had a couple of follow-up sessions as part of my training but I was now a transcendental meditator. These follow-up sessions were just to make sure I had my technique all sorted and was saying my mantra properly.

This TM thing was good stuff. I'm not sure of the science behind it, but I'm guessing that making the same sound over and over again acts like some sort of self-hypnosis.

Since learning the technique, I have stuck with it. Some days I get too busy (or can't be bothered) and miss a session, but most days I do it because it feels good when I do. As soon as I sit down, shut my eyes and start saying that mantra I can feel my shoulders get a bit less heavy. Like my worries just melt away.

And as soon as my twenty minutes is up, I feel great. It's as though I've just had a real good snooze for a couple of hours. And the truth is, I notice it if I skip a session.

Sometimes I can focus on the mantra for the whole twenty minutes with no trouble at all; other times I find my mind wanders and I start to think about stuff that is going on in my life. During the TM training you get taught that thoughts pop up from time to time and when you become aware that you have stopped saying the mantra, to just go back to it and carry on.

Every time the meditation experience is different. Sometimes I feel my hands and arms go numb and it can feel like I am floating. Believe me, I am a cynical prick, so I'm aware how ridiculous and kooky this may all sound, but this is an accurate account of my experience with TM.

For my mate Richie, transcendental meditation changed his whole life. The changes were so drastic that some of his mates even noticed them. I don't think I can claim the same level of success. No one has come to me and pointed out any difference in me like I did to Richie. But I reckon it has made me more chilled out. Stuff that would stress me out or get me all worked up prior to learning TM just doesn't worry me as much anymore. Maybe the practice has given me some perspective that was missing from my life without it? Maybe I spent $1800 when I could have just spent $25 and got a copy of that book they sell at airport bookstores about not sweating the small stuff. Who knows? But I like meditating and I think it has been a good thing for me.

And the two biggest bonuses? Not only do I still like to drink, but I reckon a session of TM the morning after a night out makes my hangover less painful.

# ☑ ARM-WRESTLE AN ALL BLACK

I've never really played rugby. I am far too soft, too breakable. Lots of guys enjoy trying to hurt other people and getting damaged in the name of sport. Not me. I think I played three seasons of schoolboy rugby before I managed to whinge enough that Mum and Dad let me quit and Dad accepted his eldest son would never play for the All Blacks, a depressing realisation for any rugby mad Kiwi parent.

I recall hating it. All I wanted to do on Saturday mornings was sit in front of our gas heater in the lounge and watch the kids' TV show *What Now* on the telly. In rugby season I would turn on the radio to Palmerston North's '2ZA—your information station' and cross my fingers that my game would be cancelled. Bear in mind, this was in the early 1980s, so we didn't have a My Sky recorder that would allow me to record *What Now*. Even video recorders were something only the very rich families had back then. So if I missed Steve Parr, Frank Flash and the *What Now* team, that episode was gone forever and that was a heartbreaking prospect for this indoorsy kid.

Walking around on that cold and often frosty rugby field I was never in the position I was supposed to be in. Other little boys in the team who actually wanted to be there and happened to be enjoying themselves would tell me off for not paying attention—dropping balls, missing tackles, not standing where I was supposed to be standing, all that stuff. That was back when they still passed the ball to me! If it could be avoided, they would always get the ball to any other player in the team.

And because I seemed to feel the cold more than the other boys, I had a tendency to keep my hands in my pockets during the match. This continued until one day when the coach, who was probably just one of the parents, pulled my parents aside and had a chat with them. That week, Mum took my rugby shorts and sewed the pockets shut. That was a devastating day.

The day that Mum and Dad finally caved and told me I didn't have to play anymore was one of the happiest of my childhood. Right up there with the day I worked out how I could play with myself in the bath without the water making a loud splashing and slapping sound.

After my short and unfruitful rugby career was knocked on the head I managed to drift though my childhood a bit more aimlessly, doing stuff I actually enjoyed doing—things like making my own binoculars to spy on the teenage girls in the cul-de-sac who had boobs. These binoculars were quick and easy to make:

they consisted of just two used toilet rolls held together with a rubber band or tape. It did nothing to make the girls I was spying on appear closer than they actually were. It just made me look like a weird kid with brown toilet rolls over my eyes.

From there I dabbled with non-contact sports—tennis, cycling and distance running. I was incredibly uncoordinated, so individual sports seemed to be my best bet—that way there were no teammates telling me off for being so shit.

I was tackled by an All Black once and it was quite a traumatic experience. I was on holiday in the Bay of Islands one summer with a good friend of mine who at the time happened to be a member of the All Blacks, Christian Cullen.

I think Christian and I got on well because his life was consumed by rugby and by being this famous All Black. So when he wasn't playing, there was nothing he wanted less than to be talking about rugby. And in me he found someone who had no interest in talking about rugby.

Also on holiday with us was Christian's teammate Tana Umaga. At the time, both guys were at the peak of their careers.

One day we were playing a game of touch rugby with a bunch of kids when Christian and Tana got bored and proposed a rule change: 'Let's make it touch for the kids, tackle for the adults.'

This revised version of the game was working well and the two All Blacks seemed to be having the time of their lives. They were tackling each other with power, pace and intensity that was actually frightening to see from up this close. The smacking and slapping sounds their bodies made when they crashed into each other made me wish I was on the sideline watching through a pair of my homemade toilet roll binoculars. These hits looked ferocious enough to snap a mere mortal in half, yet the pair of them were giggling and seemed to get great pleasure out of hurting and getting hurt. I had two goals—winning the game and self-preservation, the latter being the top priority. Then my worst nightmare happened. Christian, who was on my team, passed the ball to me. I ran a couple of paces but before I even had the opportunity to get rid of the ball and make it someone else's problem, Tana Umaga nailed me.

Generously, he tackled me with nowhere near the same pace or force he was hitting his All Black teammate with, but my fragile torso wasn't to know that. I lay on the ground winded and unable to breath. In fits of laughter, Tana got to his feet, then helped me to mine. 'You all good, bro?' he asked.

It was an unnecessary question. It was fairly plain to see I was the opposite of whatever 'all good' was. Still unable to speak and not sure of exactly what internal injuries I had sustained, I just responded by giving Tana the thumbs up.

I had no desire to be involved in that sort of confrontation ever again. I think both Tana and I dodged bullets that day—I was lucky not to be killed, he was lucky not to be charged with manslaughter.

However, I was keen to take on an All Black in a physical confrontation, one on one, man to man. I needed a contest that would allow me to walk out of the battle arena at the conclusion alive, and preferably unharmed. An arm-wrestle seemed like the best way a cottonwool kid like me could ever take on an All Black—worst-case scenario, my elbow would end up being a little bit tender from being on the bar leaner. That was an injury I could cope with!

The opportunity to tick this item off my bucket list came in August 2011, not long before the Rugby World Cup which the All Blacks went on to win.

I was at the Cavalier Tavern on College Hill in central Auckland when three of the All Blacks walked in. It was a Steinlager photo opportunity, where the guys would get behind the bar and pour a few pints and do a few interviews while photographers snapped away.

I got talking with All Black loose forward Jerome Kaino, at the time considered one of the best loose forwards in world rugby. The Samoan-born Kaino stands at just a shade under two metres tall but has a presence about him that makes him appear considerably bigger.

He is only slightly taller than me. But at 105 kilos he weighs a lot more than the 88 kilos of meat hanging off my skinny frame.

I looked to see which hand he was using to drink his bottle of the sponsor's product. Despite it being a Steinlager function he did not appear to be drinking, so I would have to ask.

He must have thought it was an odd question when from out of the blue I asked if he was left- or right-handed.

He paused a split second, then responded 'Oh, um, right-handed, bro. You?'

I am a leftie and said so. This would be perfect! I would propose a left-handed arm-wrestle. His arms were at least twice the size of mine, so for it to be anything close to a reasonable contest, my dominant side would have to be up against Jerome Kaino's weak side (if he had such a thing).

Even then, there was still no guarantee this was going to amount to anything more than a farcical mismatch—a bit like Usain Bolt having a sprint race against Heather Mills.

I went in with some flattery that was borderline flirtation. 'Physically, you're quite imposing, aren't you. You're a big guy. Could we have a left-handed arm wrestle?'

'Yeah, we can try it,' Kaino replied without even leaving a courtesy pause or giving my upper body a quick inspection to see exactly what he was about to do battle with. Never mind. I was not offended by his blatant lack of respect.

'In the unlikely event that I beat you, what do I get?' I asked, hoping he might put a jersey or some tickets to the World Cup final on the line.

Kaino paused for a second, then replied, 'You'll get a free beer.'

A Steinlager representative laughed. This would be one voucher for a complimentary beer he probably wouldn't have to hand out.

We both got ourselves in position on opposite sides of a bar leaner as a small crowd gathered around. Among the crowd were press photographers, TV journalists with camera crews in tow, some customers who just happened to have stopped by for a couple of quiets on the way home and my co-hosts on The Edge breakfast show, Jay-Jay Feeney and Mike Puru, who were recording the entire event with audio and video equipment, knowing there was a high probability something that had the potential to go viral on YouTube was about to commence.

Jerome and I linked hands on the tabletop. I took a few seconds to pivot my feet on the ground and position my elbow on the table. I can't say for sure if Jerome did the same pre-wrestle routine; I was too busy worrying about myself to take any notice of what he was doing. With members of the media circling about like hungry sharks, the last thing I wanted was a one-second slam-down. A loss was expected but if I could keep my hand away from the beer-stained tabletop for at least a few seconds, I would walk away looking like only a partial idiot.

Then my co-hosts kicked us off: 'Okay, you guys both ready? Annnd GO!'

Immediately, I could feel the pressure of this huge fist and forearm bearing down on me but I managed to hold my own and stay alive. After three seconds we were back in the start position and dead even. Already, this was a victory as far as I was concerned. From here in, every single second was a bonus point. I was shocked and slightly perplexed by my awesomeness, so in a strained voice I had to ask the question: 'I'm trying my best. Are you trying your best?'

Laughing, he replied, 'Hell yeah! I'm trying.' That was confusing—his answer indicated he was not taking me lightly, but the laughter suggested otherwise.

We battled on. Veins bulged from my neck and my face became flushed with blood. Telltale signs I was giving this everything I had.

One of the onlookers shouted out, 'Don't give in, Jerome! You should get this guy easily.'

Kaino shouted back, 'But it's my left hand.'

I could sniff blood. I could taste his fear. I still had a lot of work to do, but the greatest upset in the history of just about everything suddenly seemed possible.

Fourteen seconds in and I could hear Mike and Jay-Jay discussing what was going on. 'Oh my god, Jerome is going to get it! Dom is wavering. Jerome is going to kick his arse.'

We swayed almost at the start position for what felt like an eternity—I would have a burst of adrenaline and force Jerome's right arm to the one o'clock position, then he would manage to push me back to somewhere between the ten and eleven o'clock positions. By now we had been arm-wrestling for thirty seconds—that's about twenty-nine seconds longer than anybody in the room imagined this tussle would last.

This to-ing and fro-ing continued until 43.6 seconds had passed, when a breakthrough happened and one man managed to wear out his opponent and overpower him.

The winner, much to the surprise of everybody in the room, especially me, was me!

I had arm-wrestled an All Black and won! And not one

of those short little half-backs or show-boaty wingers. This was a proper All Black, a hard man.

Jerome Kaino ran his defeated hand over his forehead, then inspected his fingertips. 'Look at this! I'm sweating again.'

Still, I had my suspicions about the effort Kaino put in. My gut instinct is that at 43.6 seconds he just got bored and deliberately lost so he could carry on meeting and mingling with other patrons. A bit like how a dad will go easy on his young son in backyard sports.

'He's pretty strong,' Jerome exclaimed to my two co-hosts. 'He nearly popped my shoulder out of the socket, geez!'

Now he was definitely taking the piss. He had to be. Or was he?

When we'd stopped recording, Mike Puru said to Jerome, 'Hey bro, thanks for letting him win that one. He's got a bit of an ego, so he'll love this.'

Jerome interjected, 'Hey, hey, I tried my best, I really did.'

Whether he did or not, only Jerome Kaino knows and that may be a secret he will take to his grave. Although, he did post this message on Twitter the very next day:

```
I must admit @DomHarvey is a very strong
cat! #fairandsquare damit
```

Which made me think, 'Maybe, just MAYBE, I managed to beat an All Black.' What a thought.

*Jerome Kaino and I. He is the one on the left, with the 'Kaino' tattoo on his bicep.*

# ☑ TRACK DOWN MY FIRST KISS

Everyone remembers their first kiss. You know, your first proper kiss. That kiss with someone you are not related to. I reckon there are probably three details most of us never forget—the person's name, how old you were, and where the kiss took place. Here are some of the answers to these questions from my Facebook friends . . .

```
Donna, 6, she dragged me behind her dads
shed!
Jay


Tony, 14, in his bedroom with 'return of
the Mac' blaring on the radio.
Amy


Nathan, 10, disabled toilets at soccer camp.
Holli
```

Hayden, 14, St. Pats Silverstream 3rd form dance I dry retched when he stuck his tongue in my mouth.
Vicky

Clint, 11, back of the swimming pools in Hawera . . . sadly I found out later he was gay.
Deidre

Oliver, 7, the skinniest guy in our class who sucked his thumb. It was under the entrance ramp at Mt cook school wellington. He wouldn't let me go back to class until we kissed! So I pecked him on his lips and next minute the principal walked over us on the ramp! I nearly shit my pants, I thought I was going to be in detention everyday for the rest of my days at that school!
Kendra

Katie, 10, at her place in her wardrobe.
Avon

Chris, 5, boy's toilets at tikipunga primary. He even said 'I'll show you mine if you show me yours.'
Elizabeth

For me the answers are:

```
Simone, 9, the banks of the Manawatu
River.
```

I remember it vividly. We are talking a proper kiss here, a full-on grown-up 'pash' as we called it back then, both our mouths open to allow our respective tongues to engage in an aggressive wrestle, just like we had seen people do on the telly. Do bear in mind this was the early eighties, so my research was limited to a couple of episodes of *Falcon Crest* and an episode of *The Young and the Restless* I had watched one day when I was home from school sick. The way both our sets of bucked teeth banged together on impact would possibly suggest that it was her first kiss too.

At that age I had no real interest in or curiosity about the opposite sex. It was actually a grown man I was infatuated with at that time. My life revolved around my obsession with Lance Cairns—despite my blatant lack of any sort of coordination I still harboured dreams of one day putting on the beige vest and a DB Draught headband and playing cricket for New Zealand. It was another couple of years before I managed to put the pieces of the puzzle together and realised that when the coach (who was usually the teacher or a dad of a student) says things like 'as long as you try your hardest, that's what matters', it was a polite adult way of telling a kid he was rubbish.

In hindsight, I should have picked up on the many other warning signs about my lack of cricket ability . . . like how I never managed to make it past the nervous 9 and crack double figures with the bat. True story—my top score was 9, my average was 5. And batting was my strength. Even though this was primary school, where everyone gets a turn to do everything, the team managed to restrict the number of overs I bowled (using the same technique as Lance Cairns, naturally).

My batting technique involved just swinging my Excalibur (a replica of Lance Cairns' bat) as hard as I could without any real consideration for where the ball was. Sometimes my eyes would be open but not always. This meant the result was always one of these four outcomes:

1. I'd swing, connect with the ball and knock it over the boundary.
2. I'd swing, hit the ball in the air and someone would catch it.
3. I'd swing, miss and get bowled out.
4. I'd swing, miss it, and so would the wicketkeeper and the ball would roll away for four runs.

Sadly, 1 never happened. Numbers 2 and 3 were regular occurrences. And 4 happened every now and then, depending on the competence of the other team's wicketkeeper.

My usual after-school routine involved playing cricket, or practising batting or bowling, up my driveway against the garage doors. My little brother, Dan, and I spent thousands of hours out on the driveway playing cricket, and probably a comparable number of hours looking for tennis balls that had been hit into shrubs or over the fence. Seriously, in hindsight it still stuns me to this day how I could be so remarkably bad at cricket given the thousands of hours I practised.

The old lady next door was a vicious old cow. She hated us climbing over her fence to retrieve balls that went over so she would stand in her kitchen watching us and, the minute it happened, she would go outside to get the ball—but rather than throw it back to us she would take it inside with her. Some mornings we would wake up to find chopped-in-half tennis balls back on our side of the fence. What on earth would possess an elderly woman to become a tennis ball murderer?

This one particular day, though, cricket would take a back seat to romance. I was about to bowl my first-ever maiden over. Terrible sports-based pun, my apologies.

It was not chemistry or curiosity that brought our mouths together. It was Jeremy and Crystal. Jeremy Walker was my best mate. He was nine, same as me, but he had a twelve-year-old brother who had passed his vast wisdom down to his young sibling. This made Jeremy something of an enigma—he just knew stuff that no one else our age knew, plus there was this added bonus that if he got in any trouble he would threaten to have his brother beat people up on his behalf. This threat seemed so much more likely than the old chestnut the rest of us fell back on—'I'll get my dad to beat up your dad.'

Jeremy also appreciated the company of girls. He even

had a girlfriend, Crystal. Simone Lake and Crystal were best friends. And that is how one sunny summer's afternoon the four of us ended up in a bush on the banks of the Manawatu River for a well-planned kiss.

The date was arranged days in advance. Jeremy took charge and brokered the whole deal. He and Crystal kissed frequently and I suppose he thought it'd be kind of cool: he and his girlfriend and his best mate and his girlfriend's best friend all hanging out together. In hindsight I do appreciate the faith he had in me but it was never going to work—he was nine with the maturity of a twelve-year-old and I was nine with the maturity level of a seven-year-old at best.

As far as my over-protective Catholic parents were aware, I was going to Jeremy's after school for a play date, which was factual to a point. And if Mum or Dad phoned to look for me, Jeremy's mum would just say we were out on a bike ride, which, again, was factual to a point.

Jeremy had the sort of freedom that I could only dream of. It was never enough for me to say I was going out for a bike ride. My mum would interrogate me—asking where I was going, the roads I was taking and how long I would be. I was always guilty until proven innocent. Mum always just assumed I was up to something. On this occasion, she would have been right. But my alibi was so watertight and meticulously planned there was no chance of being caught out.

When the school bell rang at three Jeremy and I met up with Crystal and Simone and Jeremy reaffirmed the meeting place and time.

While he was doing this I just lurked awkwardly in his shadow, avoiding any eye contact or conversation with the girl I was about to kiss. I wasn't being intentionally rude—I just had no idea what the hell I was doing.

We biked back to Jeremy's house to prepare. Jeremy went to his brother's room and came out with a can of Brut deodorant, which we sprayed on so generously it was highly likely we would have burst into flames if the day had been any hotter.

The next step was the mouthwash. Jeremy went first and I followed. He squirted a three-centimetre length of toothpaste on his tongue then swished it around with water. I assume he learned these hygiene techniques from his older brother but since his older brother was only twelve I now wonder who *his* love mentor was.

Pash preparations complete, we biked to the Manawatu River. Jeremy was on his BMX, which was a cool bike at the time. I was on my Raleigh 20. Dad insisted I got a Raleigh 20 instead of a BMX because he thought it was a more solid, more dependable bike than a BMX. Gee, thanks, Dad. Dependable and reliable may very well be traits that are important to adults but all I wanted to do was fit in and hopefully not look like a dick. The Raleigh 20 was the kid version of a people-mover, a very sensible, practical but unsexy bike.

We soon reached the meeting spot next to the river. Jeremy arrived first, doing some sweet bunny hops and jumps on his bike, which was perfect for this sort of terrain. I arrived quite a few seconds after him on my clunky, tank-like bike complete with mudguards, a bell and a carrier on the back, perfect for a paper round but not so good for walking tracks next to rivers!

The girls were already there, just sitting on a log waiting. I dumped my bike on the ground. My bike had a stand which kept it upright but I thought it would look a lot cooler if I just dropped the bike.

The spot where we met was a bushy reserve with lots of trees and cover. It was a spot Jeremy and Crystal knew well and it seemed highly unlikely any parents, teachers or other random adults would ever catch us here.

Jeremy went over to Crystal and placed his arm around her while I stood uncomfortably next to Simone, a good metre or more still between us.

'Shall we do this?' Jeremy said. The rest of us nodded with as much certainty as you would expect from a bunch of nine-year-olds doing something they knew was naughty.

Jeremy explained how it was going to work. 'I'll count to three and then we'll start, okay?' More nodding from the girls and me.

Jeremy, who was quite a bit shorter than Crystal, then hopped onto the log the girls had been sitting on to bring himself to her eye level. I didn't find this funny at the time but looking back it cracks me up big time—it must have been like a kiddie version of Tom Cruise and Nicole Kidman having a snog.

Jeremy started his clinical count: '1 . . . 2 . . . 3.'

He and Crystal were underway. They both had their eyes shut and Jeremy had one hand on her hip while his other hand was stroking her hair.

I watched for a quick moment, maybe a second, before I went in for my kiss. I was just like Jeremy but without any of the finesse. Simone's hands were down by her sides, mine were in my pockets, and the only part of our bodies that touched was our mouths. As I've mentioned, our front teeth made a horrible clunking noise on impact. Then we settled into the kiss with our lips perfectly lined up and our tongues darting urgently around each other's mouths. After what seemed like an eternity but was probably only four or five seconds, I wondered what Jeremy and Crystal were doing and opened my eyes. They were still going, so I continued, even though I was already bored. I wondered if I was doing it wrong, because the whole exercise just felt pointless. We both pulled away from each other and the kiss ended. Stopping it was actually the most natural part of the liaison.

'I'm finished, Crystal,' Simone announced.

I followed this up with an unnecessary announcement of my own. 'Me too, Jeremy. I'm finished.'

Jeremy, still standing on the log, did not respond, and neither did his taller girlfriend. They kept on kissing. Simone and I stood there and kept on watching. And they kept on kissing. And we kept on watching.

This went on for ages—probably somewhere between five and ten minutes. I started to feel overcome with guilt about what I had done, so had this urge to race home to avoid getting found out. I picked up my bike and said my farewells. 'I'm going now, Jeremy. See you at school tomorrow.'

Jeremy continued to kiss Crystal. No pause to say

goodbye, no thumbs up or hand wave behind her back, nothing. Then I rode off on my bike and left Simone standing there without saying goodbye or even acknowledging her. What an arsehole.

Thinking back to that day, I wondered if Simone's recollection of it was much the same or totally different. Maybe she'd thought it was cool how I rode off without saying goodbye. Chicks do love a bad boy, after all.

I wanted to track down my first kiss for my bucket list because there just seems to be a certain purity and innocence to the whole thing. As you get older you realise just how young nine really is. At the time we probably all felt pretty big—we were seniors at Riverdale Primary, not far off leaving to embark on a new chapter of our lives at Intermediate. But we were just little kids.

I was prepared for a tough search if necessary—old family homes, old phone directories, private detectives, whatever it took. In the end it was a lot easier than that. All I had to do was type her name into the search box on Google, then click through to her Facebook page. Too easy!

Mark Zuckerberg and Facebook: helping creepy dudes track down their former partners since 2004.

Good old Facebook, eh? It seems like just about everybody has a page these days. It allows not-so-close friends and family to see what everyone else is up to without actually having anything to do with each other. The perfect relationship, really! It also allows voyeuristic or just downright nosy people (like me) to peer into the lives of people from our past. Nothing comes close to that guilty excitement you experience when you see that someone you thought was a dick at school is now looking way older than they actually are and balding . . . especially if it is a girl. And of course, Facebook also allows you a glimpse into the lives of past conquests to see how kind or unkind the years have been to them.

Simone's profile photo looked amazing—radiant, happy, content. It appeared as though the years had been way kinder to her than me! She was now married with a great family and her own business. Had I passed her in the street I reckon I would have still recognised her. She still had the same face—like an adult version of that pretty, but awkward and shy, little girl I kissed.

I remembered our kiss so clearly. But did Simone? Or had she been lucky enough to block it out and forget about it?

*This is me at around the time of my first kiss. I did like to hang loose . . . always with my shirt well tucked in, though.*

I considered poking her, but that just seemed inappropriate. I mean, we had only shared a kiss and that was three decades ago. It just did not seem right to blindside her with a poke from out of the blue. I decided to send her a message instead, to see if she remembered me—which she did.

It was nice to get talking to Simone again, reminiscing about old times, and eventually I broached the subject of the kiss. Simone kindly agreed to write up her version of events for this book. All in all, both stories are pretty similar:

```
My first kiss was with Dominic Harvey,
almost thirty years ago, on the banks
of the Manawatu River. A group of us
including Jeremy Walker and Crystal Budd
had decided to go to what was called
the 'Love Pit', a child-made bower of
branches nestled in the bush but within
view of the river. This was a popular
destination where kissing and smooch-
ing experiments took place, conducted
predominantly by young children at
Riverdale Primary School.
   I was nervous and apprehensive as the
four of us made our way to the Love Pit
one sunny day after school, but I wanted
to seem confident. I remember Dominic
being shy, like me (in fact, I don't
think any words were passed between
```

us), and me thinking that Dominic didn't fancy me one bit but had only come along for the ride because Jeremy had pressured him into it.

Jeremy and Crystal seemed like old hats at the kissing thing and looked very comfortable with each other as we counted ourselves down to the big moment. 3, 2, 1 . . . bang! Our teeth collided, a very awkward moment indeed, and we kissed clumsily for about three or four seconds. For both of us a very disappointing and embarrassing situation! I turned to watch Crystal and Jeremy's lingering kisses and they looked like seasoned professionals.

Jeremy then suggested we swap partners and see who could kiss the longest—this being my first introduction to what would later be known as a 'foursome'. At that moment, I turned to see Dominic take off at a rapid pace, out of the bush—was I really that bad, I thought? The feeling of rejection then was tenfold! I now realise Dominic was actually a terrified deer running for his life!

Unfortunately, there was no passion or romance about my first kiss but I'm glad this memory was shared with

> Dominic, as he continues to crack me up every morning on the radio and I still remember him being the same from Palmy school days.

I have zero recollection of the patch of grass we were standing on being called the 'Love Pit'—it sounds very grown-up. Nor do I remember Jeremy's suggestion that we swap partners and have a contest! But the other details seem to be more or less the same.

After reading Simone's version of events I picked my nephew up from school. Coincidentally, he is now nine, the same age I was when all this took place. As we walked through the grounds of his school, a few girls spoke to him—some said hi, some said bye. It did make me wonder what these little brats get up to when no grown-ups are about to supervise. Kids these days seem to grow up so much faster and have so much more exposure to information than we did when I was the same age.

We got in the car and my nephew asked, 'Dom, when we get home can I get my scooter and go down to the park to play for a while?'

'What do you want to do down there, mate?' I enquired.

'Just play cricket,' he replied.

'Who with?' I asked.

'Just some friends from my class.'

I paused.

'Will any girls be there?'

'No. I don't really like playing with girls all that much.'

That was a relief. If there was such a thing as a correct answer, that was it. Then, just as I was about to tell him he could go to the park, he spoke again, forcing me to rethink my decision. 'A lot of girls in my class have crushes on me, though.'

'You know what, buddy?' I replied. 'I think we'll just stay at home and play today, eh?'

# ☑ ASK FOR A THREESOME

You are probably thinking: 'How the hell is this something bad? What red-blooded guy wouldn't want a threesome? It sounds like a fantasy!'

I wholeheartedly agree with all of that.

But if, like me, you are a married man who is no stranger to having a thumb print on your forehead, even bringing up this topic could land you in serious trouble. Asking for a threesome could be as risky as skydiving with a chute that has been packed by a one-armed man.

If I could get this one over the line, it would be amazing and the reward would be the stuff of legends. But the potential danger was in bringing it up in the first place.

Yeah, yeah, I know about the risks—jealousy could creep in, things could be weird afterwards, the dynamics of the marriage could change, blah blah blah. But they were risks I was prepared to deal with IF they arose.

\*

So there we were, sitting in the office at home on a Friday afternoon in winter when I plucked up the courage to bring it up. 'So, you know this book I'm working on? I think we should have a threesome and I can write about it as one of the chapters.'

I sat there and held my breath, expecting the worst but hoping for the best, like a scene in a Keanu Reeves movie where he has to choose to cut the red or green wire to try and defuse the bomb.

The response came after about three seconds of thoughtful silence:

'NO. FUCKING. WAY!'

Stink! I snipped the wrong wire.

They were three of the shortest and most emphatic sentences a wife could say. And the way she said it, it was definitely three individual sentences and definitely worthy of being printed with caps lock on.

Jay-Jay's response was firm and final. I was gutted. Not with her but with myself.

My approach had been all wrong. Perhaps I should have bided my time, taken her out for dinner and brought it up as she neared the end of her second, or even third, strawberry daiquiri. It made me wonder how guys who have threesomes have threesomes. What was the secret? I know I lack the looks, charisma, sex appeal and all-round coolness that some guys possess but I honestly thought presenting the idea as 'a bit of research for my book' might just get it past the line.

What a dick—I've read enough *Cleo*s over the years to know that women need to be romanced.

I didn't expect my wife to jump at the suggestion and immediately go through her Facebook friends to bounce around names of a potential third party. But I would have been satisfied with any of the following responses:

```
'I don't know. Do you think that's a
  good idea?'
'Can we talk about this later?'
'You, me and who else?'
'Would the third person be a guy or a
  girl?'
'All right. But only if I can choose the
  person.'
```

Those last two would have made me a bit nervous, though. It could indicate she was devising some evil plan to teach me a lesson.

Like most guys I had thought about a threesome. And like most guys my threesome fantasies always involved me being the only man in the room.

Some guys may disagree with me and argue that the M-M-F combination is a good and legitimate form of male bonding. Not me though—I am greedy and not really fond of competition so it had to be F-F-M. Especially after a friend of mine shared with me a threesome horror story that I have never been able to block out.

Away on a rugby trip, my mate was out drinking with one of his teammates when they met a girl who suggested they all go back to her place. My friend and his teammate jumped at the opportunity and the three of them caught a taxi back to her place. They all sat in the back seat of the cab, where a show was put on that made it hard for the driver to concentrate on the road in front of him.

When they arrived at the woman's house they went straight to her bedroom, removed the items of clothing they still had on and got down to business.

The guys insisted on leaving the light on so they could maintain a respectable distance from each other but what happened next was unavoidable—even with ample lighting.

My friend, a fierce competitor, finished first and accidentally misfired a glob of sperm on his teammate's thigh.

Both my mate and the girl involved were able to see the comedy in what happened and laughed relentlessly. The man in white was not so good-natured about it.

'Fucking hell! Get a towel! Get a towel!' he shouted in the panicked tone you would expect from someone who just noticed a poisonous snake crawling on their leg.

Still laughing, my mate got up and grabbed something to assist with the clean-up. And that was the end of the liaison. Short and bittersweet.

I believe the taxi ride back to the hotel felt a lot longer and way less jovial than the ride to the house.

A few days after raising the topic for the first time we were driving somewhere when the nonsensical and heavily auto-tuned song 'Three' by Britney Spears came on the radio. I seized my moment and broached the subject again as naturally as I could. 'Hey, you know how this song is all about threesomes? Well, I've started writing that chapter of my book about having one.'

'Have you?' the wife replied. 'How are you going to do that? Will you just make it up?'

'Nah, I can't make it up,' I protested, as if I was penning some book of great literary importance. 'We're just going to have to bite the bullet and do it. Like Britney said—merrier the more.'

Then there was a lengthy pause. It felt like a thinking pause rather than an I'm-so-mad-at-you-right-now pause, which was promising.

I broke the silence: 'It'll be fun. I reckon you'll love it. I'll get you a bit pissed first.'

'Not happening,' she replied. 'I'm too old and too sensible now—you should have met me in my early twenties! I would have been up for it then. Plus I don't even find any of your friends remotely attractive.'

It was good news that she wasn't into any of my mates, but things weren't looking promising. Typical! I should have known this would be the outcome. One of the only things on my list that I was real keen to do and it would be the one thing I would not be able to do.

Please don't feel sorry for me, though. I didn't completely miss out on the group sex thing. Prior to getting married, there was one occasion where I made up 25 per cent of a foursome. But before you conjure up delightful soft-focus mental images along the lines of Hugh Hefner and three girls from the Playboy mansion all rolling together on a giant four-poster bed, I should warn you this encounter was far less spectacular.

I was twenty-one and still working as the midnight to 6 am announcer at 2XS FM in Palmerston North. That was all about to change though—an intern had been employed from the Christchurch Polytech radio course to take over the graveyard shift, allowing me to be promoted to the coveted breakfast slot.

*My favourite clothes when I was twenty-one. 2XS FM fluoro sweatshirt tucked into my grey Barkers trackies. Great for jogging in the dark, not so great for impressing the ladies.*

On the 7 pm to midnight shift just before me was Iain Stables. Stables went on to earn a reputation as a shock jock but back then we were both just young guys living our dreams—getting to talk on the radio and play songs for a living.

Stables had a deep voice, perfectly suited to the craft of radio. I think it's fair to say he had a face that suited the craft as well. Nevertheless, he was a phenomenal hit with the ladies. In 2011 he publicly claimed he had slept with 500 women. This may sound like an exaggerated number to some. But I reckon that could even be a conservative estimate.

On my very last night as the midnight to six announcer I was training up the new intern, Brian Reid, when Stables burst into the studio,

'Dom, do you want to go on a road trip to Otaki, mate?'

Stables was impulsive. And always up to something. Whenever he asked a question like that it never meant that weekend, or later on. It always meant right away.

I asked anyway, 'When? Now?'

'Yeah, now. We'll get the radio station van, fill it up with the Caltex card, and go down! I've got to go and see a girl and she's got a friend who likes your voice!'

There was no way I could go. I had to stay to train up the new guy and I told Stables as much.

'Nah, he'll be okay. We'll be gone for three hours tops. An hour there, stay for an hour, an hour back.'

He was very persuasive and I was hardly in a position to be turning down the opportunity to sleep with a stranger who thought I had a nice voice.

I gave Brian, the new intern, a crash course into how to work the two compact disc players in the 2XS FM studio and Stables and myself hit the road in the radio station van, listening to the broadcast on the way down to ensure the new guy didn't take the whole station off the air.

We arrived at the girl's house in Otaki and introduced ourselves.

A scenario like this would be far too uncomfortable for me to ever contemplate but Stables took charge of the situation. 'All right, we better get into this. Dom has to get back to train up this new guy.'

The girls led us down to a bedroom with two single beds. Stables hopped into one with the girl he had been chatting to on the phone during his night show. I got into the other little bed with the girl who allegedly liked the sound of my voice. I can't imagine why she liked it. Doing the midnight to 6 am slot I was restricted to three to four very short voice breaks an hour and it was a fairly tight format. So the only things I would be talking about would be info about the new music and details about upcoming station promotions—things like big digs, a raft race, concerts or kite days. I reckon even someone with a really awesome voice—Morgan Freeman, for example—would struggle to pull the chicks if all he was doing was saying things like:

```
2XS FM at 2.37 am, that's new music
for Marc Cohn, a song called 'Walking
in Memphis'. The 2XS FM annual big dig
is being held at Himatangi Beach this
```

> Sunday at 10 am. Registrations are $2 and you could win major prizes like an Akai 14-inch TV or an Ansett mystery escape. So come on down and join in the fun, registrations from 9 am. Here's Amy Grant and 'Baby, Baby' on 2XS FM.

Still, I was not going to argue if she wanted to sleep with me. I was just glad to have the opportunity.

The two single beds were separated by a small table with a radio on it, which I switched on to keep an ear on things back at the studio a hundred kilometres away.

My encounter was very brief, maybe a song and a half.

Stables and his new-found friend were considerably longer, which left me and the girl I was in the single bed with nothing to do but indulge in awkward small talk like you would have in a lift with a stranger, and watch our two friends in the next bed.

The song on the radio faded out. I remember this more vividly than the actual sexual encounter. It was 'I Saw the Sign' by Ace of Base. Then, nothing. Just the horrible static hiss of dead air. The worst sound a broadcaster can hear.

I climbed over the naked girl who liked the sound of my voice and sat naked on the side of the bed and hit the top of the radio a couple of times, as if that was going to somehow get sound coming from the speaker again. By now there had been silence for the best part of a minute and I was starting to panic.

Then from the dead air came a voice break:

> 'Ummm. Hello? Hi. This is 2XS FM and my name is Brian Reid. I'm new here and today's my first day. I'm supposed to be being trained by Dominic Harvey but him and Iain Stables have gone for a drive somewhere. If Dominic is listening or if anybody knows where he is, can you please give me a call urgently? The CD is stuck in player 2 and I can't get it out!'

We had two CD players in the studio, which were used to produce seamless music sweeps. With only one functioning, it would mean after a song played, Brian would have to eject the disc from that player, then insert the next song and cue it up. This whole process would mean there was anywhere up to forty seconds of dead air between songs.

I was naked and freaking out. My warm afterglow as a result of intercourse with a new partner had completely vanished. Now I was crippled with fear. 'I'm going to lose my fucking job. If Steve is listening, he's going to fire me for this!'

Steve was Steve Rowe, the station manager. And he was one of those bosses that would listen to his radio station at very odd hours. Combine this with the knowledge that he had hired me against his better judgement because his wife liked my CV and suddenly my future as a radio DJ was hanging in the balance.

'Don't worry about it, mate,' Stables said without even pausing what he was in the middle of. It was easy for him to say. He would be in a little bit of trouble for taking the van on such a long trip for non-work-related activity. But I would be in a world of shit for this. My promising radio career was just starting out, I had just managed to have sex with my very first fan, and now the dream would be over.

I borrowed the landline at the house and called the radio station. Fortunately, I was able to talk Brian through what he needed to do to get the stuck CD out of the player. It was a crude process that involved using a steak knife to prise open the tray. It was something that happened occasionally, so a knife was kept in the studio solely for this reason. It was a very Number 8 wire way to fix some pricey broadcast gear but it did the trick.

The problem was sorted but I still felt like I had to race back to where I needed to be, to do some sort of damage control and hopefully salvage my career.

As I sorted my items from the messy mountain of clothes on the floor I looked over to my mate.

'Stables, get dressed, bro. We have to get back.'

'Hang on, mate. I'm not ready yet.'

I couldn't believe it. I was having heart palpitations from the panic and he wanted to finish up! Fair enough, I suppose. He had arranged this big night out and was generous enough to invite me along as his wingman and I was not even courteous enough to let the guy have a moment to finish. In the end I relented, sort of.

'I'm going to wait in the van. Please be quick.'

My new lady friend walked me to the door with a bathrobe on.

I suggested we should meet up again sometime for a sequel. She indicated it would be highly unlikely that would happen again in this lifetime.

I got in the driver's seat and started the engine. After a few minutes, long enough for the van heater to warm up and for me to blast the horn a couple of times, Stables jumped in holding his pile of clothes.

We raced back at speeds no human being should ever travel in a van, let alone a van emblazoned with radio station logos.

Stables put his clothes back on and chain-smoked for a while with the window down a couple of inches before he broke the silence. 'Mate, I don't know why you're in such a rush to get back. If you're in the shit, you're going to be in the shit whether we're in Palmy or Otaki. We were having a good time there!'

He was right. I was totally envious of his blasé attitude to just about everything. He rolled through life with the attitude that most of the stuff that you worry about never even ends up occurring. This mindset has got him in trouble over the years. But it also allowed him to get away with a lot. And on this particular occasion, as my mate had predicted, nothing did happen.

Steve Rowe did not hear Brian's frantic call-out for help.

And Brian was nice enough not to tell on me. His silence cost me a box of Lion Reds, which was a very small price to pay given the trouble I would have been in if he decided to tell anyone.

And, to this day, that is my entire experience with this

group sex business—brief, incredibly stressful, not a story I like to reminisce about and certainly nothing worth boasting about.

Those among us who are sticklers for detail may argue that two couples having sex at the same time in the same room doesn't count as a legitimate foursome. As one of my mates said, 'That's a bullshit foursome! All you did was synchronised shagging.'

# ☑ DO IT ON A PLANE

As far as fantasies go, I reckon this would have to be one of the most talked about but least often actually achieved. The high chance of getting caught probably puts the more sensible half of any couple off trying it out.

But realistically, if you joined the club and then got caught, what's the worst that's going to happen? It's not like the pilot is going to turn the plane around because a couple in economy class were having a claustrophobic shag in the loo. That could make for a very funny in-flight announcement by the pilot, though.

As far as repercussions go for couples who do happen to get caught out, my guess would be that it would all depend on the mood and attitude of the airline staff member who catches you. If they're a good sort, they may give you a wink and sly grin and remind you it's against airline policy. If the staff working on your flight aren't quite so good-natured, the trolley dolly may give you a filthy look and then refuse to let you listen to your iPod or have your tray table down for the final bit of the flight. Oh wait, they don't let you do that anyway.

I've thought about this a lot. In fact, most times I fly it is something that crosses my mind. Which makes me a sick puppy, granted, but also makes me very qualified to share with you the various ways this coveted status can be gained.

There may very well be other ways. But these to me seem like the ways that will draw the least attention to yourself or your partner on the way to mile-high glory.

1. A cheeky his-and-hers hand shandy under the complimentary blanket once the cabin lights have been dimmed. For obvious reasons it is crucial that the third seat is empty, especially if the third seat is the middle one in between you and your partner. Also, to avoid drawing unwanted attention with 'the bobbing blanket', a spare hand or the thighs and knees must be used to form a type of tent framework underneath. The hand shandy will be invigorating but some of the more pedantic among us may say that it is not enough to get you membership into the coveted club.

2. Lying down on a row of those Air NZ 'cuddle class' seats. Easy and

discreet. Thrusting and noise must be kept to a minimum. And senses must be on high alert for witnesses.

3. One of those lie-flat beds in business class. These seats even give you a half-wall of privacy from other passengers. As with the cuddle class option, thrusting and noise must be avoided. Imagine you are having sex in a tent with your kids sleeping nearby.

4. The toilets. This is the location on the plane that will offer the most privacy. It is also the location where you are most likely to get busted. Chances are there will be another passenger waiting to go in when that door swings open, so be prepared to unlock it and briskly depart with your head down! (And that is if you are lucky enough to get in without being spotted and reported by a prudish or envious passenger.) These toilets offer barely enough room for one person to have a comfortable bowel movement so from a practical perspective I cannot imagine it would be the most enjoyable intercourse a couple will

> experience, but what is a little bit of discomfort for a story to gross the grandkids out with?

As I said, there may be other ways to join the club, but these four appear to be the easiest. With each of these, a long night flight will be the best option. One of those flights where you get a meal, then the cabin lights get dimmed as the passengers are encouraged to sleep.

My strategy for ticking this item off my bucket list? Option 4, the toilet on an Air NZ night flight from Brisbane to Auckland. My wife is quite conservative but she is also a very cheap drunk and I planned to shamelessly use her alcohol intolerance to my advantage.

Our flight was scheduled to board at 4.45 pm.

With all international travel you are required to check in two hours before your flight. Unbeknown to my wife, I planned to spend those two hours romancing her in a way that can only be done at an airport, sort of like departure lounge foreplay.

When the taxi pulled up I paid the fare, then fetched the trolley and loaded our bags on. Next I pretended to be interested in the smell of the perfumes in the duty-free shop. 'Mmmm, that smells good. That fragrance definitely suits you. You should buy some of this Britney Spears perfume, babe.' I think I said all the right things. And departure cards? As much as I hate these things, I filled them in too.

Then in the bookshop I found a Marian Keyes paperback and asked her if she had this title already. Her answer was irrelevant. What mattered was that I was seen to be taking an interest. This was like an episode of that reality TV show *Survivor* and I was the villain who everybody thought was the good guy. I was going to outwit, outplay and outlast in order to get me some high altitude lavatory love.

Then we took our stools at the bar in the departure lounge and ate elderly sandwiches and drank overpriced alcohol as we waited for the boarding call. This would have to be a fine balancing act—two to three standard drinks and my chances of talking her into doing something she would never usually do would be greatly enhanced. Anything more than three drinks and she would probably be deemed too drunk to board the plane.

Bing-bong, the public address system came to life and everybody stopped what they were doing in case the announcement we were about to hear was of concern to them. As soon as they realised the announcement did not affect them personally, most went back to their conversations immediately and at that moment I wondered how many other men were in the process of laying down the groundwork for membership into one of the world's most exclusive clubs. Probably not many. But I guarantee most would have thought about it at one time or another.

'This is further and final boarding call for all passengers travelling to Auckland on Air New Zealand flight NZ 734,' the announcement continued. 'Please have your passport open and boarding pass ready as you make your way to gate 80.'

We sculled back our drinks, picked up our things and made our way to the gate, where we boarded the plane, an Airbus A320. One of the smaller planes designed for short-haul international flights, this one carried 168 passengers and had only three toilets on board: one right at the front right next to the 'crew only' door through which the pilots access the cockpit and two at the back. We were seated in aisle 5, so it would be a lengthy walk of shame to get to the two loos at the back. As for the lone toilet at the front of the plane, it would simply be impossible for a couple to enter or exit that cubicle without being noticed by the prying eyes of other passengers.

I suggested we both watch a movie called *Love and Other Drugs,* starring Anne Hathaway and Jake Gyllenhaal. I had seen it before and it is a pretty shitty film. But it does feature two human beings who are better looking than most showing a lot of skin. So, combine that with a couple of alcohol beverages consumed at an altitude of 10,000 metres somewhere over the Pacific Ocean, and it could not do my cause anything but good.

Everything went according to plan. The movie, the meal service—'chuckun or byeff'—and another couple of alcoholic beverages. Once the meal trays had been taken away the flight still had more than an hour to go. My time to earn my mile-high wings had arrived. I got the Air NZ serviette saved from my meal and wrote on it:

```
Meet me at the toilet. Walk to the back
of plane in 2 minutes and I'll be in the
one on your left. Knock. x
```

I dropped the note on my wife's lap just after a very steamy sex scene in the movie. Then got up and made my way to the loos. The note was part of my strategy. I could have tapped her on the arm and talked to her but I thought a note made it all seem a little bit more exciting. Bear in mind, this is definitely not anything we had discussed or prearranged!

Both cubicles were vacant and none of the flight crew were hovering at that end of the plane. It was perfect. I locked the door and waited... and waited... and waited. After probably seven minutes I opened the door and looked out—she was nowhere to be seen. I went back to my seat. That's when I found out why I'd been stood up—Jay-Jay was sound asleep! One miniature bottle of sauvignon blanc too many.

By now she even had a slight drunk snore on. My note was still on her lap, exactly where I had left it. I carefully retrieved it, like I was playing a game of pick-up sticks, and never ever told her about my cunning plan. All my meticulous preparation had gone to waste.

It's funny how these things pan out, though. I got to cross this item off my bucket list a few weeks later. This time it was a completely spontaneous and opportunistic thing. It was in a beautiful old plane too—a DC3 built in the United States during the Second World War. This plane had 56,000 flying hours behind it with airlines including Qantas, Fiji Airways and Mount Cook Airlines.

We were in Taupo getting some McDonald's. After we got our order the wife suggested we eat it in the old aeroplane which has been converted into an extra seating area. As good luck would have it, we were all alone. We had the entire plane to ourselves.

I'll spare you all the details but let me just say that even though I ordered a Big Mac combo, this definitely wound up being a happy meal.

I am not a member of the mile-high club. But, I have done it on a plane.

# ☑ RUN THE PAINTBALL GAUNTLET

The paintball gauntlet is a favourite activity for stag parties. What happens is the guy who is getting married runs, unarmed, the length of the paintball course, while his so-called best friends all try to shoot him. They are only small balls of paint but they hurt like hell and the welts and bruises can last for a good couple of weeks.

Fortunately, I managed to avoid playing a game of paintball when I got married. I have only played the sport once in my life and that was enough to know I hated it. A notice went up on the corkboard in the radio station kitchen with a highlighted bit—the exciting news that we could all play for free. It was some new paintball place that was starting up so they were hoping to get some free plugs on the radio by treating the staff to a complimentary game.

The referee gave us all a briefing, then explained the rules, which I paid very little attention to. There was some flag in some tower somewhere on the course but all I really wanted was to shoot up some shit. I was going to be like Rambo and pretty much every other central character in a movie involving a shootout, so I would get to hurt others while everyone else miraculously missed me. Unfortunately, I found out shortly after the air horn went off to start the game that this was quite different to a Sylvester Stallone video.

I found myself a nice well-protected spot behind a 44-gallon drum, then started spraying paintballs all over the place. I don't even know if I actually hit anyone, but if I did, I definitely did not get the sort of satisfaction out of it that I anticipated I would.

Then, after maybe two to three minutes of play, I got hit! Hurt like a bitch too! The ball of paint got me right in the centre of my forehead, just above the eyebrows. I was wearing goggles and headgear but the arsehole co-worker who shot me somehow managed to find the little gap in between those two protective items. Instinctively I let out a massive groan. That's when the guy who hit me burst out laughing. For reasons I can only put down to a momentary lapse of reason, I flew into a pain-fuelled rage, dropped my gun and ran over to the colleague who found this all so amusing. After tackling him I sat on him and made him say sorry.

Through his laughter he did apologise but I did have my doubts about the sincerity of the apology, especially when he called me Abdul. I assume he thought the red welt that was forming nicely on my forehead made me look a bit like an Indian.

After that incident I was expelled from the game, which was actually quite a relief because I had no desire to continue anyway, not after that brush with death.

Actually, I had no desire to ever play again in my life.

This is precisely why I decided I should face this demon, get back out there, and experience the famous running of the gauntlet first hand. The time to go back and face my paintball demons after a self-imposed twenty-year ban had arrived.

**Where:** Lock N Load paintball (near Auckland airport)
**Date:** Friday 20 January 2012
**Time:** 0800 hours
**Shooters:** 40 Edge radio station listeners

The call had been put out on the radio early in the week to find participants to shoot me. The paintball park we chose was Lock N Load, by the Auckland airport. They were happy to host me and provide weapons and paintballs for up to forty shooters. Foolishly, I imagined we might get between five and ten shooters. Three reasons for this guesstimate:

1. Eight on a Friday morning is a bit of an inconvenient time for most.
2. Getting there would require battling insane traffic unless you lived nearby.

And this is the big one . . .

```
3. Why would anybody want to hurt me?
```

Boy, was I wrong. I arrived to quite the welcoming committee. All forty guns had been claimed. There were even shooters on stand-by. Who were these monsters? Evidently most of them were aggrieved radio listeners who had been offended at some point by something I had said. I do have a tendency to say a lot of stuff without thinking it through—you have to when you do twenty hours of live radio each week. Combine this with the fact that I am not very bright and do like to offer my opinion on matters I have very little knowledge of, and suddenly you have a recipe for getting people wound up. Some of the shooters even took the time to tell me their motivation for being there.

```
'You once said that girls called Traci,
spelt with an i, are easy. That's how
my name is spelt and I am most definitely
not a slut.'
```

```
'You once said Chad Kroeger from
Nickelback looks like the Paddle Pop
Lion. They are my favourite band. Insult
them and you insult me.'
```

```
'I drive a Rav4. I'm here because you
once said that any guy who drives a Rav4
```

> and claims to be straight must be in denial about his sexuality.'

> 'Remember the time you said security guards were people who want to be cops but had their application turned down because they're a bit odd? Well I'm a security guard and I have been waiting for this day for a long time.'

> 'Remember when you said any girl with a dolphin tattoo will sleep with a guy in three dates or less? Well, I have a dolphin swimming over my bellybutton and I was a virgin till I got married.'

There were other reasons, too, which I can no longer remember. I was so anxious about what was about to happen to me that I had no time to indulge these listeners with their little grievances. Plus, I dispute some of these complaints. If you don't think Chad Kroeger looks like the Paddle Pop Lion you need your eyesight checked.

The gauntlet run was going to take place on a course set out like an old western town—like a film set with buildings that had fronts but nothing behind them. The plan was to start at the saloon building and run down the gravel path to the little chapel at the end, probably fifty metres away. Then, after catching my breath in the chapel, I would make the return journey. While I was doing this dash the forty shooters would all be positioned along the fence about twelve metres away from me.

There were obstacles that I could hide behind—hay bales, barrels, water troughs, things like that. But since there were so many shooters lined up over the entire length of the run I thought it would be unwise to take refuge behind any of these. No matter where on the course I was, there was probably someone who had a clear shot at me. And don't they say it's harder to hit a moving target?

I was given a countdown by the bloodthirsty forty: '5 . . . 4 . . . 3 . . . 2 . . . 1!'

I took off in a sprint and was immediately engulfed in searing pain over every inch of my body. The barrage of paintballs was relentless and seemed to come from every direction. My whole body hurt and the only way to stop it was to make it to the safety of the chapel, which now seemed like it was bloody miles away.

I was wearing a hoody for protection. Obviously, I had a face mask, but I thought a hoody would offer me some neck protection. What I didn't consider was that as soon as I started to run the hood would be blown off. The shots to the neck and back of the head were winners. As were the shots that got my hands—my fingers were covered in green fluoro paint and throbbed with pain. My knees, too—who would have ever known a paintball to the side of the knee could be so excruciating?

After eleven long seconds I made it to the safety of the chapel and paused to check the damage and catch my breath.

The paintballs were still raining down. I could hear them thumping against the plywood side of the little white chapel. But for the moment I was protected—at least I thought I was. Then I was hit on the side of the neck from close range. One of the forty shooters had moved from the side fence that ran the length of the course to the back fence and had an open shot at me. Flashbacks from my last controversial paintball game twenty years earlier came flooding back. I felt like running and tackling the prick who got me with the cheap shot but decided that would be unwise. After all, he was the one who was armed. And didn't the bloke who once said, 'It's harder to hit a moving target,' also say, 'Never a good idea to take your fists to a gun fight?'

I had no option but to run straight back. Probably for the best, because as soon as I stopped running I could feel the all-over throbbing and burning getting worse. It was everywhere. Even the little bone in my ankle was sore. I remember thinking at the time, 'Who the hell would be aiming for my ankle?' It was probably the security guard guy I met earlier. That would explain why he missed out on police college—must have failed the eye exam.

I started my sprint back and immediately the flick-flick-flick-flick-flick sound of forty paintball guns going off at once started again. I ran back even faster than I had run down, covering the distance between the chapel and saloon in only nine seconds. I was hit just as often on the return trip, but because the shots to my fingers and neck already hurt so much I barely felt the pain of my new injuries, which was a bonus I suppose.

# RUN THE PAINTBALL GAUNTLET

I limped out of the western town drenched in sweat and panting. I was a broken man, much to the glee of the forty shooters who had taken time out of their busy lives for the opportunity to break me. But I had done it. I had run the gauntlet, and survived.

A couple of minutes after I'd finished, most of the throbbing subsided and only a few key areas still hurt—my kneecaps, fingers, ankle and neck—and there were deep bruises around the fleshy buttock area.

I made my way out to the car park with Leon, my boss, who had just got great pleasure out of shooting me, and Michael Kooge, who was filming video for The Edge website. There was a toot and we looked up. It was the guy in the little blue two-door Rav4 who had come to take part that morning because of an insinuation I apparently made that the Rav4 is a popular motor vehicle for gay men. He wound down the passenger window and shouted out, 'Answer me this. Who's the gay boy now?'

Then he laughed and drove off feeling pretty good about life.

On the back bumper of his Rav4 I noticed a sticker. It had a picture of a cute dog inside a love heart with the slogan, 'Life is merrier with a Yorkshire Terrier.'

Often I would draw conclusions about a grown man with such a sticker, but on this occasion I bit my tongue. As I had just found out, when my mouth causes trouble it is the rest of my body that gets punished.

# ☑ HAVE A CRACK AT WRITING EROTIC FICTION

The suggestion of including this innocuous-sounding challenge to my bucket list came up after some of my female friends got sick and tired of me criticising the 2012 book of the year, *Fifty Shades of Grey* by E.L. James.

I have not read the book, but I have flicked through it and read enough pages to know it is rubbish. Nowhere near as bad as this book you are holding right now, but still pretty bad.

Even though I struggled to see what the fuss was all about, there was no denying that *Fifty Shades of Grey* and the two other books that made up the trilogy had struck a chord with women around the world.

'How hard can it be?' I reasoned, to write some erotic fiction. Come to think of it, that very question could even count as erotic fiction in its own right!

I sat down with a glass of wine and got to work.

And, if I do say so myself, I have done well. My

multi-layered erotic fiction is romantic and passionate, but also incredibly raw and confrontational, with intense sexual chemistry between the narrator and her love interest. But that is just my assessment—you can decide for yourself.

My only criticism of my erotic fiction would be that, much like my sexual encounters in real life, my story is remarkably brief.

So here it is. You know about *Fifty Shades of Grey*. Now get a taste of *Eight Slices of Pizza*.

```
'I'm coming,' I shouted as I heard him
tapping rhythmically on my back door.
Through the frosted glass I could see
his massive package and knew it was
Harish from Hell's Pizza. I didn't usu-
ally go for Indian guys but Harish was
different—he was hotter than a Mumbai
curry.
    'Great to see you, Harish,' I whis-
pered as I handed over my money and
deliberately let my fingers linger on
his palm.
    'Open up your box, miss,' Harish
instructed me in his deliciously thick
Indian accent.
    Naturally I obliged. I lifted the
flaps and we both had a look inside.
It was greasy and moist . . . but smelt
incredible.
```

'One vegetarian pizza and lemon pepper wedges. Is this your order, miss?' Harish asked.

'Not exactly, Harish,' I replied teasingly. 'I was hoping for a mouthful of some of YOUR spicy salami.'

He knew what I was getting at. He threw me up onto the kitchen bench and tore my onesie off. He removed his belt bag and started to take off his Hell's Pizza jacket and visor.

'Please, Harish' I begged, 'leave the uniform on.'

He promised me he would be quick, explaining that the wedges get soggy if they are left too long. Such a gentleman.

Finally, we were together as one. He wanted me. And I needed him. Just like he kneads the dough to make the pizza base.

Within minutes, Harish was finished. I lay naked, breathless and panting on my formica bench while he clicked his belt bag back on and made his way towards the door.

'Harish, where are you going?' I gently spoke.

'Miss,' he replied, 'I am going to Hell.'

# ☑ WRITE A BOOK

My fourteen-year-old niece, Billie, sent me a message on Facebook:

```
Nana sez u r writing a book bout YOLO.
Soooooooooooooo cool. I'll most def read it.
```

I managed to decipher the bulk of her message but I didn't have a clue what the YOLO bit was all about.

I really do find it hard to keep up with all the acronyms the kids use these days. It seems that just as I learn what ROFL means, the kids are no longer rolling on the floor laughing anymore. Nope, by then they have all started pissing themselves as they laugh, or PMSL.

I could have just replied to Billie and asked WTF YOLO is. But doing that would expose me as being old and out of touch. I am both these things. I know it. And since I am twenty-five years older than her, Billie knows it, too. But there is no need to highlight it.

Instead I grabbed a piece of paper and tried to crack the code myself. These acronyms are usually not too hard to work out. I say 'usually' because there is the odd exception. Like the months I spent signing off my texts with an 'LOL' before my younger sister, Charlotte, put me straight on this one after my wife and I had a failed round of IVF (in-vitro fertilisation, not an acronym the kids use too much on Facebook).

The text exchange that took place went something like this:

**Me:** Bad news. No embryos survived. Very sad. LOL
**Char:** Dominic, that is NOT funny.
**Me:** I know. We are gutted. LOL
**Char:** Well why the fuck do you keep saying LOL? It's sick.
**Me:** Eh?
**Char:** I don't think joking about this is appropriate.
**Me:** LOL = Lots of love.
**Char:** Ummm no it doesn't. LOL = Laugh out loud.
**Me:** Fuck!!!! LOL

So the YOLO thing that my teenage niece was on about had me scratching my head a bit. All I could think was 'You Obviously Love Something-beginning-with-O'.

But my book was most definitely not about people who were big fans of Oprah, Oasis, Ohakune, ointment or anything else starting with that vowel.

A quick visit to the great website Urban Dictionary provided me with the answer. And my niece Billie was right. In a way my book was about YOLO.

> **YOLO = YOU ONLY LIVE ONCE**
> Acronym for You Only Live Once. Mainly used to defend doing something badass, something that takes balls, or something a person wouldn't do on a normal everyday basis.

Still, it is a pretty silly-sounding acronym. I would urge anyone contemplating getting a 'YOLO' tattoo not to rush into it. It would be terrible if you went out and got a YOLO tattoo because YOLO and then everyone stopped saying YOLO. A safer bet might be to get a *carpe diem* tattoo. It pretty much means the same thing but will make you seem a bit more intelligent. Chicks dig Latin. But, then again, why the hell would you take tattoo advice from a man who has a picture of a trampoline on the small of his back?

So, this is it, the end of an error. And I must say, I have learned a lot. These are the biggest lessons I got from this whole experience:

## Rose-tinted glasses are real

The brain is a tricky old thing. With the right amount of time, even things which were horrible can be looked back at fondly—like being beaten up by a girl. The three minutes Daniella Smith and I shared in the boxing ring were absolute terror for me. And the damage her fists did to my torso caused me discomfort which lasted long after the fight. But the bruises heal, the swelling goes down, and then you can look back and laugh. I can't see it ever happening in this lifetime, but if I ever got back into the ring with Diamond Daniella it would be because I was wearing rose-tinted glasses when I agreed to such a rematch. I can only hope that she has a personal policy about not hitting a man with glasses.

## Memories last longer than the pain

By getting out of your comfort zone and doing something a bit daring or risky for a few minutes, you actually give yourself a lifetime of memories. And the bigger the risk, the bigger the reward. In other words, the more anxious and scared you are before doing something, the more memorable it will be.

## Facing your fears doesn't mean you conquer them

Whoever came up with that idea was full of it. It's a nice slogan for a Nike poster but it's simply not true. A lot of us fear getting injections, but facing them doesn't mean they become any less scary.

## Usually things aren't as bad as you imagine them to be

In the process of writing this book I experienced a lot of 'Is that it?' moments. Sometimes we build things up in our minds to the point where most of the fear comes from our own imaginations rather than the actual 'thing' itself.

## Doing interesting things makes you a more interesting person

This one is probably a no-brainer for most people but it was an epiphany for me. Because I love a good comfort zone and have a fairly predictable routine, my contributions to conversations are often limited to stuff I have read on the internet or seen on the telly. While doing these things and writing this book, if someone said to me, 'So, what have you been up to lately?' instead of replying with the stock standard, 'Nah, nothing much, eh,' I was able to come up with something far more exciting.

## The best experiences are shared experiences

Most enjoyable things are made more enjoyable if they are shared with someone else, the exception possibly being a bowl of ice cream—nobody wants to share that!

On the flipside, terrible experiences are easier to get through if there is someone else doing it with you. I'd be a terrible liar if I said the trip to the gay sauna was anything other than terrifying. But there is no doubt it was made way less scary thanks to my wingman, Robert

Scott, coming along with me. And it has given the pair of us old mates something new to laugh about—the sauna visit gets brought up pretty much every time we catch up.

**I am still an idiot**
All these lessons I learned are probably quite obvious. In fact, it is highly likely you already knew all these things instinctively. But chances are you are not an idiot. For me to figure this stuff out I had to lose a large sum of money in a sports bet, visit a dominatrix, eat at a buffet until I was sick and go cross-dressing.

My name is Dominic Harvey and I am still an idiot.